p 117

Complete — to be fused; F.A + Credit Agreements combined into a complete whole. [conflate gossip w/ real news.]

Noumenal — (in metaphysics a noumenon is a posited object or event that exists independent of human sense +/or perception) Reality — opposite to phenomenon — no direct access to noumenal — feedback from noumenal. Noumenal / Phenomenal relationship by which observations are informed. Gain that

Toleration, power and the right to justification

MANCHESTER UNIVERSITY PRESS

CRITICAL POWERS

Series Editors:
Anthony Simon Laden (University of Illinois, Chicago),
Peter Niesen (University of Hamburg) and
David Owen (University of Southampton).

Critical Powers is dedicated to constructing dialogues around innovative and original work in social and political theory. The ambition of the series is to be pluralist in welcoming work from different philosophical traditions and theoretical orientations, ranging from abstract conceptual argument to concrete policy-relevant engagements, and encouraging dialogue across the diverse approaches that populate the field of social and political theory. All the volumes in the series are structured as dialogues in which a lead essay is greeted with a series of responses before a reply by the lead essayist. Such dialogues spark debate, foster understanding, encourage innovation and perform the drama of thought in a way that engages a wide audience of scholars and students.

Published by Bloomsbury

On Global Citizenship: James Tully in Dialogue
Justice, Democracy and the Right to Justification: Rainer Forst in Dialogue

Published by Manchester University Press

Cinema, democracy and perfectionism: Joshua Foa Dienstag in dialogue
Democratic inclusion: Rainer Bauböck in dialogue
Law and violence: Christoph Menke in dialogue
The shifting border: Ayelet Shachar in dialogue

Forthcoming from Manchester University Press

Autonomy gaps: Joel Anderson in dialogue

> "Nothing contributes more to peace of soul than having no opinion at all." — Georg. Lichtenberg —
>
> "The haste / a fool is the slowest thing in the world." — Thomas Shadwell —
>
> "Self-respect w/o the respect of o's is like a jewel which will not stand the daylight." — Alfred Nobel —

Toleration, power and the right to justification

Rainer Forst in dialogue

Rainer Forst

with responses from:
Teresa M. Bejan
John Horton
Chandran Kukathas
Patchen Markell
David Owen
Daniel Weinstock
Melissa S. Williams

Manchester University Press

Copyright © Manchester University Press 2020

While copyright in the volume as a whole is vested in Manchester University Press, copyright in individual chapters belongs to their respective authors, and no chapter may be reproduced wholly or in part without the express permission in writing of both author and publisher.

Published by Manchester University Press
Altrincham Street, Manchester M1 7JA
www.manchesteruniversitypress.co.uk

British Library Cataloguing-in-Publication Data
A catalogue record for this book is available from the British Library

ISBN 978 1 5261 1632 1 hardback

First published 2020

The publisher has no responsibility for the persistence or accuracy of URLs for any external or third-party internet websites referred to in this book, and does not guarantee that any content on such websites is, or will remain, accurate or appropriate.

Typeset by Newgen Publishing UK
Printed in Great Britain
by TJ International Ltd, Padstow, Cornwall

Contents

List of contributors	*page* vii
Series editor's foreword	ix
Anthony Simon Laden	
Preface	xiii
Rainer Forst	
Abbreviations of the works of Rainer Forst	xv
Part I Lead essay	1
1 Toleration, progress and power	3
Rainer Forst	
Part II Responses	21
2 What's the use? Rainer Forst and the history of toleration	23
Teresa M. Bejan	
3 Let's get radical: Extending the reach of Baylean (and Forstian) toleration	46
Chandran Kukathas	
4 Tales of toleration	69
John Horton	
5 Overcoming toleration?	94
Daniel Weinstock	
6 On turning away from justification	117
Melissa S. Williams	
7 Power, attention and the tasks of critical theory	139
Patchen Markell	

8	Power, justification and vindication *David Owen*	150

Part III	Reply	165
9	The dialectics of toleration and the power of reason(s): Reply to my critics *Rainer Forst*	167

Index 221

Contributors

Teresa M. Bejan is Associate Professor of Political Theory and Fellow of Oriel College at the University of Oxford. Her dissertation was awarded the American Political Science Association's Leo Strauss Award for the best dissertation in political philosophy in 2015 and was published as *Mere Civility: Disagreement and the Limits of Toleration* by Harvard University Press in 2017. She has also published peer-reviewed articles in *Political Theory*, *Journal of Politics*, *British Journal of Political Science*, *Review of Politics* and other journals.

Rainer Forst is Professor of Political Theory and Philosophy at Goethe University Frankfurt and is co-director of the Research Centre 'Normative Orders' and of the Centre for Advanced Studies 'Justitia Amplificata'. In 2012, he was awarded the Gottfried Wilhelm Leibniz Prize of the German Research Foundation. Among his works that have recently appeared in translation are *The Right to Justification* (2012), *Toleration in Conflict* (2013), *Justification and Critique* (2014) and *Normativity and Power* (2017).

John Horton is Professor Emeritus of Political Philosophy at Keele University. He is the author of *Political Obligation* (2nd edn, 2010) and has written extensively on contemporary political philosophy, especially on toleration, political obligation and *modus vivendi*.

Chandran Kukathas is Dean and Lee Kong Chian Chair Professor of Political Science at the School of Social Sciences, Singapore Management University. His research interests include the history of liberal thought, contemporary liberal theory and multiculturalism. Among his publications are *Rawls: A Theory of Justice and Its Critics* with P. Pettit (1990), *The Liberal Archipelago: A Theory of Diversity and Freedom* (2003), 'The Case for Open Immigration' (2005) and 'A Definition of the State' (2014).

Patchen Markell is Associate Professor of Government at Cornell University. He is currently finishing a book on Hannah Arendt's political thought, called *Politics Against Rule: Hannah Arendt and The Human Condition*. He is also one of the general editors of the Critical Edition of the Complete Works of Hannah Arendt (Wallstein Verlag). His recent publications include 'Politics and the Case of Poetry: Arendt on Brecht' (in *Modern Intellectual History*, 2016) and 'Unexpected Paths: On Political Theory and History' (in *Theory & Event*, 2016).

David Owen is Professor of Social and Political Philosophy at the University of Southampton. He has published widely on Nietzsche and post-Kantian critical theory, the ethics and politics of migration, and democratic theory. His most recent work includes 'The Right to Nationality Rights' (2018), 'Realism in Ethics and Politics' (2018) and *What is Owed to Refugees?* (Polity, 2020).

Daniel Weinstock is James McGill Professor of Philosophy at McGill University. He is Director of the McGill Institute for Health and Social Policy and was awarded the 2017 Charles Taylor Prize for Excellence in Policy Research by the Broadbent Institute. Among his publications are *Philosophy in an Age of Pluralism: The Philosophy of Charles Taylor in Question* (1994), 'Towards a Normative Theory of Federalism' (2001) and 'On the Possibility of Principled Moral Compromise' (2013).

Melissa S. Williams is Professor of Political Theory at the University of Toronto. She has published extensively on issues of democratic theory and edited numerous important volumes in political theory. Her publications include *Voice, Trust, and Memory: Marginalized Groups and the Failings of Liberal Representation* (2000), '10 Nonterritorial Boundaries of Citizenship' (2007), 'A Democratic Case for Comparative Political Theory' with M. Warren (2014) and 'The Ethics of Indigenous Rights' with T. Harrison (2018).

Series editor's foreword

Rainer Forst's emergence, over the last twenty years, as one of the leading voices of his generation of critical theorists, is due primarily to his work concerning two related concepts: justice and toleration. This volume focuses on his work on toleration. (Another volume, *Justice, Democracy and the Right to Justification*, in the Critical Powers series, takes up his work on justice.) Although the idea that toleration is a generally praiseworthy attitude is no longer a contested one, as it was in the seventeenth century, this does not mean that debates over toleration are of merely historical interest. As ongoing debates about abortion, headscarves, veils and burqas, same-sex marriage, extremist political parties, and the right of religious people to withhold services demonstrate, questions about the appropriate grounds and scope of toleration are still live political issues.

As Forst reminds us in his lead essay, any particular conception of toleration involves providing an account of the source and scope of three component features of the basic concept: objection, acceptance and rejection. That is, in tolerating, say, a behaviour or attitude, I must simultaneously object to it while nevertheless accepting it (not trying to ban or eradicate or outlaw it). At the same time, I have to work out where the limits of my toleration lie: that is, what attitudes or behaviours I regard as beyond the pale, and thus not only object to, but also reject. The history of toleration, and the question of whether that history is a history of progress, then, depends on how we understand the struggles over the scope and source of these features. Forst's monumental *Toleration in Conflict* traces out the dialectical path of these struggles as debates over conceptions of toleration and their justification. Here, he rehearses some of these steps on the way to what he describes as a reflexive and critical conception of toleration. He then indicates how we can use such a conception both as a yardstick of progress regarding forms of toleration and also as a basis for answering the pressing problems of toleration we still face as citizens of diverse democratic societies.

Forst's first move is to distinguish between what he calls a permission and a respect conception of toleration. According to the permission conception of toleration, toleration is the attitude that a dominant authority takes towards a minority group that it permits to live according to their faith or other beliefs, all within limits set out by that authority. On this conception, toleration thus crucially involves treating those tolerated as second-class subjects or citizens. In contrast, the respect conception of toleration starts from an idea of the equal respect that free and equal democratic citizens owe one another. Here, citizens agree to tolerate one another as a mark of respect while nevertheless not thereby expressing esteem for each other's views. Toleration on this conception involves the mutual recognition that our shared institutions must be based on norms we can share as free and equal persons, and that this requires that we allow our fellow citizens to live out their own conceptions of the good life. The respect conception of toleration places the determination of the source and scope of objection, acceptance and rejection in the hands of democratic citizens. Nevertheless, the shift from a permission to a respect conception of toleration does not resolve struggles over the particular demarcation of the concept and its implications for contested policies. Rather, it ushers in a different set of struggles over the proper grounds for working out the lines between what is and is not tolerable.

It is in interpreting those struggles and offering a normative account of their basis and grounding that Forst ties his work on toleration to his work on justice. In both cases, he argues that the morally defensible conception must rest on what he calls the right to justification. That is, whatever lines a democratic society draws between what it tolerates and what it finds intolerable, those lines themselves must satisfy demands citizens make that they be justified in ways that are general and reciprocal. In particular, this means that the decision to draw the lines in a certain manner cannot rest solely on any particular religious or other comprehensive ethical worldview.

Since many of the commentators challenge this attempt to ground a normative account of toleration for its rationalist basis, it is worth here briefly outlining what sort of foundation the right to justification provides for Forst's theory. Forst describes his theory as Kantian, and by this he tends to mean two things. First, the right to demand and the duty to provide justifications involves a requirement to offer *reasons* to one another for our actions and institutions. Not everything I say to defend what I do will count as a justification. In particular, reasons must be general – applicable to all – and reciprocal – acceptable by all. To offer a justification for my action or attitude, then, is to offer an explanation and defence that cannot be reasonably rejected. This is the sense in which the theory is rationalist: the normative force of justifications lies in their appeal to reason, and the right we have to demand justifications rests on our status as beings of practical reason. However, and this is the second feature of his account, Forst also understands the idea of an 'appeal to reason' in a distinctly Kantian way: reason is a not a fixed property or set of principles, but rather a faculty of critique. That means that the approval of reason does not come from establishing a claim's connection to a prior, fixed, grounding, but through opening up that claim to criticism and seeing if the claim can withstand it. This makes the very practice of demanding and giving reasons one that can change and develop over time, and whose particular rules can always be challenged. Note, however, that these two features of the account of reason push in different directions. The first, on its own, suggests a more or less fixed foundation, a solid ground from which to evaluate and judge any particular scheme of toleration. At the same time, the second feature pushes towards a more open-ended account, so that the determination of what is reasonable and thus justified is always open to contestation and struggle, thus preventing, for instance, those resting on a privileged position within oppressive power relations from arrogantly insisting that their position rests unassailably on the foundation of reason.

Forst's favoured, critical theory of toleration involves one way of working out a proper balance between these opposing propensities. It also adds a further wrinkle that is worth mentioning, as it involves the third term of the volume's title, and is the specific subject of a number of the commentaries here. This is Forst's account of what he calls 'noumenal power'. For many theorists, power is essentially causal: it involves the capacity to change how people act. On such a view, the space of reasons is independent of power relations, and a concern with rational justification can seem to be blind to the effects of power. Forst views power as noumenal, however: he places it within the space of reasons. For Forst, power is precisely the ability to influence the actions of others by shaping the space of reasons they inhabit (he contrasts power with violence, which he takes to be the purely causal attempt to influence others without shaping the space of reasons they inhabit). Making power noumenal does not so much sanitise power as it makes reason itself a social, and socially embedded, realm. And it means that, for Forst, merely arguing that claims to toleration must appeal to reason is never the end of the story. For, what counts as a reason within a particular social setting is itself in part the result of particular power relations, and since these themselves can be challenged, struggles over toleration are not merely debates about how to derive a theory from set premises, but struggles over the very space of reasons in which claims to toleration are made.

A great deal of the critical focus of the commentaries and Forst's responses turn on just how Forst balances the two pulls of his Kantian picture, and whether his account of noumenal power can do the work he needs it to do. While this takes many of the discussions here into rather deep philosophical waters, the chapters remain focused on the very practical and live questions toleration continues to raise for us as members of democratic societies.

Anthony Simon Laden

Preface

Rainer Forst

This book was a long time in the making. It called for a great deal of tolerance on the part of my dear friends and colleagues, some of whom had written their contributions quite a while ago, in order finally to see our exchange through to publication. However, the plan for the volume kept changing as new chapters appeared that we wanted to include, and when all were finally in, it took me longer than I originally thought to come up with a proper reply. My only hope is that I have not completely failed in my attempt to do justice to the detailed critiques with which I was presented.

I owe a huge debt of gratitude for the honour and pleasure of having this volume appear in the series 'Critical Powers'. First of all, I am indebted to my critics – Teresa Bejan, John Horton, Chandran Kukathas, Patchen Markell, David Owen, Daniel Weinstock and Melissa Williams – for their brilliant pieces. Secondly, I am indebted to the editors of the series, Tony Laden, Peter Niesen and David Owen, who were so kind as to encourage me to do a second volume in the series, which in the meantime has moved to Manchester University Press.[1] David Owen in particular was the driving force behind all of this, for which I am extremely grateful to him. Caroline Wintersgill was generous enough to use her marvellous editing skills to make this a better book. And Ciaran Cronin was, as usual, the best and most perceptive translator one could wish for. Paul Kindermann, Felix Kämper and Amadeus Ulrich did a superb job in preparing the manuscript for publication.

Some of the chapters collected here go back to a conference on my work held at the University of York in June of 2011. It was organised by Matt Matravers and David Owen, and I am immensely grateful to them for their initiative and efforts. The Morrell Studies in Toleration Program at the University of York has been the most important centre for the development of contemporary theories of toleration, and it was a great honour to have the opportunity to discuss my work there.

A few of the other chapters were written for a workshop on my work held at Rice University in Houston, Texas, in November 2015, which was organised by Christian Emden and Don Morrison and was sponsored by the Boniuk Institute. I am likewise extremely grateful to Christian and Don for that honour and for the inspiring discussions with the great colleagues they invited on that occasion.

I would like to dedicate this book to my dear friend Glen Newey, who tragically passed away in 2017. Glen was one of the greatest political philosophers of our generation, and his work on toleration, which he first developed at York, has set the standards for everyone else working in this field today. Our profession – and our lives, too – are so much the poorer without his voice, his brilliance and his irony.

Note

1 The first volume was published by Bloomsbury Press in 2014 under the title *Justice, Democracy and the Right to Justification* and contains articles by Amy Allen, Simon Caney, Eva Erman, Tony Laden, Kevin Olson and Andrea Sangiovanni.

Abbreviations of the works of Rainer Forst

CoJ   *Contexts of Justice: Political Philosophy Beyond Liberalism and Communitarianism*, trans. J.M.M. Farrell (Berkeley: University of California Press, 2002)
J&C   *Justification and Critique: Towards a Critical Theory of Politics*, trans. C. Cronin (Cambridge, MA: Polity Press, 2014)
JDRJ *Justice, Democracy and the Right to Justification: Rainer Forst in Dialogue* (London: Bloomsbury, 2014)
N&P   *Normativity and Power: Analyzing Social Orders of Justification*, trans. C. Cronin (Oxford: Oxford University Press, 2017)
RtJ   *The Right to Justification: Elements of a Constructivist Theory of Justice*, trans. C. Cronin (New York: Columbia University Press, 2011)
TiC   *Toleration in Conflict: Past and Present*, trans. C. Cronin (Cambridge: Cambridge University Press, 2013)

Part I

Lead essay

1

Toleration, progress and power

Rainer Forst
(Translated by Ciaran Cronin)

I The promise and dialectics of toleration

We are not the first generation to live in societies marked by profound differences in forms of life and morals. For a long time, Christians in particular struggled with how to live together without seeing the actions of others as primarily the devil's handiwork. Today, we can still gain an inkling of how extreme such conflicts could be when questions of abortion are discussed. But also controversies over same-sex marriage or the right to adopt for same-sex couples, circumcision on religious grounds, Islamic dress codes, the vilification of religious leaders or whether fascist parties should be outlawed point to conflicts that catapult us back as if on a time journey into the historical epochs in which the concept of toleration was coined.[1] This concept remains so attractive because it promises to make it possible to live with such differences *without* being able to or having to resolve them.

Even this brief review of the ongoing history of conflicts over toleration shows how much sense it makes to examine the two concepts of toleration and progress together. For we think, or at least hope, that our societies have become more tolerant since the times of the Wars of Religion and the bloody persecution of minorities. By adding the third term 'power' to 'toleration' and 'progress' in my title, however, I want to suggest that we are dealing with a complex history in which one should not be too quick to invoke the concept of progress, because conflicts over toleration are always situated in the context of relations of social power in which forms of domination are reproduced and undergo change. Here 'domination' refers not only to forms of intolerance, because sometimes domination also operates by granting toleration.² This is why the correct theory of toleration must be critical: it must subject the various forms and justifications of toleration to critical examination and bring a genealogical perspective to bear on the constant amalgamation of norms and relationships of domination. A history of toleration therefore has to be a dialectical one. It tells a story of the rationalisation of arguments for toleration (each of which has its limits and can become inverted into intolerance), but also of the advancing rationality of power, which is sometimes opposed to toleration, but is often also bound up with it.³ We are still part of this dialectic.

II The concept of toleration

I will first discuss the concept of toleration. It is important to recognise that this concept is itself the subject of social conflicts and is not a neutral party that stands above the fray.⁴ Some cases in point: while some people think that right-wing political activities should be banned because they violate the limits of democratic toleration, others regard this as intolerant; while some people tolerate circumcision, others consider it to be intolerable, even when boys are involved; some people are in favour of tolerance⁵ towards same-sex partnerships, but not of equal rights, whereas others regard this as intolerant and repressive.

So not only is it a matter of controversy how far toleration should extend, but some of the examples cited also raise the question of whether toleration is even a good thing, on the grounds that, at the one extreme, it can go too far or, at the other, legitimise the denial of equal rights. Isn't toleration even the hallmark of an asymmetrical policy or a cunning form of rule through the disciplining of minorities, following Kant's dictum that the name of toleration is 'arrogant',⁶ or Goethe's saying: 'Toleration should be a temporary attitude only; it must lead to recognition. To tolerate means to insult'?[7] What we need here is a historically informed, critical philosophy whose task it is to examine our store of concepts and which asks: What exactly does the concept of toleration mean in the first place?

Tolerance denotes an attitude that, analytically speaking, involves three components – with which we can already clear up a series of misconceptions, for example, the mistaken notion that toleration has something to do with judgement-free arbitrariness or indifference, as in Nietzsche, for whom toleration was the 'inability of saying yes or no'.[8] When we say that we 'tolerate' something – for example, a friend's opinion, the smell of a particular food, or the action of a group – we do so only when something bothers us about the opinion, the smell or the action in question. And indeed, the first component of toleration is that of *objection*.[9] We object to the beliefs or practices that we tolerate because we believe that they are wrong or bad. Otherwise, our attitude would be one of indifference or affirmation, not one of tolerance.

However, toleration also necessarily involves a second component, that of *acceptance*. It specifies reasons why what is wrong or bad should nevertheless be tolerated. Tolerance involves striking a balance between negative and positive considerations, because the reasons for acceptance do not cancel the reasons for objecting but are *prima facie* on the same level and, in the case of toleration, tip the balance. The objection, however, remains valid. The (apparent) paradox of how one can accept something to which one actually objects should not be overemphasised, because there is nothing out of the ordinary in looking at things from two sides and seeing reasons for accepting something that one finds problematic. This is not to deny, of course, that there is an important problem here, since with this constellation the social conflict is imported, as it were, into the attitude of tolerance itself. It requires one in a certain sense to transcend or bracket one's own negative opinion.

Finally, a third component must be kept in mind, that of *rejection* – thus once again one involving negative reasons. These negative reasons mark the limits of toleration, so that they must, of course, be more serious and stronger than the first-mentioned reasons for objecting, since they cannot be trumped by acceptance considerations. In an ambitious, democratic conception of toleration (which I will discuss in greater detail below), these reasons must be ones that can also be offered to those affected by the rejection (i.e. those whose beliefs or practices are not tolerated). They justify why limits have to be drawn from an impartial vantage point, for if the limits of toleration were completely arbitrary, tolerance would not be a virtue and would succumb to the (much-discussed) paradox of toleration that it always also represents the vice of intolerance. Therefore, it can be a virtue only if its components are based on good reasons. Limitless tolerance, on the other hand, would be absurd because it would also have to tolerate all forms of intolerance, including its own negation, and thus place itself in question.[10]

The task of toleration is to bring these three components into the correct normative order. The reasons for objecting to, accepting or rejecting a belief or practice can have different origins. All three can have religious sources, such as when one objects to a different religion as false but tolerates it in the spirit of religious peace and harmony until it leads to blasphemy. The reasons can also be of different kinds, however, such as when a religious objection is confronted with reasons of acceptance and rejection that appeal to human rights – for example, reasons to accept based on the right to freedom of religion and reasons to reject grounded in the right to bodily integrity. It is important to notice that these reasons themselves are not part of the concept of toleration, which is *dependent* on other normative resources.[11]

This analysis already makes it clear that toleration is not always the correct recipe against intolerance. Racism, for example, is a widespread cause of intolerance. But when we call for 'tolerance' as a response to racist attacks, what are we doing? Do we want 'tolerant racists', that is, people who remain racists, only do not act according to their beliefs? No, we should instead work towards overcoming racism; and that means that in this case the reasons for objecting are already the problem. There was a time when the model of overcoming reasons for objecting led

Enlightenment thinkers to argue that the appropriate response to religious strife was to work towards a religion of reason; but this proved to be unfeasible, because they expected something from reason that it is not able to deliver – namely, to provide ultimate answers to speculative questions. Religiously based reasons for objecting cannot be overcome in this way.

Nonetheless, the problem of the tolerant racist alerts us to an important insight into social progress: an increase in toleration is often a sign of progress, since those who are foreign or different are accepted with less narrow-mindedness; but sometimes less toleration is a mark of progress. Thus, racism itself should not be an object of social toleration, since it has a tendency to become entrenched in everyday life and to give rise to violence. This does not mean that every expression of racism should be prosecuted, but that such expressions should be socially ostracised. It is an important matter whether the limits of toleration are drawn socially or legally.

But ultimately progress can also mean that the reasons to be tolerant at all should cease to apply: there should not be any racist reasons for objecting, or any considerations that degrade people. This also applies to attitudes towards homosexuality. To tolerate homosexuality is one thing; but no longer to regard it as grounds for toleration is quite another. Both would constitute progress compared to social intolerance; however, the latter would constitute the greater progress: no more toleration, but no more rejection either, but instead indifference – just togetherness in diversity, without tolerance or intolerance.

III Conceptions of toleration

To continue the analysis, we must distinguish different *conceptions* of toleration that have evolved over the course of history. Here I will confine myself to two.[12] The first I call the *permission conception*. We encounter it in the classical toleration laws, such as in the Edict of

Nantes (1598), which states: '[N]ot to leave any occasion of trouble and difference among our subjects, we have permitted and do permit to those of the Reformed Religion, to live and dwell in all the Cities and places of this our kingdom and country under our obedience, without being inquired after, vexed, molested, or compelled to do any thing in religion, contrary to their conscience.'[13] Toleration on this conception is an authoritarian attitude and practice which grants minorities the permission to live according to their faith, albeit within a framework determined unilaterally by the permission-giving side. All three components – objection, acceptance and rejection – are in the hands of the authorities, and those who are tolerated are marked and indulged as second-class citizens, and depend on the protection of the monarch. This is the notion of toleration that Goethe and Kant have in mind in their criticism, because here being tolerated also means being stigmatised and dominated. This form of toleration represents a complex combination of freedom and discipline, of recognition and disrespect, which calls for a Foucauldian analysis of the 'governmentality' at work in this context of power.[14]

Here we touch on another important point about toleration and progress, namely the ambivalent character of progress. On the one hand, an edict like the Edict of Nantes (the same applies to other toleration laws such as the English 'Toleration Act' of 1689 or Joseph II's 'Patents of Toleration' of 1781) represents an important step towards ensuring the security and social betterment of a minority (even if this was also precarious and often of short duration); on the other hand, it manifests the inequality of this group and its extreme dependence on the good will of the monarch (and on existing constellations of power). Thus, such an edict represented clear progress – and just as clearly a policy of domination and unequal treatment (and sometimes also of blackmail, if we think, for example, of the conditions under which Jews were 'tolerated' in Christian countries).

However, to the truth of a dialectical history of toleration there also belongs the fact that in the course of the modern democratic revolutions a different notion of toleration has developed that is horizontal by comparison with the vertical permission conception – namely, the *respect conception*. The key idea informing this conception is that toleration is an attitude of citizens towards each other who know that they do not agree when it comes to central questions of the good and proper life, but who nevertheless accept that their shared institutions must be based on norms which can be shared by all as free and equal persons and do not simply stipulate the values of one group and make them into the law. The objection component remains subject to the scope for definition of individuals or their communities; but the components of acceptance and rejection are determined in a process of legitimation that aims at norms that can be justified in general way – namely, *independently* (in a relevant sense) of the particular, non-generalisable beliefs of individuals. Tolerance is the virtue of tolerating beliefs and practices with which one disagrees, but which do not violate any principles that reflect the equality and freedom of all. The person of the other is *respected* as someone who enjoys equal political and legal rights; what is *tolerated* are his or her beliefs and actions.

IV Justifications of toleration

In the reconstruction of the justifications offered for toleration since antiquity that I develop in *Toleration in Conflict*, I distinguish a total of twenty-five justifications, which often appear in different variations over the course of history.[15] The dominant lines of thought are, firstly, humanist justifications (from Nicholas of Cusa to Lessing), which seek to reconcile the differences between religions by tracing them back to core religious, or at least ethical, agreements, and, secondly, arguments (from Augustine to Locke) that accord central importance to freedom of conscience, that is, the idea that authentic convictions must not be coerced or cannot be coerced, but must come about freely. The third line comprises justifications (from Castellio through Bodin and Bayle to Kant) based on a secular morality of reciprocal normative justification coupled with a notion of 'reasonable disagreement' in religious questions. Here I can only mention briefly the most relevant points regarding these conceptions.

When it comes to showing due regard for the contributions of major thinkers of toleration, it is important to recognise the force as well as the limits of their arguments. John Locke is a good example. In his famous 'Letter on Toleration' (1689), he argues for a conception of the separation of Church and state according to which the state has the task of ensuring earthly justice, while it is left up to individuals to seek their salvation in their religious communities and to entrust themselves to God. This radicalisation of the two-kingdoms doctrine as it was developed from Augustine through Luther is made possible by a radicalisation of the idea of freedom of conscience. According to this doctrine, the individual must not and cannot cede authority over questions of faith to others, because God alone may decide these questions and because true faith can only come from inner conviction and cannot be brought about through pressure or even coercion: 'Faith is not faith without believing.'[16] Accordingly, everyone must also pursue his or her own path to salvation and not trust others who may be pursuing other interests.

Locke did not invent these arguments but only connected them in a pointed and systematic way. They can already be found among early Christian thinkers. Augustine, in particular, argues for freedom of conscience and for the separation of the kingdoms, although not without according the Church a special role on earth. But the proposition 'credere non potest homo nisi volens' [man cannot believe against his will][17] stems from Augustine, as well as the admonition that nobody should think that one can be coerced into following God, because He does not want false believers. However, it was the same Augustine who in his later years withdrew this doctrine when faced with the conflicts with the Donatists[18] – and formulated the very arguments with which the Anglican clergyman Jonas Proast would later create difficulties for Locke. Augustine in his later writings justifies the 'good coercion' by invoking the biblical parable of the guests who are forced to enter the banquet, and asks whether, when one sees that someone is jeopardising his salvation, it is not one's solemn Christian duty to lead him away from the wrong path. Although coercion – even to the extent of *terror* – is not suitable for implanting the truth, it is, Augustine now argues, suitable for tearing people away from false doctrines. Augustine relates how many Donatists who had been forbidden to exercise their religion by the Church, and as a result had returned to the truth, had confirmed this to him. True freedom of conscience is therefore not the freedom to follow whomever or go wherever one wants, but the freedom to embrace the truth, and only the one truth. Incidentally, it was not until the Second Vatican Council that the Catholic Church recognised a conception of freedom of conscience that no longer involved such restrictions.

Thus Locke's argument that conscience must not be subjected to coercion and also that it is not coercible is problematic, as he later recognised himself[19] – all the more so when one considers the methods that human beings have developed to manipulate conscience and beliefs and to produce convictions in those subjected that the latter regard as true and authentic. The free conscience is not an epistemic fact of nature and, as Augustine's later theory shows, it is not a self-evident theological requirement. For to put it in Hegelian terms, not only the 'consciousness of freedom' undergoes progress but also the many means and possibilities of exercising power and domination over people's minds and of perfecting unfreedom that is no longer perceived as such.[20]

There is another respect in which Locke's justification of toleration is incomplete. By placing such strong emphasis on freedom of conscience, he draws the boundaries of toleration where he thinks that this freedom is not granted – that is, among Catholics who are prepared to bind their conscience to a temporal (ecclesiastical or political) authority, and among atheists, since they lack any conscience at all. To remove God 'even in thought',[21] according to Locke, would be to dissolve the bonds of human society. This is a notion of the limits to toleration that runs right through the history of Christian societies up to the present day: someone who does not accept divine justice will not be a reliable moral person on earth.

In mentioning these problems with Locke's approach, my intention is not to diminish this great philosopher from a contemporary perspective, but instead to point out that we can learn something here about the ambivalent character of progress. An advance in the justification of toleration often draws upon older sources and frequently inherits their problems or gives rise to new ones – and may draw the boundaries of toleration in ways that cannot be justified. In my book I tried to write such a dialectical history of justifications of toleration and pointed out how such justifications can become inverted into their opposite.[22]

It was a contemporary of Locke, the Huguenot Pierre Bayle, who recognised and avoided the problems of Locke's approach – in a critique of the late Augustine, not of Locke's theory – and formulated the logic of the respect conception of toleration.[23] If both parties to the conflicts in France of his time, Catholics and Protestants, insisted that their ideas should apply to everyone and accordingly be dominant, then according to Bayle any crime could in principle be portrayed in the name of religion as a pious deed. Whoever accepts this moral truth makes a correct use of reason – as *raison universelle*. Hence, human reason, Bayle argued, must be able to find a language in which an injustice, such as that of forced conversion or of expulsion or torture, can really be called an injustice. This language of morality and justice must be the same for everyone and, based on the power of practical reason, it must be able to correct the distortions and disguises resulting from religious partisanship.

At this point, we must combat the misunderstanding that such a conception of toleration founded on reason is 'intellectualist'.[24] On the contrary, it is a matter of a historically situated form of genuinely *practical* reason shaped by the experience of concrete conflicts and human violence. Anticipating Kant, Bayle took the view that, apart from all of the religious teachings that unite, but also divide, people, there must exist a practical reason that requires them to seek social cooperation based on norms that can be justified between them as free and equal individuals. Thus Bayle not only argued, like Bodin and others before him, for a secular state, but also consistently argued for a secular morality that was not anti-religious, but was generally valid because it was not based on religious principles. When we speak of progress in toleration, we must take the development of this morality as our yardstick. This progress occurs in small historical steps wherever existing relations of toleration and their justifications are subjected to critical examination and a new, more inclusive, reciprocal and general level of justification of toleration is formulated and realised.

V Toleration and justice

We might now be tempted to assume that Bayle's respect conception is the one that guides us today and imagine ourselves to be at the forefront of historical progress. However, we would be mistaken if we believed that in our democratic age we had overcome the first, hierarchical permission conception in favour of the second, respect conception. For in many contemporary disputes we find proponents of both conceptions in conflict, and the permission conception reappears in majoritarian garb. While some people think that minarets and mosques (or, as in some places, mosques without minarets) should be tolerated provided that they adhere to the guidelines laid down by Christian majorities, others insist that it is a basic right among equals to have suitable places of worship. While some people think that, although toleration forbids proselytising, it does not require the removal of crosses or crucifixes from public classrooms or courtrooms, others insist on their removal in the name of equal respect. The same applies to Muslim headscarves, same-sex marriages and the like. Should same-sex partnerships be 'tolerated' only within a framework laid down by a heterosexual majority, or can they demand equal respect and fully equal rights?

The normatively dependent concept of toleration itself *does not* tell us what we should cling to here for orientation. And many values or principles suggest themselves – freedom and autonomy, on the one hand, social stability and peace, on the other. Depending on where the emphasis is placed, we arrive at different conclusions. I think that we should adhere to the principle of *justice*. For what else is the question of what position and rights minorities have in a society except a question of justice? What is at stake here is a form of justice that calls on us to rethink and, if necessary, to abandon traditional conceptions in the sense of materially equal respect. The central connection between justice and toleration consists in the following question: Does my *objection* to a practice rest on reasons that do not merely reflect my ethical or religious position that others, after all, do *not* share and do not have to share, but on reasons that are sufficient to proceed to *rejection* – hence, for example, to justify putting a stop to this practice by legal means? Is the objection to circumcision, same-sex marriage, wearing a religious symbol, building a place of worship, etc. sufficient to make an argument that can be upheld among equal citizens and that can be fairly asserted vis-à-vis those affected – also and especially if one belongs to a majority? In these questions, being in the majority is not decisive, because questions of toleration are traditionally ones about the position of minorities.

What do I have to accept in order to answer these questions in accordance with the respect conception? This touches on a difficult epistemological point, because toleration is often accused of requiring one to question one's own position in a sceptical way. But this is not the case. Bayle's conception of toleration does not require you to doubt the truth of your own religion, but only that you know that religious-ethical beliefs are *neither* verifiable *nor* falsifiable by rational means alone. They are located within the domain of what John Rawls called 'reasonable disagreement'[25] and are therefore, as Bayle put it, *dessus de la raison*,[26] beyond the scope of reason, as it were, but are not necessarily irrational (unless they involve superstition). Reason is compatible with many ethical and religious positions among which it cannot and must not decide itself.[27] This does not mean, as some fear, that reasons for objecting are 'privatised', because they continue to be articulated in social space. It only means that, when it comes to general political norms, a certain intersubjective justification threshold of reciprocity and generality is accepted.

In the attitude of tolerance in accordance with the respect conception I must accept that I owe others who live with me under a shared system of norms reasons for such norms that can be shared between us *morally* and politically, and in particular do not stem from the fund of *ethically* and religiously contested convictions. We call this ability to recognise corresponding reasons in theoretical and practical-political use and to seek them together in discourse, as I said, *reason*. And so, tolerance, correctly understood, is a virtue of the public use of reason. If there is any moral progress in the history of toleration, and that is a real 'if', it consists of the insight into the deontological difference between moral norms and ethical values.

Thus, the justification of toleration that I consider to be superior to the others is *reflexive in nature*: it regards that justification of toleration as correct which is based on the principle of justification among free and equal individuals itself. It does not employ any controversial comprehensive doctrines or ethical values, but only the rational principle of mutual, critical justification, in which every person affected always has a veto regarding the reciprocal and general character of the justification used. In this way, arguments are filtered out that transport privileges and one-sidedness: someone who argues for equal rights to marry for same-sex couples does not defend a privilege, but attacks one without creating a new one. Those who criticise the crucifix on the classroom wall do not want to replace it with their own symbol, but want to overcome a symbolic privileging of a particular religion. And anyone who advocates tolerating the wearing of a burka does not have to see it as an expression of an autonomous religious decision. However, he or she knows that one cannot impose a one-sided meaning on this symbol and that in this case the right to personal freedom carries greater weight than a certain idea of the *ordre public*, to which some people in France, for example, appeal as the basis of a legal duty to show one's face openly.[28] And if circumcision practices are to be seen as intolerable, we need good reasons for regarding them as bodily injuries, which distinguishes female from male circumcision. People can be bothered by minarets if they feel to be, but they must not ban them, not even by referendum.

If we want to talk about genuine progress in toleration, the central question is how to develop a secular moral language in which those affected can present and discuss their claims – and in which there is a willingness also to treat minorities as equals. A secular state cannot do this without a corresponding conception of justice shared by its citizens. The form of reason that is called for here has learned to make some central distinctions, in particular those between ethical-religious life plans which are not generalisable and moral norms which are generally binding, and thus at the same time between what reason can and cannot accomplish in the religious domain. It is able to distinguish between faith and superstition – and prevents mixtures of faith and reason, for example of the doctrine of creation with the theory of evolution – but it cannot set the true faith apart. Reason knows that it is not sufficient to provide 'ultimate' answers to metaphysical questions of the good and sanctifying life; but it also knows that it does not have to be sufficient in that way to provide us with orientation in the world of action and thought. The secular morality associated with the respect conception is not a 'secularistic' one that colonises or marginalises religion; but neither is it one that religion can fully appropriate as trump.[29]

VI A critical theory of toleration

When people call for 'progressive' religions today – for example, with reference to Islam – we should remind ourselves of European history. It is not the case that 'Christianity' arrived at such an attitude of respect of its own accord. The truth is rather that unconventional and ostracised thinkers such as Bayle, and many others could be mentioned, pointed to the blind spots in Christian teaching and called for them to be changed. It was the power of criticism, more than the power of faith, which led to advances. And these advances were always accompanied by ambivalences, new power constellations, restrictions on freedom and hierarchies. But as long as reason is a factor that musters this power of critique, the question of progress remains alive. It is ultimately the question raised by those who do not want to accept a boarded-up, normatively sealed world, even if they are only a few.

As we have seen, the question of toleration is situated within a complex social network of power, simply in virtue of the obvious fact that every argument for toleration, if justified, is directed against intolerance, which occupies the space of social reasons and justifications in such a way that the faith of one group is regarded as true and rightly dominant, while those of other faiths seem to have succumbed to a greater or lesser extent to error and to be socially dangerous, unreliable, etc. Struggles for toleration take these noumenal power relations as their starting point – in quite different ways, but necessarily in the space of justifications. For whether they offer an immanent critique of the dominant religion (on the grounds that, for example, it rests on a narrow interpretation of Christianity) or reject it as grossly immoral, as Castellio did when he argued against Calvin that 'To kill a man does not mean to defend a doctrine, but to kill a man',[30] the actual struggle always takes place in the space of social reasons. Of course, this is not a purely 'noumenal', spiritual conflict, but instead a real social struggle. But without a change in the space of reasons, no form of toleration will come to exist where intolerance previously prevailed.

Not only the justification and the policy of intolerance manifest themselves as a relationship of domination, but also, as mentioned above, some policies of permission toleration. Insofar as certain 'dissenting' groups are tolerated, they are stigmatised as deviant and are disciplined even when they are granted freedoms (subject to clear limitations). These freedoms are not genuine rights, but only conditionally granted spaces of freedom that can be restricted again at any time. This is not how equal rights are realised. The slogan 'Toleration yes, marriage no', which was used in Germany to prevent same-sex marriage, speaks a clear language in this respect.

As we saw in relation to Locke, in a dialectical, critical theory of toleration a third factor must be borne in mind. For limits are also built into the justifications for toleration that can lead to conditions of domination: Who has the 'free conscience' whose protection is being claimed, which religion belongs to the core of the humanist essence, where does the blasphemy that can no longer be tolerated begin, etc.? Therefore, the normative core of a critical theory of toleration must rest on the principle of justification itself, because in this way every particular justification of toleration can be questioned concerning its blind spots and exclusive implications. This reflexive justification must also be able to ask itself whether it contains assumptions about reason, for example, that cannot be justified among free and equal persons. So the question of justification never comes to an end, and where it is posed in a radical way, social progress is being demanded and, if all goes well, it will be realised. But the horizon of such progress always remains open – and its achievements fragile.[31]

Notes

1 I analysed these and other toleration conflicts in my *TiC*, ch. 12. Further analyses of such conflicts can be found in J. Dobbernack and T. Modood (eds), *Tolerance, Intolerance and Respect: Hard to Accept?* (Basingstoke: Palgrave Macmillan, 2013).

2 Such relations between toleration and power are discussed by Wendy Brown and me in our book *The Power of Toleration: A Debate* (New York: Columbia University Press, 2014).

3 The model for such a dialectical history is provided by Jürgen Habermas, *Theory of Communicative Action*, 2 vols, trans. T. McCarthy (Boston: Beacon Press, 1984, 1987); see my reflections on this in the introduction to *TiC*.

4 G. Newey, *Toleration in Political Conflict* (Cambridge: Cambridge University Press, 2013), in particular, underscores this political dimension of the concept.

5 *Translator's note*: Note that here and in what follows 'Toleranz' is translated as 'tolerance' when it refers to a subjective attitude, stance or virtue, whether of an individual or of a collective (such as a government or a social group), otherwise as 'toleration' (e.g. when discussing 'Toleranz' as a theoretical concept or a government policy).
6 I. Kant, 'An Answer to the Question: What is Enlightenment?', in Kant, *Practical Philosophy*, ed. and trans. M. Gregor (Cambridge: Cambridge University Press, 1996), p. 21, Ac. 8:41.
7 J.W. Goethe, *Maxims and Reflections*, trans. E. Stopp, ed. P. Hutchinson (London: Penguin, 1998), p. 116 (translation amended).
8 F. Nietzsche, *Nachgelassene Fragmente* 1885–1887, in *Kritische Studienausgabe* 12, ed. G. Colli and M. Montinari (Munich and Berlin: dtv/de Gruyter, 1988), p. 432.
9 My analysis of the components of toleration follows – in essence, if not in every detail – Preston King, *Toleration* (New York: Allen & Unwin, 1976), ch. 1.
10 I discuss these paradoxes of toleration in *TiC*, p. 23f. On this, see also J. Horton, 'Three (Apparent) Paradoxes of Toleration', *Synthesis Philosophica*, 9:1 (1994), 7–20.
11 I discuss the idea of normative dependence in *TiC*, § 3.
12 I discuss four conceptions of toleration in *TiC*, § 2.
13 Edict of Nantes, cited in Carter Lindberg (ed.), *The European Reformations Sourcebook*, 2nd edn (Oxford: Wiley, 2014), p. 193.
14 See *TiC*, § 10 *et passim*. See Wendy Brown's critique in her book *Regulating Aversion: Toleration in the Age of Identity and Empire* (Princeton: Princeton University Press, 2006).
15 *TiC*, § 29.
16 J. Locke, *A Letter Concerning Toleration*, ed. J. Tully (Indianapolis: Hackett, 1983), p. 26.
17 Augustinus, *Johannis Evangelium*, in Patrologiae cursus completus, series latina, ed. P.G. Migne, vol. 35 (Paris, 1845), pp. 2 and 26.
18 Cf. *TiC*, § 5.
19 *TiC*, § 17.
20 Cf. R. Forst, 'Noumenal Power', *The Journal of Political Philosophy*, 23:2 (2015), 111–127.
21 Locke, *Letter Concerning Toleration*, p. 51.

22 *TiC*, especially § 29.
23 See *TiC*, § 18.
24 L. Tønder, *Toleration: A Sensorial Orientation to Politics* (Oxford: Oxford University Press, 2013), pp. 11 and 28.
25 J. Rawls, *Political Liberalism*, expanded edn (New York: Columbia University Press, 2005), p. 55. See my interpretation of Rawls in 'Political Liberalism: A Kantian View', *Ethics*, 128 (2017), 123–144.
26 P. Bayle, 'Second Clarification', in Bayle, *Historical and Critical Dictionary: Selections*, ed. and trans. Richard H. Popkin (Indianapolis: Hackett, 1991), p. 409. French: P. Bayle, 'Choix d'articles tires du Dictionnaire historique et critique', in Bayle, *Oeuvres diverses*, vol. suppl. ed. by E. Labrousse, 2 vols (Hildesheim, 1982), p. 1223.
27 See *TiC*, ch. 10.
28 See the case before the European Court of Justice, S.A.S. v. France (July 1, 2014; Appl. No. 43835/11).
29 R. Forst, 'Religion and Toleration from the Enlightenment to the Post-Secular Era: Bayle, Kant and Habermas', in *N&P*, pp. 77–104.
30 Castellio, *Contra libellum Calvini*, quoted in E.M. Wilbur's translation, *A History of Unitarianism: Socinianism and its Antecedents* (Boston: Beacon Press, 1972), p. 203.
31 Many thanks to Paul Kindermann and Felix Kämper for their helpful remarks on an earlier version of this text.

Part II

Responses

2

What's the use?
Rainer Forst and the history of toleration

Teresa M. Bejan

I Introduction

As a leading member of the 'fourth generation' of the Frankfurt School of critical theory, Rainer Forst is now rightly considered one of the foremost political philosophers of his generation. His intellectual prominence owes not a little to the uncommon ambition, critical purchase and analytical power he brings to the discipline. Forst has eschewed the narrower questions and distributive justice cul-de-sac of much recent normative theory in favour of a critical vision of justice as the elimination of domination and arbitrary relations of rule.[1] This 'picture' of justice rests, in turn, on his conception of human beings as *animalia rationalia* – that is, as 'reason-deserving, reason-requiring, reason-giving' and hence as '*justifying* beings' who are owed and owe others, in turn, reasons for the exercise of power over them.[2]

Since the early 1990s, Forst has built a complete, constructivist moral, social, and political theory grounded in this 'basic right to justification'.[3] Our understanding of this system has been enriched in recent years by a series of critical exchanges, in which Forst's fellow critical and analytic theorists have challenged his system in part or in whole.[4] One criticism has come up again and again – that Forst's system is unduly rationalist, even 'absolutist', in its moralism, hence insensitive to its own historical and cultural particularity.[5] In particular, Amy Allen and Seyla Benhabib have charged Forst with a form of Enlightenment triumphalism and a coercively linear and progressive view of history at odds with earlier generations of the Frankfurt School. For Allen, this masks the particular European and *Christian* origins of the rationalist morality Forst presents as transcendent and universal – hence its own continuing imbrication with domination. Benhabib argues that Forst forgets the fact that 'the universalistic moral point of view, captured by the "right to justification", is a *contingent* achievement of human history ... [and historical] struggles against slavery, oppression, inequality, degradation, and humiliation throughout centuries'.[6]

While Forst has embraced the 'moralist' charge on the grounds that 'one cannot relativize the fundamental claim of human dignity',[7] when it comes to charges of ahistoricism and a 'blinkered Enlightenment unenlightened about itself',[8] he evidently rankles. His response is always the same – to direct his critics to his 'toleration book', in which he himself 'tr[ied] to show ... by analysing centuries of social struggles, that the idea and practice of universal morality is a *historical achievement*'.[9] But one must not conflate questions of genealogy with those of validity.[10] Against what he sees as the 'conservatism' implicit among some contextualists, he insists that the nature of that historical achievement lay precisely in the ability of historical actors (including Martin Luther, Sebastian Castellio, the Levellers and Pierre Bayle) to radically *transcend* their own contexts of justification and engage in revolutionary forms of critique.[11]

What Forst refers to with all due modesty as his 'toleration book' was anything but modest. What began as Forst's *Habilitationsschrift* in Frankfurt first appeared in German as *Toleranz im Konflikt: Geschichte, Gehalt, and Gegenwart* in 2003, and the slightly abridged 2013 English version, *Toleration in Conflict: Past and Present* (*TiC*), still clocks in at over 600 pages (longer than his supervisor's *Habilitation*, *The Structural Transformation of the Public Sphere*).[12] *TiC* is a masterpiece that flagrantly violates the informal division of labour between political theory and the history of political thought that has become essential to the self-conception of political philosophy as an essentially un- or anti-historical pursuit.[13] As a testament to Forst's intellectual historical *bona fides*, the English edition was published in the

Cambridge *Ideas in Context* series edited by James Tully and Quentin Skinner himself.

Given its size, scope and the depth of its engagement with the long history of religious toleration in the West from antiquity to the twenty-first century, it is not surprising that Forst's critics have not engaged with it in all of its detail and have been tempted to see his historical engagements as orthogonal to the philosophical system developed in his more recent work. But this is a mistake. Not only is the 'respect conception' identified in *TiC* as 'the correct form of toleration', as a fundamental expression of our respect for others as 'justifying beings', it is also normatively essential for the ongoing practice of mutual justification in ethically diverse societies.[14] In his most recent collection, *Normativity and Power*, Forst goes farther, presenting *TiC* as exemplary of his method of critical theory. Such a theory, Forst argues, must be aimed at emancipation through inquiry into 'the rational form of a social order that is both historically possible and normatively justified … and why the existing power relations within (and beyond) a society prevent the emergence of such an order'.[15] Thus on this view, 'any meaningful discourse concerning normative orders' must be 'predicated on … inter-disciplinarity', through which 'the perspective of philosophy' can be connected with 'those of social science and history without succumbing to reductionism'.[16]

Such declarations make the historian of political thought's heart swell, and I count myself among the converted when it comes to the importance of interdisciplinarity without reductionism for political theory. Moreover, *TiC* has been crucial to my thinking about toleration and to the development of my own 'historically informed' approach to political theory more generally.[17] In this chapter, I will revisit Forst's 'toleration book' in light of these reaffirmations of its normative and methodological significance and explore what it tells us about what theorists might have to gain – or lose – by following his lead. Doing so raises important questions about what we *do* when we turn to the past for present purposes, and what exactly we find when we look there.

II An historical achievement

Plenty of theorists pay lip service to interdisciplinarity, but Forst has proven himself uniquely willing to put his money where his mouth is. *Toleration in Conflict* offers a sweeping philosophical history – or what Forst calls a 'critical history of argumentation' (*Argumentationsgeschichte*) – so as to recover 'the central arguments which were offered for an attitude or a policy of toleration in their socio-historical and philosophical contexts' and examine them critically 'with reference to their systematic content and their role in the conflicts of their time'.[18]

Forst's important insight – now widely shared by other theorists and historians – was that toleration is a necessarily 'contested' concept, not in its *essence* (as W.B. Gallie might have it), but in its interpretation.[19] As a balancing act between its distinctive 'objection', 'acceptance' and 'rejection' components, the concept is compatible with a wide range of *conceptions* of toleration, which come into conflict on particular questions and can then be justified in different ways.[20] Because of this conceptual and justificatory complexity, Forst argues, arguments for toleration therefore cannot be adequately understood when stripped from the particular contexts – and *conflicts* – in which they are made. To understand toleration (like justification itself), one must look not only to theory, but to practice as well – in this case, the vast historical terrain over which contestations about the nature and limits of religious tolerance raged in Western Europe for the better part of two millennia.

Toleration in Conflict is divided into two parts. After a brief theoretical introduction in which Forst introduces the competing conceptions of toleration and the superior 'respect conception' that alone can resolve its (apparent) paradoxes, he then embarks on a historical narrative tracing the various conceptions of toleration and the myriad justifications offered for and against it from late antiquity. Forst aims to show his readers how these were shaped by the historical conflicts – over power, politics, religion, etc. – and sociopolitical contexts in which they occurred. In doing so, he stresses (as Glen Newey and others have done), that calls for toleration are not *neutral*.[21] Rather, they are made generally by parties to a dispute – that is, by interested individuals and groups with partial, even partisan, perspectives. Thus, as Forst presents it, the historical narrative that comprises well over half of the book is not simply window-dressing; rather, it establishes the essential point that arguments for toleration are not made from nowhere, and so for this concept, at least, theory and practice must always go hand-in-hand.[22]

Here, one might note another aim underlying Forst's historical project that becomes clear only in the second theoretical part of the book in his lengthy discussion of Rawls's *Political Liberalism*.[23] That is, to make good on Rawls's offhand remark in that work, that 'the historical origin of political liberalism (and of liberalism more generally) is the Reformation and its aftermath, with the long controversies over religious toleration in the sixteenth and seventeenth centuries'.[24] As the historical account of early modern toleration debates in ch. 5 of *TiC* demonstrates, Forst agrees. Yet he insists that, although it is 'a child of toleration', liberalism (whether Lockean or Rawlsian) must not be viewed as the historical endpoint, or 'culmination' of toleration discourse. Rather, it can – and indeed must – be understood, criticised and ultimately perfected with reference to its conceptual foundation.[25] Thus, recounting the long history of toleration – culminating in the fully moral and rational 'respect conception' that emerges only with Pierre Bayle – is not simply an illustration of the proper method of critical theory (as opposed to analytic liberal theory) for Forst. It establishes the end point of his political and moral philosophy, as a fully liberal, truly tolerant and socially democratic society in which the basic right to justification will, at last, be fully met.[26]

Since *TiC*, Forst has focused his energies on developing that vision. Looking backward however, it is clear that in 2003 Forst was well ahead of his time, pioneering moves that have now become standard in the ever-expanding toleration literature – including the turn to history itself.[27] Still, Forst remains exceptional in his willingness to stray from the beaten path. His historical narrative is populated by a rich array of philosophers and theologians, heretics and saints, prophets and sectarians that puts many a historian of political thought (including this one) to shame. While hitting the canonical high points, he expands our horizons through his sustained engagement with the thought of more marginal figures (like Abelard, Ramon Llull, Reimarus or Roger Williams), or reading famous thinkers through their more obscure works. His discussion of Locke is devoted mainly to *A Letter Concerning Toleration*'s many sequels, and of Bodin to the bit of unpublished esoterica known as the *Colloquium of the Seven on the Secrets of the Sublime* – a text, it so happens, that would be singled out by Rawls as well in his posthumous essay, 'On My Religion', although Forst did not know this at the time.[28] And although the historical narrative does 'culminate', more or less, with Kant, Forst's unabashed preference for Bayle, along with his open acknowledgement of the limitations of both (in Bayle's case, the neglect of democracy, and in Kant's, the intolerant conception of 'rational religion'), complicates any charge of Enlightenment triumphalism.[29]

With hindsight, Forst appears ahead of his time in another key respect. *TiC* pushes back explicitly against self-professed critics of toleration, who by the late 1990s were quickly forming a cottage industry.[30] By the time *TiC* was published in German, the consensus position among political theorists who agreed on little else was that the time had come to move 'beyond toleration' and replace it with something more positive – be it recognition, acceptance, esteem for difference, or mutual respect.[31] While Forst's critical-historical account reveals significant sympathy with more radical critics like Stanley Fish, for whom toleration is always a discourse of power, he was adamant that one must not throw the baby out with the bathwater.[32] Just because the deficient 'permission conception' of toleration – a conditional permission of acknowledged evils that exercises disciplinary power by exchanging persecution for more subtle and insidious forms of social control – entails domination, does not mean that all conceptions of toleration must.[33]

Forst's solution, as we have seen, was not to move 'beyond' tolerance, but to reconceive of toleration *itself* as an expression of 'mutual respect' and 'recognition of others as our moral and political equals'.[34] It does this, he argues (drawing on both Habermas and Rawls), by making a categorical distinction between our 'ethical' grounds for objection and 'moral' reasons for acceptance – namely, the recognition of people's equal moral status as 'justifying rational beings', apart from their particular ethical (often religious) commitments.[35] The second, theoretical part of the book is thus devoted to showing how this conception of toleration and its corresponding justification must become our basis for critique as uniquely capable of resolving the paradoxes that had made toleration into the notoriously vexed – and suspect – concept it had become.

While toleration-as-respect would seem to run afoul of the common sense of toleration captured by Isaiah Berlin (following Herbert Butterfield) as 'imply[ing] a certain disrespect: I tolerate you and your absurd beliefs and your foolish acts though I know them to be absurd and foolish',[36] for Forst, that was the point. Only through the respect conception could we overcome Goethe's dictum, 'Dulden heisst beleidigen' [To tolerate is to insult] and rescue toleration from its critics once and for all.

III Practical problems

Forst's own achievement in recovering toleration-as-respect as an *historical* achievement is considerable. But how, exactly, did he get there? *Normativity and Power* presents *TiC*'s historical approach not as a curious diversion, but as exemplary of critical theory as such, by overcoming 'the traditional dichotomies between "realistic" and "ideal" approaches in political philosophy'.[37] Such theories, he tells us elsewhere, must shuttle back and forth between social and historical reflections on the 'power of justifications' in social reality to abstract, moral reflection on the 'justification of power'. We must do both, Forst insists, because human beings are not simply *animalia rationalia* or 'justifying beings' after all. We are also 'beings who tell stories', including stories *about* justification, and those justification narratives also constitute the 'space of reasons' in which we find ourselves.[38]

On this view, historical work thus serves not only as *Argumentationsgeschichte*, but '*Geschichten-geschichte*', if you will, by offering a critical history of different, often competing, narratives of justification. According to Forst, such histories reveal, in turn, that 'in moments of critique' existing orders and narratives of justification are open not only to 'immanent' critique, but something more radical, in which wholly new narratives are introduced and 'tes[t] the boundaries of what is seen as justifiable' at all.[39] As examples, he cites the Levellers, in re-casting the King's authority as contractual rather than *jure divino*, or Martin Luther, in first dubbing the Pope 'the Anti-Christ', followed by Bayle's unprecedented example of a society of atheists.[40] Thus much of the point of doing history, for Forst, is to show that radically transcendent critique is possible, and political theorists must engage with our history, in part, to remind ourselves of the possibility of breaking free.

Forst develops this argument in response to Allen and Benhabib, and in doing so he admits that rather than a tale of 'contingency' (Benhabib) or insuperable 'embeddedness' (Allen), *Toleration in Conflict* is a tale of *progress* – a description he had avoided in the earlier work.[41] But *Normativity and Power* fully embraces that characterisation:

> Although history should not be viewed as a linear and progressive sequence in which higher and more egalitarian justification structures are successively established, the historical dynamic of ever more wide-ranging demands for justification can nevertheless be reconstructed … *Progress* becomes apparent in such a dialectical conception of history in overcoming inadequate justifications for social relations and in the establishment of improved discursive relations of justification; but the persistence of asymmetric justification narratives and corresponding orders likewise becomes apparent.[42]

As he explains in the accompanying footnote: 'I have explored this in *Toleration in Conflict* through a systematic, historical analysis of the demand for toleration and legal equality.'[43]

For Forst, then, the history of toleration *is* a tale of progress – not of Reason (as Enlightenment authors like Voltaire or Kant might have it), however, but of ever more wide-ranging demands for justification in the face of arbitrary power. Thus quite a lot rests, both in Forst's recent methodological reflections as in *TiC* itself, on its character as a work of *history*, which derives its authority from being an authentic record of events, people and arguments in the past *wie es eigentlich gewesen ist* (Ranke). Forst does not say much about this – nor, indeed, do many of the political theorists eager to make use of historical authors and exemplars in their works – but in order for his history to do the critical and normative work he wants it to, it must be *good* history. But was the 'history of toleration' really (*eigentlich*) as Forst presents it?

While *TiC* had the benefit of being 'ahead of its time' as an historically informed work on toleration, it came out before the fleet of new, revisionist works on toleration by historians that have fundamentally changed how we view that history.[44] Like Forst's book, these remain (with very few exceptions) works of Western European history, informed by the sense that the problem of toleration somehow *belongs* to the inhabitants of Western liberal democracies, as the 'children' of early modern toleration debates, even if it is not limited to them. Many reflect the lingering 'Locke obsession' in toleration studies by focusing on early modern England;[45] still, others range more widely across northern and central Europe and to the European colonies of the New World.[46] And while Forst would have little patience for the equivalence some of these historians draw between toleration and persecution as alike forms of 'charitable hatred',[47] their shift in focus from the 'vertical' dimension of toleration as a relationship between states and subjects to its 'horizontal', interpersonal dimension as a social practice of coexistence would seem highly congenial to his own understanding of toleration as a virtue and duty we owe as persons and citizens to our fellow justifying beings.

In doing so, however, these historical accounts highlight contexts conspicuously absent from Forst's narrative – contexts one might think should be more central, given his stated normative and methodological commitments. As an intellectual historian, Forst considers his historical thinkers in the context of the high-level political and religious controversies of the pre- and early modern European 'states' in which they lived. As an example, consider *TiC*'s fifth chapter on 'Natural Law, Toleration, and Revolution' which canvasses early English defenders of toleration, including Locke, before turning to Pierre Bayle. It begins with a potted history of Church–state relations in England from the Reformation to the Civil War, before turning to more and less detailed discussions of works by the Levellers Overton and Walwyn, then John Milton, William Penn and Roger Williams before turning to Locke. Locke is sandwiched, in turn, by a chronology of his own many writings on toleration, followed by a legal overview culminating in what Forst refers to as the 1689 'Toleration Act' and the deficient 'permission' model it instituted. We then turn to the relative retreat of toleration in France, from which Bayle fled and his brother was killed, as the context for his own *Dictionnaire* and *Philosophical Commentary*.[48]

That these summaries would not placate a historian will not come as a shock to Forst – the question is, rather, what are they *doing* for his narrative beyond lending some colour or context to the works produced? Presumably, the point is a deeper one about the relationship between theory and practice, but the method of juxtaposition does little to spell out the concrete connections in each case. Forst is too sophisticated to peddle the old Whig line that the so-called Toleration Act (actually entitled 'An Act for Exempting their Majestyes Protestant Subjects dissenting from the Church of England from the Penalties of certaine Lawes') put Locke's 'theory' into 'practice' (it did not). Yet how Locke's own thinking was shaped by not only the *laws* and formal *policies*, but also the social *practices*, of toleration of his day – not only as a young man in Interregnum Oxford, Restoration London, and then in exile around the Netherlands (in which Church–state settlements looked quite a bit different in Antwerp than they did in Rotterdam or

Amsterdam), or how he practised it himself – go unexplored. The same can be said of Forst's favourite, Bayle. How did these men experience toleration? What sort of difference did they encounter in their own lives, in which contexts, and how might this have informed how they envisioned the demands of their different 'respect' conceptions – and where they drew the line?[49]

Such a fine-grained and humanistic form of contextualism would be difficult to do on the scale of Forst's ambitions. But surely, if it is to tell us anything about 'social reality' and the actual '*power* of justifications' (both as arguments and narratives), as Forst suggests, intellectual history must have some contact with social and cultural history, as well. More particularly, if theories and practices of justification must be considered together as he suggests – and with an eye out for radical breaks with what came before – Forst's neglect of the British colonies of North America is particularly strange. The various 'experiments' with toleration (and persecution) conducted there took place in the face of 'deep' religious, cultural and linguistic differences, in which many of his *dramatis personae* were personally and actively involved. Forget Hobbes and Locke's armchair involvement with the colonies of Virginia and Carolina! When Forst discusses Penn and Williams (the founders of Pennsylvania and Rhode Island, respectively), he does so solely in the English context.[50] This indifference to his subjects' practical engagements – and encounters with radical difference – is frustrating, but it applies in Forst's treatment of the Old World, too. For example, Michel de Montaigne travelled all around Europe and worked for years as a diplomat between Catholic and Protestant factions in France, dealing with difference and practising toleration daily, while writing the *Essais*, but for Forst his understanding of toleration is a product of modern scepticism and new forms of subjectivity developed against a 'backdrop' of political and religious upheaval.[51]

To make clear: my point is not to fault Forst for failing to make a long book even longer, but rather to note, *given his commitments*, what perhaps should have made it in. Despite his stated aims, Forst's history remains highly theoretical. What 'counts' as context is captured in a series of high-altitude snapshots of state laws and policies (and the political elites behind them[52]), which then feature mainly as *inputs* of the theories that follow. These develop in a largely *reactive* way as demands for further justification. Yet this approach is strange for a number of reasons – first, it seems at odds with Forst's insistence that we ourselves are participants in the history we recount.[53] In his own history, however, the only vantage points open to us are those of the philosopher or the politician, which are presented as fundamentally separate.

This clearly undersells the practical purchase of toleration theory in the medieval and early modern periods, and indeed vice versa. Yet grappling with the complexities of this interaction would complicate the two-track narrative Forst, in fact, pursues. After the Stoics, he treats the 'practice' side of toleration throughout as purely a top-down matter of law and state (or Church) policy, rather than the first- and inter-personal (and extra-legal) everyday business of 'unmurderous' coexistence.[54] When the interpersonal *is* re-introduced, it comes (via Kant) through the 'legislative' point of view, whereafter the two tracks are united through the – mainly theoretical – democratisation of the modern state. This is in keeping both with Forst's theory of modernisation as a dual process of rationalisation (both of politics and morality) *and* his theoretical commitment that 'the decisive perspective from which the issue of toleration should be dealt with is that of the citizens as *legislators*, who ... are simultaneously the *subjects* of these laws'.[55] Yet it obscures the wide array of other, more pressing, perspectives from which even we moderns are called upon to tolerate every day. And given this, one might also worry that Forst's insistence that the 'correct' thing to do whenever we encounter differences or people of whom we disapprove is to imaginatively adopt the perspective of self-legislator may be 'one thought too many', as it were.

It seems that the salient form of toleration in such cases will remain the habitual forbearance, the mental (and physical) toughness, of 'putting up' with it and not asking why.[56] Yet Forst worries that such habits of sufferance are vestiges of the retrograde 'permission' conception, and as such, they must be something we will – or should – outgrow. As a matter of political theory, I am not so sure;[57] but certainly as a matter of intellectual history, *thinking* about and *doing* toleration in this way, every day, represented a highly salient context for the production of the early and late (and indeed post-) modern theories Forst canvasses. His decision to leave it out suggests a worrying pre-determination as to what the 'trajectory' of modernity must be.

IV Forst's *Fundamenta*

But of course, we *do* know what the trajectory of modernity must be, and Forst owns as much: it is the discovery and ever-more-rigorous application of the respect conception of toleration, grounded in the basic right to justification. Forst will later call this his '*fundamentum inconcussum*' or unshakeable foundation.[58] While many commentators have noted that for a purported anti-foundationalist and constructivist, Forst talks a lot about foundations,[59] his particular choice of words here is highly suggestive.

Pace Descartes: as a student of the long history of toleration, Forst knows full well that the *fundamenta*, or 'fundamentals', were one half of a key distinction made by 'eirenic' writers such as Erasmus and Sebastian Castellio (building on medieval theologians like Abelard and Ramon Llull),[60] so-called for their desire to restore concord to Christendom by reconciling Protestants to the Catholic Church. These writers distinguished the 'fundamentals' of faith from 'things indifferent' or *adiaphora*. While Aquinas and others adapted this initially Stoic distinction to separate actions that were intrinsically evil, like blasphemy, from neutral ones like plucking a blade of grass, after the Reformation Erasmus and others revived the Stoic emphasis on the indifference of 'externals' to stress that the *fundamenta* of Christianity lay in the sincerity of our beliefs *in foro interno*, along with sacraments like baptism and communion with an explicit basis in Scripture. As Forst himself notes, this was a way of restoring harmony to the Church by seeking unity in diversity and stressing that the differences on the basis of which Luther and other heretics justified schism were, strictly speaking, indifferent. Thus, they could be afforded 'latitude' because they were not worth disagreeing about at all.[61]

The same move would be made in later debates by proponents and critics of toleration alike. The latter saw latitude as an effective way of bringing in (or 'comprehending') as many dissenters as possible within the state Church, leaving only a weak and eminently persecutable remnant outside. The most infamous example is Hobbes's peculiarly minimalist form of Christianity in which the belief that 'Jesus is the Christ' and sacramental obedience to the Sovereign were the only *fundamenta*. Forst calls out the Enlightenment (and Kant) for effectively secularising this 'humanist ideal of religious unity' and so reintroducing intolerance of 'superstition' in their efforts to unite mankind through the *fundamenta* of Reason and 'rational religion' as a basis for morality.[62] Faced with the same charge, Forst argues that his *fundamentum* is (foundationally) moral, not ethical, as a condition of practical reason to which all of us adhere as moral agents rather than a secular liberal creed. Like John Bowlin, however, I remain sceptical that this distinction can be made as neatly as Forst would like.[63] Moreover, I am not convinced that any purely 'moral' commitment to respecting others as justifying beings can be made to do the social and political work that Forst wants it to.[64]

To take only one example, Forst specifies a right to 'freedom of expression' as one of the first, determinate institutional implications of the right to justification.[65] But as the history of toleration shows, religious insult statutes akin to modern hate speech laws were widely adopted in the early modern period not simply as a prudential proscription of 'fighting words', but as an expression of *respect* for dissenters' 'tender consciences'. The fact that these statutes were used to persecute dissenters, in turn, does not change the fact that they were – and are still today – justified as expressions of mutual respect in Europe, and challenged on the same grounds in the United States. The difference of liberal democratic culture in both places when it comes to what 'respect' entails is a product not of reasoned arguments, but of (yes) contingent historical factors – above all the high proportion of uncivil evangelical Christians that emigrated to British North America in the seventeenth century (Europe kept the philosophers).[66]

I do not highlight this history to conflate genealogy with validity – I certainly do not think that the evangelical origins of American 'free speech fundamentalism' give us any reason to reject it. But I do consider this to be a prime example of what an engagement with history can and must do for a political theorist – namely, in helping her become self-critical about her own commitments, particularly those that function as *fundamenta inconcussa* because they seem so obvious and, well, *ours*. Forst himself recognises this in his recent pleas for the importance of interdisciplinarity: 'In order to achieve progress … it is indispensable to *de-reify* conventional philosophical definitions of concepts that suppress their practical, political character.'[67]

While Forst certainly does use history to great effect in 'de-reifying' the concept of toleration in *Toleration in Conflict*, the same cannot be said of the concept of 'respect', the meaning of which is meant to shine forth with Kantian clearness the moment it is introduced. So, too, with 'justification' (in German, *Rechtfertigung*).[68] This – as Amy Allen and Doug Thompson both note and Forst knows well – derives from the Latin *justum facere* (to make right or just).[69] This, in turn, became central to Christian soteriology; fallen human beings are 'justified' through Christ's suffering on the Cross, to which they attest or participate either through 'works' (virtuous actions and sacramental observances) or 'faith'. As a good Lutheran, it seems fitting that Forst would adopt the latter approach. Is the affirmation of the 'basic right to justification', like Hobbes's 'Jesus is the Christ', Forst's *unum necessarium* through which all our social and political sins can be made right?

Again, and all joking aside, the point of recovering the historical (or theological) contexts in which modern concepts, including Forst's own, were forged is *not* to discredit or debunk. It is, however, to highlight the (often unstated) *affective* work that these concepts do in our political theories, as specifying 'what we can agree on' as a basis for community.

Forst, like Habermas, derives the substance of the consensus underlying this creedal communion from what we are all (implicitly) committed to it by the mere act of asking for and offering justifications.[70] But the work that supposed consensus does in the theory is the same as Rawls's 'overlapping consensus' on a political conception of justice – to find unity in diversity on the basis of which diverse citizens can come together in a stable, well-ordered and respectfully tolerant society over time.[71]

V Conclusion

That Forst's preferred foundation and its corresponding conception of toleration should emerge victorious in his historical account is not surprising; in both *TiC* and in his later works, he wears his Hegelianism and Whiggery on his sleeve. Historical authors are described as 'children' or 'typical' of their time,[72] who take steps 'forward' or 'backward' relative to the preordained trajectory of the respect conception. Still here, the historically minded political theorist might worry that the historical narrative on offer is designed to satisfy our wishful thinking, containing nothing more than what we hoped or expected to find in the first place. What is the use, we might ask, of doing history *or* genealogy, if we are not going to learn anything more from our encounter with the past than what we knew already going in?

Forst might respond once more that such pre-determinations are a function of the inevitable partiality of the historian or theorist, who is by necessity a participant – and partisan – in the process she describes. Forst thinks of himself *qua* critical theorist as a partisan of emancipation. He describes those historical figures whom he credits with radically breaking from or transcending their own contexts of justification – whether Castellio, the Levellers or Pierre Bayle – as 'Progressives' and as such, they are his heroes.[73] Still, forget for a moment whether, in fact, the 'sides' in the history of toleration can be so clearly drawn.[74] Notice that this sets significant limits on what we can *learn* from an encounter with past ways of thinking and acting. Have we really nothing to learn from the persecutors, or from those who Forst identifies as tolerant in the 'incorrect' way, beyond the fact that they were wrong – and on the wrong side of history, besides?

Throughout this chapter, I have indulged myself in Forst's approach by contextualising *Toleration in Conflict* as an historical artefact and event by depicting it as both 'ahead' and 'behind' the times in which it was produced. By way of conclusion, I will simply note that, in the most important respect, Forst's 2003 tome was absolutely the child of a particular moment in the mid-1990s – that is, in the 'respect conception' itself. Forst completed his doctorate under Habermas in 1993, and while many political theorists were using the demand for 'mutual respect' as grounds for *rejecting* 'mere toleration' at that point, Forst's theory embraced an equivalence that was becoming increasingly widespread in popular discourse. This is the conflation of toleration with respect – as in the Southern Poverty Law Centre's influential 'Teaching Tolerance' programme launched in 1991, the LA Museum of Tolerance's 1993 call for tolerance as 'respect [for] human dignity', and culminating in the UNESCO Declaration of the Principles of Tolerance in 1995 that begins simply, 'Tolerance *is* respect, acceptance and appreciation of the rich diversity of our world's cultures, our forms of expression and ways of being human.'[75]

I have pushed back against this *reductio ad respectum* – the determination to turn every good thing in moral and political life into a form of neo-Kantian respect for persons – in my own work on toleration, and I am not alone.[76] My chief concern here, however, is that, as a pioneering, influential and inspirational work in my own genre of historically informed political theory (the importance of which to my own work cannot be exaggerated), *Toleration in Conflict* ultimately reifies its central concepts, and so cannot get to grips with any of the potential challenges to its preconceptions posed by the historical figures Forst surveys. It therefore rules out one of the most important and rewarding things an engagement with history *can* do. As Annabel Brett puts it: 'intellectual history does not merely unravel the structure of what we have inherited but [it] can also unearth what we have lost: ways of speaking and of seeing the world, once current, now exotic and (perhaps) full of possibility'.[77] If we close ourselves off in advance to that possibility because we already know where we are going – and who got lost along the way – really, what's the use?

Notes

1 See his *RtJ*.
2 *RtJ*, p. 61 and 'The Right to Justification: Moral and Political, Transcendental and Historical. Reply to Seyla Benhabib, Jeffrey Flynn and Matthias Fritsch', *Political Theory*, 43:6 (2015), 822–837.
3 His ambition in building this system is matched by the openness and grace with which he acknowledges his debts to others – including Jürgen Habermas (under whom Forst completed his doctorate in 1993), as well as Iris Marion Young, 'relational egalitarians' like Elizabeth Anderson and Samuel Scheffler, and John Rawls, particularly of 'the Kantian constructivism period in the early 1980s'. See Rainer Forst, 'Two Pictures of Justice', in R. Forst, *JDRJ*, pp. 7–9, and Forst, 'Reply to Seyla Benhabib, Jeffrey Flynn and Matthias Fritsch', 823.
4 See the contributions by A. Sangiovanni, A. Allen, K. Olsen, A. Laden, E. Erman and S. Caney in *JDRJ*; also S. Chambers, S.K. White and L. Ypi, 'Roundtable on Rainer Forst's *Justification and Critique*', *Philosophy and Social Criticism*, 41:3 (2015), 205–234; and S. Benhabib, M. Fritsch and J. Flynn, 'The Right to Justification by Rainer Forst', *Political Theory*, 43:6 (2015), 777–837.
5 E.g. S.K. White, 'Does Critical Theory Need Strong Foundations?', *Philosophy and Social Criticism*, 41:3 (2015), 207–211.
6 A. Allen, 'The Power of Justification', in *JDRJ*, p. 78 and S. Benhabib, 'The Uses and Abuses of Kantian Rigorism: On Rainer Forst's Moral and Political Philosophy', *Political Theory*, 43:6 (2015), 777–792.
7 R. Forst, 'A Critical Theory of Politics: Grounds, Method, and Aims. Reply to Simone Chambers, Stephen White and Lea Ypi', *Philosophy & Social Criticism*, 41:3 (2015), 228.

8 J. Habermas, *An Awareness of What Is Missing: Faith and Reason in a Post-Secular Age* (Cambridge: Polity, 2010), p. 18.
9 Forst, 'Reply to Benhabib, Flynn, and Fritsch', 827f.
10 To suggest that 'the basic claim of being respected morally is only valid within a particular ethical-cultural horizon of "European Enlightenment modernity"' within which it is supposed to have developed would be to exclude all 'people in non-European societies past and present' from emancipation and 'the realm of justification'. Forst, 'Justifying Justification: A Reply to My Critics', in *JDRJ*, p. 183.
11 Forst, 'Justifying Justification: A Reply to My Critics', p. 184.
12 Misleadingly, the central term dropped from the original subtitle (*Gehalt*) means 'meaning' or 'substance'.
13 J. Floyd and M. Stears, *Political Philosophy versus History? Contextualism and Real Politics in Contemporary Political Thought* (Cambridge: Cambridge University Press, 2011). Of course, Forst is not alone in this – John Rawls and Quentin Skinner alike have been known to cross the divide, and the Frankfurt School historically denied it.
14 Forst, *TiC*, pp. 29f., 536. As such, Forst notes that even Habermas has embraced it – see his 'Religion and Toleration from the Enlightenment to the Post-Secular Era: Bayle, Kant, and Habermas', in *N&P*, pp. 77–104.
15 Forst, *N&P*, p. 1. See also Forst, 'A Critical Theory of Politics: Grounds, Method, and Aims', 227.
16 *N&P*, p. v, my emphasis.
17 For 'historically informed' political theory, see A.R. Murphy, *Conscience and Community: Revisiting Toleration and Religious Dissent in Early Modern England and America* (University Park: Penn State University Press, 2001), p. ix and T.M. Bejan, *Mere Civility: Disagreement and the Limits of Toleration* (Cambridge, MA: Harvard University Press, 2017), p. 14.
18 *TiC*, p. 13.
19 *Ibid.*, p. 34.
20 Preston King, *Toleration*, new edn (Oxon and New York: Routledge, 2012).
21 G. Newey, *Virtue, Reason and Toleration: The Place of Toleration in Ethical & Political Philosophy* (Edinburgh: Edinburgh University Press, 1999).
22 In *N&P*, Forst will suggest that this goes for all philosophical concepts, which must be 'de-reified' through contextual inquiry. I return to this point below.

23 Forst observes that 'no other work in recent political philosophy has accorded the connection between justice and toleration greater prominence ... [and] earned a special place it he further development of the modern discourse of toleration'. *TiC*, p. 468.

24 J. Rawls, *Political Liberalism*, expanded edn (Cambridge, MA: Harvard University Press, 2005), p. xxiv. Forst cites this claim approvingly in the introduction to ch. 5, 'Natural Law, Toleration, and Revolution', *TiC*, p. 171.

25 *TiC*, p. 171.

26 See *ibid.*, ch. 12: 'The Tolerant Society', pp. 518–573.

27 See, for example, Murphy, *Conscience and Community*; G. Remer, *Humanism and the Rhetoric of Toleration* (University Park: Penn State Press, 2010); J. William Tate, *Liberty, Toleration and Equality: John Locke, Jonas Proast and the Letters Concerning Toleration* (New York: Routledge, 2016); J.R. Bowlin, *Tolerance Among the Virtues* (Princeton: Princeton University Press, 2016); Bejan, *Mere Civility*; D. I. Thompson, *Montaigne and the Tolerance of Politics* (New York: Oxford University Press, 2018).

28 J. Rawls, 'On My Religion', in Rawls, *A Brief Inquiry into the Meaning of Sin and Faith* (Cambridge, MA: Harvard University Press, 2009), p. 266; Forst, *TiC*, p. 151.

29 Forst reaffirms this point in his essay 'Religion and Toleration From the Enlightenment to the Post-Secular Era: Bayle, Kant, and Habermas', in *N&P*, pp. 77–104.

30 For the original, see H. Marcuse, 'Repressive Tolerance', in R. Paul, P. Wolff and B. Moore, *A Critique of Pure Tolerance* (Boston: Beacon Press, 1965); M. Minow, 'Putting Up and Putting Down: Tolerance Reconsidered', *Osgoode Hall Law Journal*, 28:2 (1990), 409–448; K. McClure, 'Difference, Diversity, and the Limits of Toleration', *Political Theory*, 18:3 (1990), 361–391; S. Fish, 'Mission Impossible: Settling the Just Bounds between Church and State', *Columbia Law Review*, 97 (1997), 2255; and for a late entry, W. Brown, *Regulating Aversion: Tolerance in the Age of Identity and Empire* (Princeton: Princeton University Press, 2008).

31 See A. Gutmann and D. Thompson, 'Moral Conflict and Political Consensus', *Ethics*, 101:1 (1990), 64–88, and *Democracy and Disagreement* (Cambridge, MA: Harvard University Press, 2009); Amy Gutmann (ed.), *Multiculturalism* (Princeton: Princeton University Press, 1994); M. Walzer, *On Toleration* (New Haven: Yale University Press, 1997); and A. Galeotti, *Toleration as Recognition* (New York: Cambridge University Press, 2002).

32 See his discussion of Fish in *TiC*, pp. 23–25.
33 *Ibid.*, pp. 6–7. Forst makes his own debt to Foucault explicit in his historical analysis of the permission conception over time. E.g. *TiC*, pp. 224, 236, 333, 540–541.
34 *Ibid.*, pp. 18, 31.
35 *Ibid.*, pp. 29–30 and *passim*.
36 I. Berlin, 'John Stuart Mill and the Ends of Life', in Berlin, *Four Essays on Liberty* (Oxford: Oxford University Press, 1969), p. 184.
37 Forst, *N&P*. See also his reply to Ypi in Forst, 'A Critical Theory of Politics', 226–227.
38 Forst, 'On the Concept of a Justification Narrative', in *N&P*, pp. 55f.
39 Forst, 'A Critical Theory of Politics', 226.
40 *Ibid.*, 226, and *N&P*, pp. 59–60.
41 He raises the possibility that one *might* tell the history of toleration as a history of 'the progress of reason', but declares that he will not. *TiC*, p. 13.
42 *N&P*, p. 66, my emphasis. See also the following chapter, 'On the Concept of Progress', pp. 69f.
43 *N&P*, p. 66, n. 29.
44 See, for example, J. Coffey, *Persecution and Toleration in Protestant England, 1558–1689* (New York: Longman, 2000); Murphy, *Conscience and Community*; J.R. Collins, *The Allegiance of Thomas Hobbes* (Oxford: Oxford University Press, 2005), J. Marshall, *John Locke, Toleration and Early Enlightenment Culture: Religious Intolerance and Arguments for Religious Toleration in Early Modern and 'Early Enlightenment' Europe* (New York: Cambridge University Press, 2006); A. Walsham, *Charitable Hatred: Tolerance and Intolerance in England, 1500–1700* (Manchester: Manchester University Press, 2006); and S. Sowerby, *Making Toleration* (Cambridge, MA: Harvard University Press, 2013).
45 J. Laursen and C. Nederman, *Beyond the Persecuting Society* (Philadelphia: University of Pennsylvania Press, 1998), pp. 2–4.
46 P. Zagorin, *How the Idea of Religious Toleration Came to the West* (Princeton: Princeton University Press, 2003); B.J. Kaplan, *Divided By Faith: Religious Conflict and the Practice of Toleration in Early Modern Europe* (Cambridge: Belknap Press, 2007); C. Beneke, *Beyond Toleration: The Religious Origins of American Pluralism: The Religious Origins of American Pluralism* (Oxford and New York: Oxford University Press, 2006); E. Haefeli,

New Netherland and the Dutch Origins of American Religious Liberty (Philadelphia: University of Pennsylvania Press, 2013); and S. B. Schwartz, *All Can Be Saved: Religious Tolerance and Salvation in the Iberian Atlantic World* (New Haven: Yale University Press, 2014).

47 E.g. Walsham, *Charitable Hatred*.
48 *TiC*, pp. 172–187, 209–211, 233–239.
49 What he calls 'Locke's Fear' – that promises and oaths can have no hold upon an atheist – is presented simply as an intellectual and imaginative failure in contrast with Bayle. *TiC*, pp. 223–224, 239.
50 *Ibid.*, pp. 182–185, 206–208.
51 *Ibid.*, pp. 146, 152–153. For the importance of this context, see Thompson, *Montaigne and the Tolerance of Politics*.
52 Memorable interludes feature Maria de Medici and the Holy Roman Emperor Joseph II.
53 Against Benhabib, he insists that the critical theorist must take a moral, and hence a participant's, perspective on history 'because it is *our* history. We *are* that history ... [and] have no liberty to stand outside of it'. Forst, 'Reply to Benhabib', 827–828, emphasis in the text. See also *N&P*, p. 6.
54 Of which Kaplan offers many fine examples in *Divided By Faith*.
55 *TiC*, p. 519.
56 Thompson, *Montaigne and the Tolerance of Politics*.
57 See Bejan, *Mere Civility*, ch. 5.
58 Forst, *RtJ*, p. 5.
59 Allen, 'The Power of Justification', 67; White, 'Does Critical Theory Need Strong Foundations?'
60 Discussed in *TiC*, ch. 2.
61 Bejan, *Mere Civility*, pp. 32–33.
62 *TiC*, pp. 286–313; *N&P*, p. 93.
63 Bowlin, *Tolerance Among the Virtues*, p. 49.
64 I have highlighted what I take to be the lethal vagueness of 'mutual respect' as a moral, social, and political principle – especially when it comes to questions of toleration – in *Mere Civility*. Here, I agree with Benhabib that Forst's 'criteria of reciprocity and generality are too vague and cannot lead to an agreement on a list of basic rights' – let alone indicate with any concreteness the institutional and legislative consequences they should have. Benhabib, 'The Uses and Abuses of Kantian Rigorism', 786.

65 Forst, 'Reply to Benhabib', 822.
66 Bejan, *Mere Civility*, p. 172.
67 *N&P*, p. 2.
68 This means we lose Forst's nice play on words, *Das Recht auf Rechtfertigung*, in English.
69 Allen, 'The Power of Justification', 78; Thompson, *Montaigne and the Tolerance of Politics*, ch. 3.
70 See Sangiovanni on Forst's adaptation of Habermas's use of 'speech-immanent obligations'. Andrea Sangiovanni, 'Scottish Constructivism and the Right to Justification', in *JDRJ*, pp. 42–44. The source of solidarity, on this view, becomes the shared deliberative or justificatory field.
71 Bejan, *Mere Civility*, pp. 158–159.
72 See, for example, the characterisation of Roger Williams at *TiC*, p. 185 and *passim*.
73 Forst, 'Reply to Benhabib', 828.
74 After all, in the early modern period, one man's 'persecution' (e.g. fines for recusancy) was another man's tolerationist alternative (to boring his tongue or burning him at the stake).
75 'About Teaching Tolerance', *Teaching Tolerance*, accessed 6 October 2017 (www.tolerance.org/about); 'Vocabulary and Concepts', Museum of Tolerance, Los Angeles, accessed 15 January 2020 (www.museumoftolerance.com/education/teacher-resources/vocabulary-and-concepts); and 'Declaration of Principles on Tolerance', UNESCO, accessed 22 November 2017 (http://portal.unesco.org), my emphasis. Cf. Balint, *Respecting Toleration*, p. 80, and Thompson, 'Introduction: Negotiating Toleration', in *Montaigne and the Tolerance of Politics*.
76 Bejan, *Mere Civility*; Balint, *Respecting Toleration*; Thompson, *Montaigne and the Tolerance of Politics*.
77 A. Brett, 'What is Intellectual History Now?', in D. Cannadine (ed.), *What is History Now?* (Basingstoke: Palgrave, 2002), p. 127.

3

Let's get radical: Extending the reach of Baylean (and Forstian) toleration

Chandran Kukathas

Tis pleasant enough, and very glorious to the Christian Name, to compare the Griefs of the Orthodox, and their Complaints against the Pagan and Arian Persecutions, with their Apologys for persecuting the Donatists. When one reflects on all this impartially, he'l find it amount to this rare Principle; I have the Truth on my side, therefore my Violences are good Works: Such a one is in an Error, therefore his Violences are criminal.

Pierre Bayle[1]

'Shut up!', he explained.

Ring Lardner

In *The Right to Justification* Rainer Forst tells us that that social context in which humans find themselves is called 'political' when it is 'an order of justification' – an order which consists of norms and institutions that are to govern their lives together in a justified or justifiable way.[2] The most important normative concept that applies to this order, he tells us, is that of *justice*. Justice 'overarches' every form of political community, demanding reasons why some have rights, and asking how it is determined who possesses what claims, and how persons stand in relation to one another as authors and addressees of justifications. Political and social justice, he argues, should be understood as grounded in a single right: the right to justification.[3] In his other philosophical writings, as well as in sections of *The Right to Justification*, Forst has also gone to great lengths to emphasise the significance of toleration, which he also sees as fundamental to the good society, and much of his work has been an attempt to show how important it is to adopt the right understanding of toleration if we are indeed to live in a society in which the right of justification is taken seriously. To this end, he has drawn extensively on the thought of Pierre Bayle, offering an insightful and illuminating interpretation of Bayle's theory of toleration in order to criticise not only Locke's better known arguments, but also modern-day doctrines which have unwittingly relied upon them and been led astray.

My aim in this chapter is to examine Forst's use of Bayle and to argue that he has underappreciated the force of Bayle's challenge, and the radical nature of its implications for our understanding of political order, and of the place of justice in our thinking. The issue here is not merely one of interpretation, though this is where we shall begin. The larger question at stake is the defensibility of the conception of political order that Forst wishes to elaborate. My contention is that Forst goes badly wrong in placing justice at the centre of his theoretical analysis, and in suggesting that tolerance is, in the end, a 'normatively dependent concept' – that it is not an ideal in its own right but a 'virtue of justice'.[4] Taking Bayle seriously has important, and radical, implications for the way we think about justice, and politics more broadly. While Forst has begun to see Bayle's importance, he has turned away from him at the critical juncture and gone back to the more conventional understanding of politics he looked like challenging.[5]

I begin in section I with an account of Bayle's theory of toleration, drawing attention to the distinctiveness of his view, and reviewing the main objections that have been raised against him both by his contemporaries and by modern commentators. In section II, I turn to Forst's account of Bayle's contribution to show how he has sought to incorporate Bayle's thought into a deeper understanding of toleration. Section III then considers Forst's theory of toleration more critically, arguing that he has not embraced Bayle to the extent necessary for the incorporation to be of any great consequence. Section IV then goes on to argue that the root of the problem lies with the subordination of toleration to justice and offers reasons for thinking that toleration is not a virtue of justice but supplies the foundations for justice. Section V then goes on to suggest that this requires thinking about justice in a very different way, one which gives it a much more modest place in our thinking about political order generally. I conclude with some wider reflections on where this leaves Rainer Forst's conception of justice as the right to justification.

I Pierre Bayle's theory of toleration

Bayle's theory of toleration arises out of his preoccupation with the question of whether possession of the truth justifies religious persecution. He addressed this issue directly in his *Philosophical Commentary*,[6] which appeared in 1686: a time when French Huguenots were moving in their thousands to Holland to escape persecution at the hands of the Catholic state. The people Bayle addressed here included not only French Catholics but also his fellow Calvinists, both of whom held that possession of the truth *did* justify persecution, and that they would be right to use force against the other because they knew what was right while their opponents did not. Bayle held, against his religious compatriots and his persecutors alike, that all coercion in religious matters was inconsistent with reason and, so, wrong. The case for righteous persecution by the light of reason he found wanting, and the theory he proposed as an alternative was the doctrine of mutual toleration, according to which those who disagree on matters of faith, while entitled to attempt to persuade one another of what each takes to be the truth, have no right to use force to attempt to convert an erring conscience to what is asserted to be the true faith.

Bayle develops his argument through a critique of the literal (and dominant) reading of the Gospel of Luke, 14.23, which recounts a parable of a Lord who commands his servant to 'compel' his invited but reticent guests to come into his house to enjoy his hospitality. No less an authority than St Augustine had read this passage as evidence that Jesus Christ held it to be justifiable to use compulsion or force to bring unwilling people into the true church. Bayle, however, insists that the only plausible interpretation of Christ's word 'compel' is not 'force' but 'persuade'. Coercion in religious matters was inconsistent with reason and inconsistent with the spirit of Christianity. The natural light of reason reveals that the use of force to bring about conversion is wrong, and Christ could not have intended by his use of the word 'compel' to suggest that he wished us to persecute.

Bayle's theory holds that reason should guide our interpretations of scripture, that the literal reading of scripture, particularly in this case, is contrary to reason, as well as to the spirit of the Gospels, causes confusion of vice and virtue, gives infidels a pretext for expelling Christians from their lands, leads to crimes in the name of Christianity, depriving it of an important argument against other religions (notably, Islam), makes the complaints of the first Christians against their persecutors invalid, and makes it impossible to end the dispute between persecutors and the persecuted. Implicit in the doctrine of compulsion is a doctrine of violence, which is, he thinks, quite contrary to Christ's teachings. Much of Part II of the *Philosophical Commentary* attempts to answer those who think either that he has exaggerated the violence implicit in compulsion, or that he has failed to appreciate the utility of violence, which is needed to preserve order (as the Fathers of the Church, and indeed, the Old Testament, recognised). The outcome is a positive theory of toleration which is an alternative to the theory of righteous persecution, and to the ideas of 'half-tolerationists' who think that '*general toleration*' is absurd.

At the core of Bayle's theory is the thought that the erroneous conscience has the same claims to respect as an enlightened one. Those who are in error have the same rights as those who are blessed with true understanding if they are sincere in their belief in the rightness of their convictions. Disputes between one and the other cannot be resolved by invoking the superior rights of truth because the truth is precisely what is disputed. Each therefore has an equal claim to toleration by the other.

Since one must be in error, the erroneous conscience must have a claim equal to that of the enlightened one.

Central to Bayle's thinking is his view that an act is never more sinful than when it is undertaken in the conscious belief that it is wrong. An innocent act of wrongdoing is excusable; an otherwise right act is contemptible if committed in the belief that it is wrong. This does not, however, mean that one can evade responsibility for wrongdoing by trying to remain ignorant. Wilful negligence and self-deception can be grave sins which render a person culpable even when his actions are the result of error. Equally, it is seriously wrong to force, or even tempt, a person to go against his conscience, whether by threat or inducement. In the end, our actions must be judged not by their real qualities but by our intentions – by our purity of heart. Sincerity is more important than truth.

Persecution, and intolerance or half-toleration more broadly, is not tenable because any principle of persecution will always rebound upon the orthodox. If the case for intolerance is sound, it can be deployed equally effectively by the heretic. In Part III of the *Philosophical Commentary*, Bayle shows this is something St Augustine failed to appreciate, at least in his later writings: the consequence of his doctrine of intolerance could only be to arm all sects against one another.

Now, Bayle's theory does confront two serious difficulties. The first is a problem of internal consistency: having insisted at the outset that reason should be our guide, and that we are blessed by God with access to its natural light, how can he then coherently assert that disputes between truth and error are incapable of resolution? Indeed, if he thinks that reason can reveal to us that persecution is wrong, why can it not also reveal to us other truths? According to Walter Rex, by the end of Bayle's argument 'the criterium of natural light has virtually disappeared and the fallible but absolute judgment of conscience has been put in its place.'[7] He had begun by maintaining the priority of philosophy over theology, but in the end his rationalism gave way to fideism, if not complete scepticism. The second is a problem of plausibility, arising out of paradox. If we are indeed obliged to act as conscience dictates, because to act against conscience is to sin, then the person who sincerely believes that he ought to use force to compel religious obedience, does not sin in persecuting – and indeed is obliged to persecute. 'The argument of the erring conscience has now worked back upon itself and partially destroyed Bayle's argument for tolerance.'[8]

In Rex's judgement, Bayle was not able to resolve the problems at the heart of his doctrine and his contribution was in laying the groundwork for future defences of toleration – by developing arguments, refuting objections and suggesting routes down which later writers might travel. Thus, for example, Diderot was able to uphold the principle of toleration by asserting that intolerance was unjust, cruel, immoral, and an insult to piety and to human dignity. Bayle could not make such a move, constrained as he was by the need to work with traditional Christian concepts.[9] In the end, 'the theme of tolerance had to await the age of Enlightenment to come into its own'.[10]

Is this really the full extent of Bayle's contribution to the understanding of toleration: paving the way for the (very different) theories to come? In fact, Bayle's theory of toleration is more robust than Rex suggests, and what he provides is not merely a clearing in which to construct a philosophy of toleration but a doctrine that is distinctive and compelling in its own right. The real question, as we shall see, is whether we are prepared to embrace that theory and its implications, for its radical nature makes it difficult to accept without at the same time abandoning a number of settled convictions which are built into our way of thinking.

To see this, we should begin by recognising that Bayle's theory neither rests upon nor descends into scepticism. Leave aside that Bayle always rejected scepticism, not merely in religion but in general.[11] We have the capacity to reason and to discern truths, including truths of morality, and Bayle repeatedly returns to this theme in the *Philosophical Commentary* after devoting the first part to the defence of the natural light as a gift of God. Yet this is not to say that we are infallible, that we can come to discern the truth without effort, or that we can spare ourselves the burden of careful and painstaking inquiry when the truth is at issue. Once we recognise this, it becomes clear that the possibility of knowledge does not imply the impossibility, or even the unlikelihood, of disagreement or error. Equally, the possibility of knowing the truth supplies the warrant for continuing to examine and re-examine matters more closely when things look uncertain, or when disagreement persists.

If we can know the truth through the exercise of reason, and yet we also regularly disagree about the truth, Bayle's theory tells us, the right course of action cannot be for one of us to demand that the other accept his understanding of the truth, much less for one to try to compel acceptance of a particular view. If it is reason that enables us to find the truth, and at least one party has not seen it, the answer can only be to resort to further exercise of our capacity for reason. The fact of disagreement does not undermine or contradict Bayle's claim that we have the capacity to know the truth through reason; on the contrary, if there were no disagreement it would be a better conjecture that truth is not the outcome of rational inquiry. Bayle sees truth as the outcome of a process to which reason is central; and reason could have no role unless there is something with which to engage and overcome in the pursuit of truth: error. To engage our capacity for reason, however, we must disengage our capacity for (and propensity to) violence. The exercise of force is inconsistent with the exercise of reason.

Bayle's theory of toleration is a theory of mutual forbearance from the exercise of violence, one against the other. It is necessary to make reasoning possible. But how are we to establish that our efforts at reasoning have reached a successful conclusion? When does reasoning end? Implicit in Bayle's view is that it does not, for it is an ongoing *process* rather than a *procedure* or technique.[12] Conclusions of reason are themselves only aspects of the process of reasoning, for they do not terminate the activity and remain themselves open to further assessment, challenge and modification.

It is with this in mind that we should consider Bayle's attitude to the conscientious persecutor. If it is sinful to do what one holds to be wrong, the righteous persecutor who does sincerely hold that he ought to persecute is indeed obliged to persecute. If he declined to do so despite his conviction he would act immorally, even if rightly. Our attitude towards him should be one of disapproval for his moral weakness, tempered with relief that his weakness has prevented him from doing wrong. On the other hand, if the righteous persecutor wished to act on his convictions, particularly if he has not tried to deceive himself in order to indulge a wicked desire, we have to respect the sincerity of his conviction even as we ought to try to persuade him of the error of his thinking. Our response to the persecutor, conscientious or vicious, should be to resort to reason. If we think the persecutor is in the wrong and is not amenable to reason, we would then be justified in taking action to prevent him from persecuting others. Indeed, if we ourselves are convinced (conscientiously believe) that we ought to persecute the persecutor, then we do not sin if we exercise force in this way (as we are indeed obligated to do).

Is this view as implausible or as self-contradictory as some, like Rex, have suggested? Let me suggest that Bayle's view is essentially sound, even if he does err at the critical moment. His error, however, is not the one Rex identifies but an error of an entirely different kind.

Bayle is right to the extent that he says that we should always return to reason. Even when confronted by those who decline to do so, our first recourse must be to reason, which means that we must tolerate – we must resist the temptation to use force. If we take reason at all seriously, we must assume that it has the capacity to illuminate and to persuade. He is also right to suggest that we can only rightly act as conscience dictates and that this imperative ought to be respected inasmuch as we ought not to try to force people to act against conscience. To say otherwise would be to imply that it would be acceptable to tell people to do wrong (as against trying to persuade them that they are mistaken about what they think is right). The tension that now arises is between two seemingly incompatible propositions: the first that reason should guide us, the second that conscience should. What if they tell us different things?

Rex's conclusion is in effect that the problem cannot be solved until we accept that toleration has its limits, which can be identified by reason. Reason can tell us that intolerance is unjust, and an insult to human dignity, so those who wish to persecute even in all sincerity have no claim upon our patience. Otherwise we would have to tolerate the intolerant.[13] What I think Bayle senses, however, is that reason cannot settle the limits of toleration to the extent that it licenses the use of force to establish those limits. Reason cannot legislate: it cannot serve to justify the use of violence.

Now, Bayle does not argue this explicitly, which is why Rex concludes that Bayle's thought is a failed attempt to defend toleration within a Christian framework, but one that brilliantly illustrates the tension between reason and faith in the theology of the time. The Enlightenment resolved the tension by invoking reason to put faith (in this case in the form of the persecuting religious authority) in its place.

Yet perhaps Bayle did not go down this route because he could discern (however dimly) its difficulties. The main difficulty is what to do when these conclusions of reason are challenged by others whose reasoning leads to altogether different results. Bayle's commitments to the principle of respect for conscience, and to the idea that reason reveals to us the wrongness of using force rather than persuasion to change belief, make it difficult for him to think reason could justify the suppression of reason.

The one mistake Bayle makes, if this analysis is correct, is to argue that it would be justifiable to use force to prevent the attempt by some to persecute others, even if it would not be justified to use force to change the minds of persecutors. If force cannot be justified by a claim to be in possession of the truth, it is hard to see how the use of force can be justified in any circumstances.

If this is indeed the thought behind Bayle's overall argument, its implications are radical and significant. The use of violence could never be justified by appeal to reason. Even if the proclaimed purpose of violence were to be to uphold reason it would not be justified. Claiming to have truth on one's side is of no use when the truth is the subject of contention. To offer truth as a justification is to beg the question. In order to appreciate just how significant is this argument of Bayle's we should look more deeply into his theory of toleration. The best way of doing this would be to look at Rainer Forst's reading of Bayle, which does much to establish just how important Bayle is.

II Rainer Forst on Bayle on toleration

Rainer Forst is one of the few contemporary thinkers writing on toleration (and justice) to have recognised the distinctiveness and significance of Bayle's theory. For our purposes, however, what is important is that Forst attributes to Bayle responsibility for the development of a particular conception of toleration he describes as the reflexive conception of toleration.

In the history of thought there are three prominent conceptions of toleration. The first, Forst tells us, is the 'permission conception', according to which 'toleration is a relation between an authority and a dissenting, "different" minority (or various minorities)'.[14] Toleration here means that the authority or majority gives qualified permission to the minority to live as they wish provided it accepts the dominant position of the authority or majority. The Edict of Nantes, the Toleration Act after the Glorious Revolution of 1689, and the Toleration Patents of Joseph II in 1781 were examples of this kind of toleration. Toleration here is non-reciprocal – the more powerful party simply condones the activity of the weaker. Toleration is a grant from the powerful to the powerful to the powerless, but is nonetheless a form of exercising and preserving power.[15]

The second form of toleration Forst calls the 'respect conception', according to which the tolerating parties recognise one another in a reciprocal, 'horizontal' way, despite their differences. Historically, this respect was grounded in some kind of shared moral conception, such as a notion of individual rights that persons shared by nature. This notion of toleration was, however, circumscribed by these moral conceptions, and those who did not share in the relevant moral understanding could not claim them. Thus, those who were atheists, typically, could not claim a right to toleration since atheists could not claim the rights that were accorded to those who belonged to the community of believers. Toleration here depended upon a shared morality.[16]

In an earlier paper Forst suggested that there were two other conceptions of toleration also worth noting. There was the *coexistence conception* of toleration, in which the object of toleration was to secure peace, understood as a *modus vivendi* among similarly powerful groups.[17] And there was the *esteem conception*, which requires a stronger level of respect amounting to esteem for the ways of life of the other parties.[18]

Bayle, Forst suggests, introduced an altogether new understanding of toleration. Locke, and other 'respect' theorists of toleration, had excluded atheists and Catholics from among the tolerable for fear that their beliefs kept outside the realm of common morality. Bayle, however, suggested that no such common conviction was necessary, for even a society of atheists was possible. Mutual toleration was possible among people of different religious beliefs, who could nonetheless share convictions about mutual respect that ruled out the exercise of force to compel religious belief. Bayle's justification for toleration, Forst argues, avoids the weaknesses in the liberalisms of Locke, Mill and, more recently, Kymlicka, because it does not require any commitment to a particular view of personal autonomy as a precondition of the good life. Grounding toleration in autonomy, Forst maintains, makes it difficult to tolerate traditional ways of life that do not exhibit the right kinds of autonomy.[19] What Bayle offers is a theory of toleration that is not subject to these difficulties.

Bayle's theory, according to Forst, is a reflexive theory that is a kind of combination of the permission and respect conceptions. Politically, it is like the permission conception, but socially it calls for the toleration of respect. Bayle's understanding of toleration was able to make room for the toleration of atheists, and also to do what Locke struggled to do in his first *Letter concerning Toleration*: supply an answer to the challenge of Proast (who was himself only rehearsing St Augustine) who argued that intolerance could indirectly serve to secure the good by creating the conditions under which the right doctrines might be adopted.

Bayle's greatness has, for most of the history of political thought, gone unrecognised. One of Forst's most important contributions has been to recover his insights and to try to incorporate them into a modern analysis. So far so good.

Sadly, however, Forst goes one step too far (or has one thought too many). Having rescued Bayle's contribution from relative obscurity, he proceeds to interpret it in a way that deprives it of much of its critical power, and turns toleration from a revolutionary into a cautious, and even conservative, doctrine. We need to consider why, and how.

III Forst's theory of toleration

Forst wants to offer what he calls a neo-Baylean justification of toleration, which he thinks is superior to others for being a *reflexive* conception. Rather than resting on a particular idea of salvation or notion of the good, it is grounded on the very principle of justification, 'a higher-order principle of the demand to give adequate reasons for claims in the political realm'.[20] It is at this point, however, that Forst abandons the spirit of Bayle's enterprise, and forgoes an opportunity to take the theory of toleration down the more radical, critical, path Bayle's theorising revealed.

The Bayle that Forst presents is a Bayle who has been Kantianised and Rawlsified in the course of an attempt to address the question: what are the limits of toleration?[21] Another way of presenting this question would be to say: when, or for what reasons, may we cease to tolerate? For the question itself implies that there are limits; the issue is, where do they lie? Forst's answer, in a nutshell, is that we may do so when we have justified our actions to others. Herein lies the problem; as we shall see.

How are we to justify ceasing to tolerate? To answer this question, we need first to understand why we need such a justification. Forst's explanation begins by identifying three paradoxes of toleration: the paradox of the tolerant racist, the paradox of moral tolerance, and the paradox of drawing the limits.[22] We should consider these in turn.

The paradox of the tolerant racist arises when we are forced to concede that the racist who curbs his desire to discriminate against 'inferior races' is virtuous, since he has behaved 'ethically' by suppressing his prejudices. Indeed the more racist his convictions, the more virtuous he will turn out to be for being tolerant. But this understanding of toleration turns blind prejudice into an ethical judgement and is surely not acceptable, according to Forst. We need therefore to start not with irrational prejudice and hatred but with judgements that have an intelligible and acceptable basis before we can talk of tolerance. Racists cannot exemplify the virtue of tolerance.[23]

The paradox of moral tolerance arises if both the reasons for objection and the reasons for acceptance are called 'moral', for then it seems that it is morally right to tolerate what is morally wrong. It would become morally right to tolerate immoral acts, such as racists attacks, for example. Solving this paradox requires making some kind of distinction between different kinds of 'moral' reasons, 'some of which must be reasons of a higher order that cannot be trumped and which ground and limit toleration'.[24]

The paradox of drawing the limits arises out of the idea that, 'since toleration is a matter of reciprocity, those who are intolerant need not and cannot be tolerated'.[25] But this idea, Forst says, is not only vacuous but dangerous, for the definition of intolerant is all too often one-sided and intolerant. Moreover, since those who are intolerant of the intolerant are themselves, by definition, intolerant and so deserving of intolerance. In this case, toleration ends as soon as it begins.[26]

We can only find the limits to toleration, Forst argues, and recognise tolerance as a virtue, if we can draw the limits in some non-arbitrary, impartial way. 'The reasons of rejection must be morally justified reasons.'[27] From this he draws a critically important conclusion: toleration is a normatively dependent concept. 'By itself it is too empty and indeterminate to answer the question about the character of the reasons of objection, acceptance, and rejection.'[28] It needs to draw on other resources if it is to have any substance, content and limits. What this means is that it has to rely on a conception of *justice*. Toleration is not a virtue in its own right, but a normatively dependent concept – one that depends on a conception of justice.

It is at this point that Forst's theory of justice takes centre-stage: the theory of justice as the right to justification. Justice circumscribes the limits of toleration.

The question, however, is whether toleration in this account has a role of any consequence or is a virtue of any great significance. What work does toleration do in this moral universe? And where, one might ask, is Bayle?

The answer, I think, is that toleration is of no great significance, and has entirely lost purpose and, so, its lustre. As for Bayle, he's gone back to Rotterdam, to continue writing books no one would read. Or is turning over in his grave.

If we accept Forst's account of the relationship between justice and toleration, there is nothing for toleration to do. All the work is done by justice. In the theory of social and political morality, toleration is superfluous. It remains a virtue to be sure, but one with about as much importance as punctuality, being well-groomed, and charm.[29]

The only issue now is whether this matters. In the first issue of the *Journal of Political Philosophy*, in a paper entitled 'Autonomy as a Good: Liberalism, Autonomy and Toleration', Deborah Fitzmaurice argued that it did not. Once we realise that the good of autonomy guides our assessment of how to regulate relations among citizens, toleration becomes quite unnecessary. There's no sense in getting excited about a normatively dependent concept.

But I thought then that Fitzmaurice was wrong in explicitly prioritising autonomy to the exclusion of toleration, and think now that

Forst is wrong inadvertently to eviscerate toleration by subordinating it to justice. We need to consider why.

IV Justice and toleration

Toleration is not the handmaid (or the butler or batman) to justice but is itself the master principle. Toleration is in play when people resist the temptation to exercise power, particularly in the form of force or violence, to alter the conduct or circumstances of others whose activity is deemed unacceptable. To tolerate is to decline to suppress or censure that of which one disapproves. Why is this principle fundamental?

I think Bayle saw that it is fundamental because to exercise force is to abandon reason, and a commitment to reason and reasoning is fundamental if right conduct is our intention. And right conduct has to be our intention if we are to be moral. Acting rightly means acting according to conscience; but acting according to conscience does not mean indulging our whims and behaving capriciously – it means acting according to what we genuinely *think* to be right. Reason is therefore vital if we are to act conscientiously. Reason cannot be in play, however, when force is exercised. Force must be forsworn for reason to hold sway, and the condition in which force is held at bay is a condition of toleration.

This is a very powerful idea, which is, in fact, given clearer expression in Kant in his discussion of "The Discipline of Pure Reason in Respect of its Polemical Employment".[30] According to Kant, reason depends for its workings – for its very survival – on the existence of a realm of freedom: a realm in which criticism of or challenge to even the conclusions reached through reason itself can never be suppressed. He writes:

> Reason must in all its undertakings subject itself to criticism; should it limit freedom of criticism by any prohibitions, it must harm itself, drawing upon itself a damaging suspicion. Nothing is so important through its usefulness, nothing so sacred, that it may be exempted from this searching examination, which knows no respect for persons.

Reason depends on this freedom for its very existence. For reason has no dictatorial authority; its verdict is always simply the agreement of free citizens, of whom each one must be permitted to express, without let or hindrance, his objections or even his veto.[31]

This realm of freedom is nothing less than a condition of toleration. It is a condition in which force may not be exercised to suppress any contention, criticism or challenge, for it is a condition in which no power has the authority to suppress any idea. There is nobody to whom one might appeal to suppress any dissenting idea: not to the majority opinion, nor to the views of an elite, nor even to reason itself – for Reason, like the Pope, has no divisions, and no authority to enforce anything. Such authority as reason possesses it does in virtue of its recognition by persons who are free to subject any of its determinations to critical scrutiny. Reason, in Kant's account, as Onora O'Neill explains, 'has no transcendent foundation, but is rather based on agreement of a certain sort. Mere agreement, were it possible, would not have any authority. What makes agreement of a certain sort authoritative is that it is agreement based on principles that meet their own criticism. The principles of reason vindicate their authority by their stamina when applied to themselves'.[32] Criticism, and the toleration criticism needs if it is to be sustained, are essential if the authority of reason is itself to be sustained. Indeed, in Kant's thought, the 'development of reason and of toleration is interdependent ... Practices of toleration help to constitute reason's authority'.[33]

It is important to recognise here that this argument for the importance of toleration is not, like John Stuart Mill's, for example, an argument about the tendency of toleration and free discussion to lead to the truth. Nor is it an argument that toleration will enable us to grasp truth more securely, say, by coming to a greater awareness of still-defended falsehoods. Even as Kant insisted that 'there can, properly speaking, be no polemic of pure reason',[34] he was all too aware of the existence of 'disingenuousness, misrepresentation, and hypocrisy even in the utterances of speculative thought, where there are far fewer hindrances to our making, as is fitting, frank and unreserved admission of our thoughts, and no advantage whatsoever in acting otherwise.'[35] It is not an argument that toleration is a useful convention. Toleration is necessarily involved in any context in which reason operates. And reason is banished when toleration is compromised or abandoned.

Because this is not a consequentialist argument, it does not depend upon contingent or empirical considerations. It cannot be argued, for example, that mild intolerance will not undermine reason, just because a single infraction cannot bring down the entire edifice of reason. But that is not the point. The point is that a condition of tolerance defines the existence of reason. Analogously, we might say that an absence of fighting defines the existence of peace. To be sure, one small fight will not necessarily bring an end to an enduring peace within or among nations, but it remains true that if there is fighting there is, in that context, no peace. Where there is no tolerance, there is, in that context, no reason – only force.

This brings us to the issue of what 'toleration to uphold reason' might amount to in practical terms. There is toleration that upholds reason when there is no force exercised to impede the communication among persons that is essential to the working of reason. It is worth bearing in mind here that the mere absence of force impeding communication does not mean that such communication will always produce good results. Reasoners may be in the grip of error or may simply reason poorly. Moreover, as Kant noted, people are prone to be deceitful, and misrepresent not only themselves but also their most speculative thoughts. Yet 'what could be more prejudicial to the interests of knowledge than to communicate even our very thoughts in a falsified form, to conceal doubts which we feel in regard to our own assertions, or to give an appearance of conclusiveness to grounds of proof which we ourselves recognize to be insufficient'.[36] Nonetheless, reason is upheld when force is eschewed; and in the end, it will only be through processes of reasoning that error, deceit and sophistry are identified.

But what does it mean to say that force is not exercised? It means that no physical power is brought to bear on a person to compel him to accept the rightness of a determination he disputes, or to perform an action he repudiates. When no force is exercised to compel belief or action, we might say that the principle of toleration is obeyed to the letter and reason holds sway. However, it is only when we also eschew more subtle forms of the exercise of power – deceit, manipulation, cajolery – that the principle of toleration is obeyed in spirit, and reason is upheld or honoured.

This argument in favour of toleration defends it by describing it as that moral stance which is most consistent with a respect for reason. It takes a stance that forswears the use of force in favour of rational engagement: dialogue in favour of censure, persuasion in favour of suppression. Another way to look at the matter would be to say that toleration is a doctrine of peace. What requires further explanation, however, is precisely what kind of peace this might be.

Peace may come in many forms, yet not all are equally secure or equally desirable. The peace of the graveyard, as Kant intimated, can be nothing more than a satirical notion,[37] as would be the peace that followed a nuclear holocaust. Equally, the peace endured by a terrorised populace would scarcely be worth commending, even if it were a peace of sorts. The peace of toleration is not the peace of exhaustion, nor the peace of cowed submission. The peace of toleration is the peace of reason: the peace that obtains when there is a commitment to resolving all questions not by resort to force but by recourse to reasoning.

Now, the temptation here is to say that this condition of toleration, which is also, by its very nature, a condition of peace, is best accounted for as a construction of justice. This thought should be resisted. The initial problem with regarding toleration as given shape and content by justice is that this is inconsistent with a proper conceptual understanding of toleration. To tolerate is to refrain from suppressing that of which one does not approve. Justice, by its nature, must be something of which we approve. If justice determines the boundaries or the scope of toleration, then toleration becomes a requirement that we only accept that of which we approve and may rightly suppress that of which we do not approve. If this is the case, then toleration becomes redundant. If toleration means doing what justice demands, it has to mean not accepting – tolerating – that of which we do not approve. Now, to be sure, this only means not accepting – tolerating – one particular class of those things of which we do not approve: those things we define as unjust. But this is a pretty important class. The move to define toleration in terms of justice thus would, at best, turn toleration into a demand that we not suppress things of which we do not seriously disapprove. And it would turn toleration into a relatively insignificant virtue, if it remained a virtue at all.

But there is still more at stake than this. Toleration is important not because we sometimes disagree about trivial matters but because we often disagree about things that are of fundamental significance. It is important because we often disagree about how we should live: because we disagree about justice. (To relegate toleration to the status of the virtue of accepting trivial differences with others would be to trivialise toleration.) Toleration cannot simply be a matter of justice because we actually disagree about what is justice. The question is: What should we do when we disagree about justice? The answer implicit in the doctrine of toleration is that we should not seek to enforce our view of justice when we are powerful enough to do so.

Now it might be retorted at this point: but surely we will disagree about toleration no less readily than we will disagree about toleration – about its value and its scope? An appeal to toleration does not resolve the problem of moral disagreement. Yet this is where the analysis of toleration as an aspect of a commitment to reason and to peace becomes crucial. For what toleration demands is that, in the face of disagreement, we retreat to reason – or, better still, we refuse to retreat from our commitment not to abandon reason. It demands that we resist the temptation to use power to suppress those views with which we disagree, even if we regard them as unjust. Confronted between a choice of upholding (what we think is) justice and upholding reason, we choose reason. Every time. What this means is that, in the face of serious disagreement we opt not to use force to bring about the arrangements we would like to see but continue to reason with those with whom we disagree. We opt not to return to the state of nature or the state of war: that state in which reason and reasoning have no public place or standing.

But does this mean that a commitment to toleration must also mean abandoning any commitment to justice? Does it mean that we simply confront an invidious choice: justice or toleration? In the end, that is not quite how matters should be viewed; for there is also reason why a commitment to justice itself demands a commitment to toleration. If justice is, as Plato tried to show, not simply the view of the stronger but the construction of reason, a commitment to justice would require a determination not to yield to the temptation to abandon reason in favour of force. A commitment to justice cannot mean refusing to tolerate disagreement about justice; it can only mean tolerating even what one regards as unjust so as not to abandon the condition that makes the pursuit of justice possible. This means, above all, forsaking force and pursuing peace. It means forsaking force in favour of toleration. It means forsaking force in order to reason. Justice is something whose understanding can only be pursued in peace. This is not the peace of the grave; nor the peace of the truce or balance of power; nor the peace of justice (for this would give us only an empty tautology); but the peace of toleration.

V Justice and political order

The implications of this way of thinking are radical. If toleration is taken seriously, it is difficult to justify any authority with the capacity to close off discussion or bring peaceful contestation to an end by the forcible imposition of a solution. Authority brings reasoning to a halt. Even if authority is exercised after the most extensive consultation, debate and dialogue; after each and every person is offered justifications, and justifications for those justifications; after every effort is made to take seriously the objections and reservations of those to whom the justifications are offered; the fact remains that, unless the outcome of this process is complete agreement, force will be used to establish – to enforce – some conclusion. We might try to convince ourselves that those who remain unpersuaded but are compelled to submit to our conclusions have been treated justly because we have offered them justifications for our actions, and that we have taken account of their reasonable objections (ignoring only their unreasonable ones). But they will probably view our protestations of justice with Ring Lardner's quip firmly in mind: 'Shut up', they explained.

A Baylean theory of toleration takes us in a direction that would make us much more sceptical about political power, and about the exercise of force more generally. For it is not a theory of toleration that can be co-opted by justice: it is not a normatively dependent notion but fundamental. At its most radical it counsels non-violence even in the face of attack. Its tendency is not authoritarian but anarchistic. Its recommendation is not righteous self-assertion, or the pursuit of justice, or even resistance, but the injunction to 'resist not evil'. Our first duty as human beings is not, as Rainer Forst suggests, to look for constructive justifications to offer our fellows for the enforcement of justice[38] but forbearance from the exercise of violence.

What is uncertain, of course, is whether this can supply the foundation of any kind of political order. I suspect that the answer may be 'no'. But here I am inclined to say two things. First, so much the worse then for political order. Second, perhaps we should devote less time and energy to finding justifications for political order and accept that even those that claim to be just – perhaps *especially* those that claim to be just – necessarily rest on very troubling foundations.

Notes

1 P. Bayle, *A Philosophical Commentary on These Words of the Gospel, Luke 14:23*, ed. J. Kilcullen and C. Kukathas (Indianapolis: Liberty Fund, 2005), p. 134.
2 *RtJ*, p. 1.

3 *RtJ*, p. 2.
4 R. Forst, 'Tolerance as a Virtue of Justice', *Philosophical Explorations*, 4:3 (2001), 193–206.
5 I have discussed other radical implications of Bayle's thought in 'Toleration without Limits: A Reconstruction and Defence of Bayle's *Philosophical Commentary*', in C. Laborde and A. Bardon (eds), *Religion in Liberal Political Philosophy* (Oxford: Oxford University Press, 2017).
6 Bayle, *A Philosophical Commentary on These Words of the Gospel*.
7 Walter Rex, *Essays on Pierre Bayle and Religious Controversy* (The Hague: Martinus Nijhof, 1965), p. 181.
8 *Ibid.*, p. 181.
9 *Ibid.*, p. 189.
10 *Ibid.*, p. 188.
11 See the discussion in J. Kilcullen, *Sincerity and Truth: Essays on Arnauld, Bayle and Toleration* (Oxford: Oxford University Press, 1988), pp. 101f.
12 A procedure always has a definite beginning and an end. A process is open-ended.
13 I am extrapolating from Rex's discussion, which is more concerned on the whole to identify tensions in Bayle's thought than to advance a solution. However, his remarks on the advances made by Enlightenment thought I have taken to mean he favours the position I have ascribed to him. Rex does not, for example, use the language of tolerating the intolerant. Responsibility for this interpretation of Rex is mine.
14 *RtJ*, p. 140.
15 *Ibid.*
16 *Ibid.*, pp. 141f.
17 R. Forst, 'Pierre Bayle's Reflexive Theory of Toleration', in Melissa Williams and Jeremy Waldron (eds), *Toleration and its Limits*, NOMOS XLVIII (New York: New York University Press, 2008), p. 80.
18 *Ibid.*, p. 81.
19 *RtJ*, p. 145.
20 *Ibid.*, p. 149.
21 See R. Forst, 'The Limits of Toleration', *Constellations*, 11:3 (2004), 312–325.
22 Forst, 'Tolerance as a Virtue of Justice', 194–5.
23 *Ibid.*, 194–5.
24 *Ibid.*

25 *Ibid.*
26 *Ibid.*
27 *Ibid.*
28 *Ibid.*, 196.
29 One is tempted to add: Toleration has passed on. It is no more. It has ceased to be. It's expired and gone to meet its maker. It's a stiff! Bereft of life, it rests in peace. Its metabolic processes are now history. It's off the twig! It's kicked the bucket, it's shuffled off its mortal coil, run down the curtain and joined the choir invisible. It is an EX-CONCEPT.
30 I. Kant, *The Critique of Pure Reason*, trans. N.K. Smith (London: Macmillan, 1978), A739/B767–A769/B797, pp. 593–612.
31 Kant, *Critique of Pure Reason*, A739/B767, p. 593.
32 O. O'Neill, *Constructions of Reason: Explorations of Kant's Practical Philosophy* (Cambridge: Cambridge University Press, 1989), p. 38. I have not only drawn on O'Neill's discussion of Kant but also owe to her the argument that toleration is central to Kant's understanding of reason.
33 *Ibid.*, p. 39.
34 Kant, *Critique of Pure Reason*, A750/B778, p. 600.
35 *Ibid.*, A750/B778, p. 599.
36 *Ibid.*, A750/B778, p. 600.
37 I. Kant, 'Perpetual Peace', in *Kant's Political Writings*, ed. H. Reiss (Cambridge: Cambridge University Press, 1979), p. 93.
38 Forst, 'Tolerance as a Virtue of Justice', 204.

4

Tales of toleration

John Horton

Among the many significant contributions that Rainer Forst has made to political philosophy, his work on toleration has been amongst the most searching and original. Through a rich, detailed and sensitive excavation of the history of the theory (and, to a lesser extent, practice) of toleration, primarily in the West, he has developed a distinctive re-reading of that history, which then helps to shape what is a powerful philosophical and normative analysis of toleration.[1] Ultimately, if I have grasped his ambitions at all correctly, Forst seeks nothing less than a historically informed understanding of the meaning and moral basis of toleration as a political value, which when so understood can also play a substantial role in resolving, or at the very least significantly narrowing the space for legitimate disagreement about, many of the disputes concerning the requirements and boundaries of toleration in cases where these are a matter of serious contention. And, while predominantly theoretical, his work is refreshingly replete with examples of the implications of his theory for practice.

I want to begin, therefore, by readily acknowledging that Forst has unquestionably made a major contribution to rewriting the history of theorising toleration in the West. As he would be the first to accept, he is not alone in this, but nonetheless his work is, in my view, the most important and wide-ranging. In particular, he offers a distinctive and valuable corrective to an overly Anglo-centric version of the story of toleration, according to which, and admittedly caricaturing somewhat, England gave the world toleration and the United States then took it forward. It is a narrative that has been called 'the story of the three Johns', as on this view, the key figures in the story of toleration are John Locke, John Stuart Mill and John Rawls.[2] Forst's historical work provides a much more nuanced and sophisticated alternative to this unduly limited and ultimately misleading account.

A particularly notable feature of Forst's account is how, for him, it is Pierre Bayle, a somewhat marginal figure in the Anglo-centric story, rather than Locke, who provides the basis for an account of toleration that is much more relevant to a robust and defensible normative theory of toleration suitable for the contemporary world.[3] He is, perhaps, occasionally inclined to overstate the extent to which Bayle's views can be seen a forerunner of his own and, indeed, whether they are quite so radically 'advanced' compared to those of Locke. For instance, Bayle, too, clearly refused to extend toleration to Catholics when he argued that a religion that 'coerces conscience' has in turn no right to toleration, as Forst himself on at least one occasion admits.[4] More commonly, though, he omits to mention this in his predominantly upbeat portrayals of Bayle's view on toleration.[5] Moreover, it is at least arguable that Locke's reason for denying them toleration – because Catholics, and in his day not without some plausibility it should be added, were held to owe their allegiance to a foreign power – represents less of an attack on anything that is essential to Catholic religious belief than did Bayle's reasoning, which seems to strike at the heart of Catholic doctrine. However, this is largely a matter of nuance and does not in any fundamental way undermine his revisionist history of the idea of toleration in the West.

In addition to this work of historical reconstruction, which is deserving of far more attention than I am able to give it here, Forst has also done some very useful spadework by way of the currently unfashionable and underestimated task of conceptual clarification. While his account of the structure of the concept of toleration is, as he acknowledges, not very different from that of several other writers, he sets forth that structure with notable clarity and precision, and with his own particular focus. Toleration is, for Forst, an attitude or practice that is necessary and appropriate only with respect to a certain kind of social conflict. Crucially, toleration does not resolve such conflicts in the sense that the conflicting parties come to agree about what they had previously disagreed. Rather, toleration contains and moderates the conflict. The conflict is not made to disappear, but toleration defuses its social destructiveness. Toleration, therefore, makes possible peaceful coexistence among those who disagree. To see how it does this we need to understand the conceptual structure of toleration.

The three core elements in Forst's account of the structure of toleration are: the objection component, an acceptance component and a rejection component. That is: there must be an initial objection to some act or practice, but also some offsetting reasons – the acceptance component – that 'do not cancel out the negative reasons but are set against them in such a way that, although they trump the negative reasons … and in this sense are higher-order reasons, the objection nevertheless retains its force'.[6] But, in addition, the limits of toleration, the rejection component, also needs to be specified; this is 'the point where there are reasons for rejection that are stronger than the reasons for acceptance' and intolerance will be the appropriate response.[7] It is also worth remarking, as Forst elaborates, that this has the implication that in any normative discussion of toleration:

> There are *two boundaries* involved: the first lies between (1) the normative realm of those practices and beliefs one agrees with and (2) the realm of the practices and beliefs that one finds wrong but can still tolerate; the second boundary lies between this latter realm and (3) the realm of the intolerable that is strictly rejected. There are thus three, not just two normative realms in a context of toleration.[8]

Any appropriate deployment of the concept of toleration, therefore, necessarily involves distinguishing between that which is endorsed and that which is objected to but tolerable, on the one hand, and, on the other, between what can be tolerated and that which is rejected, and therefore intolerable. Although Forst does not quite put it this way himself, the tolerable can be understood as a kind of middle ground between the unobjectionable and the intolerable.

There are other conditions of toleration, such as voluntariness – toleration must be voluntary if it is to be distinguished from mere sufferance or endurance – but the only one on which I wish to comment, and which is implicit in the passage quoted earlier, is the idea that toleration is what Forst calls a 'normatively dependent concept'. By this he means:

> that by itself [toleration] cannot provide the substantive character of the reasons for objection, acceptance, and rejection. It needs further, independent normative resources in order to have a certain substance, content and limits – and in order to be regarded as something good at all. In itself, therefore, toleration is not a virtue or a value; it can only be a value if backed by the right normative reasons.[9]

For instance, one does not display the virtue of tolerance if one tolerates the intolerable or if one permits something that one disapproves of on grounds that are themselves morally objectionable. One cannot, therefore, arrive at any substantive value or virtue of toleration simply from recounting the formal properties of the concept: it is always deployed in a normative context, the content of which is supplied by norms and values other than that of toleration itself. I stress this point about the normative dependence of toleration for two reasons. First, because I believe it is both important and correct to say that judgements about toleration always stand in need of some normative content that cannot be derived from the concept itself. To be in favour of toleration in general or per se is not to be in favour of anything in particular. But, secondly, I do so because it is less clear to me that there is always something which answers to the description of 'the right normative reasons'; at least if this means, as it appears to for Forst, that there is some set of uniquely correct and cognitively ascertainable set of normative reasons that justify the proper application of the concept. It is this quest that quite specifically shapes Forst's whole understanding of the project of normatively justifying toleration. For he sees the principal normative task precisely to be one of setting out 'the right normative reasons' for toleration. That is, a normative theory of toleration, on this very ambitious agenda, should give it the right content, explaining in general terms what should be tolerated, what should not be tolerated, and why.

It is in part through the process of historical recovery and in larger part through careful normative analysis that Forst identifies four principal conceptions of toleration. These he calls: the permission conception, the coexistence conception, the respect conception (which admits of two forms – formal equality and qualitative equality) and the esteem conception. I shall very briefly explain each of them. The permission conception, which has some claim to be the classic understanding, 'designates the relation between an authority or a majority and a minority (or several minorities), which does not subscribe to the dominant system of values. Toleration here means that the authority (or majority) grants the minority the permission to live in accordance with its convictions so long as it – and this is the crucial condition – does not question the predominance of the authority (or majority)'.[10] Effectively, the authority or the dominant majority agrees to resist suppressing the minority; but that is pretty much it. In particular, there is no implication that the tolerated group has equal standing with the tolerant group.

Like the permission conception, the coexistence conception presents toleration as an appropriate means of ending or avoiding conflict and pursuing one's own ends and does not itself represent a value or rest on strong values. Toleration is justified primarily in pragmatic and instrumental terms. What changes, however, is the constellation formed by the subjects and objects of toleration. For now, an authority or majority and a minority or minorities do not confront one another but groups of approximately equal strengths who recognise that they must practice tolerance for the sake of social peace and in their own interests. They prefer peaceful coexistence to conflict and consent to the rules of a modus vivendi in the shape of a mutual compromise.[11]

Here because of the rough equality of power between the two groups, each group tolerates the other, rather than it being a one-way process.

On this conception the 'toleration relation is thus no longer a vertical one, as in the permission conception, but a horizontal one: those who exercise tolerance are at the same time also tolerated'.[12] Under both these conceptions, however, toleration essentially tracks the balance of power relations in any given situation, rather than any normative notion of reciprocity: what is fundamental is that neither the permission nor the coexistence conceptions 'lead to a form of mutual recognition which goes beyond the sufferance of others and rests on farther-reaching moral or ethical considerations'.[13]

By contrast with the permission and coexistence conceptions of toleration, the respect conception

> proceeds from a morally grounded form of mutual respect on the part of the individuals or groups who exercise toleration. The tolerating parties respect one another as autonomous persons or as equally entitled members of a political community constituted under the rule of law. Although their ethical convictions about the good and worthwhile life and their cultural practices differ profoundly and are in important respects incompatible, they recognise one another – and here an alternative with far-reaching consequences presents itself – as ethically autonomous authors of their own lives *or* as moral and legal equals in the sense that, in their view, the basic structure of political and social life common to all ... should be governed by norms which can be accepted by all citizens alike without privileging any single 'ethical community' (e.g. a religious community).[14]

The key point here is that there is an acknowledgement – recognition – by the tolerator that the tolerated have an equal moral and political standing, and not based on a mere equality of power, as in the coexistence conception. Instead, toleration is based on the idea of equality of mutual respect and recognition. This conception has two variants: formal equality and qualitative equality. The former is built on a sharp distinction between the political and the private, 'according to which ethical (i.e. cultural or religious) differences ... should be confined to the private realm, so that they do not lead to conflicts in the political sphere'.[15] This approach involves a kind of political abstinence: we keep these differences out of politics. Qualitative equality, on the other hand, requires that 'persons respect each other as political equals with a certain ethical-cultural identity that needs to be respected and tolerated as something that is (a) especially important for a person and (b) can provide good reasons for certain exceptions from or changes in existing legal and social structures'.[16] On this interpretation of the respect conception, therefore, there is no attempt to keep cultural or religious differences out of politics, but instead political processes mediate them in a manner that ensures equal respect.

Finally, there is the esteem conception of toleration, which 'involves a more demanding form of mutual recognition than the respect conception, for, according to it, toleration means not only respecting the members of other cultural or religious communities as legal and political equals but also esteeming their convictions and practices as ethically valuable'.[17] On this view, therefore, although there will necessarily still be a negative element in judging the worth of what is tolerated (as it would not be toleration at all without some negative judgement), it will also in some ways and to some degree be positively valued for what it is. The worry about this conception, of course, is that what is being expected from supposed *toleration* may be hard to distinguish from attitudes of broad approval or admiration. After all, many good things also have negative aspects among their features, yet it would seem odd in most such cases to think of these as less than unqualified goods as objects of toleration.

Of these four conceptions it is the permission and respect conceptions that are most developed in Forst's discussion of toleration, with the latter, in its qualitative form, being the conception that Forst, himself, endorses. The former functions as something of a stalking horse – sometimes, unfortunately, in practice the best that is possible, but a conception that ideally should be transcended by the respect conception. While he relates these conceptions grow out of his historical narrative about the development of ideas of toleration in the West, Forst does not tie them in any tight way to particular times and places – they are ideas that can temporally overlap and coexist and be found in a variety of different cultures and contexts. Yet, in his own words, they can also be read as embodying 'two stories about toleration, a dark and pessimistic one and a bright and optimistic one'.[18] It will come as no surprise that, for Forst, it is the permission conception that embodies the dark and pessimistic tale, while the respect conception represents the bright and optimistic story. For, whereas the permission conception, although obviously an advance on all forms of intolerance, implies the kind of hierarchical relations of dominance and subservience that led Goethe, Paine and Kant and others in the past and Wendy Brown in our own day to be highly disparaging of the very idea of toleration,[19] the respect conception enshrines a notion of reciprocity between individuals or groups that is based on a more worthy ideal of equality of persons. On this view, it is the '*moral notion of the person as a reasonable being with ... a right to justification* [that] is fundamental. This right to justification is based on the recursive general principle that every norm that is to legitimise the use of force (or more broadly speaking, a morally relevant interference with other's [sic] actions) claims to be reciprocally and generally valid and therefore needs to be justifiable by reciprocally and generally non-rejectable reasons'.[20] And, crucially, everyone is both entitled to and can be required to give such a justification.[21]

There are both normative and epistemological elements to the right to justification. As it bears on toleration, the normative component 'lies in the principle of justification itself, while the *epistemological* component consists of an insight into the finitude of reason: reason is not sufficient to provide us with the one and only, ultimate answer about the truth of the good life which would show that all other ethical beliefs are false'.[22] This is the key to understanding the distinction between the moral and the ethical, which in turn underpins the division between those objections that are a legitimate basis for coercive intervention against some action or practice, and those that are not. For the right to justification entails that:

> One must be willing to argue for basic norms that are to be reciprocally and generally valid and binding with reasons that are not based on contested 'higher' truths or on conceptions of the good which can reasonably be questioned and rejected. *Generality* then means that the reasons for such norms need to be shareable among all persons affected, not just dominant parties.[23]

It is the distinction between the moral, which appeals to the general and the shareable, and the ethical, which is particular and lacks generality, that is central here. For, the validity of *ethical* values for a person depends upon the affirmation of these values through this person in his or her ethical identity, and if this identity is not possible, the argument based on such values has no moral, categorical force to it. In disputes about the validity of a *moral* norm, however, one is required to raise, accept or reject normative claims that pass the test of reciprocity and generality.[24]

Where fundamental values are at stake, only principles or norms that 'cannot be reciprocally and generally rejected' can be legitimately imposed on those subject to them. This involves what Forst calls 'relativisation without relativism'. Thus,

> in contexts of justification in which universal obligations are at stake, toleration requires that one refrain from imposing one's own ethical convictions without appropriate justification precisely when one continues to believe that these convictions are true and right. Even if these evaluative convictions do not overcome the threshold of reciprocity and generality with the required reasons, it by no means follows that they can no longer be regarded as true or right and that they are ethically devalued, but only that they do not provide a sufficient reason, at least in this situation, for general normative regulation. *This* is the crucial insight of toleration.[25]

Therefore, 'the limits of toleration are reached when others are denied their basic right to justification in general, or, alternatively, this right is flouted in particular cases'.[26]

Being somewhat inclined to scepticism about bright and optimistic stories, and especially feeling that dark and pessimistic ones are more likely to capture the truths of politics, I want now to raise some doubts about Forst's tale. Not, as I said earlier, doubts about the historical story – I shall simply bracket that – but, rather, about the normative story. Although Forst might not entirely concur with this disconnect, and conceding that his historical narrative is heuristically effective, it does not seem to me that the normative story is in any fundamental respect dependent upon the historical narrative. So, my focus will be on that normative story, and in particular on the respect conception of toleration. Moreover, I use the expression 'raise some doubts' rather precisely, because most of what I go on to say is essentially interrogative in character: it largely raises some questions rather than purporting to offer conclusive counter-arguments. However, it would be disingenuous to imply that all this is merely a request for further information or clarification, although there certainly is an element of that. For some of the questions have a distinctly sceptical inflection, and are accompanied by more than a suspicion that once an effort is made to dispel these doubts, a number of tensions and potential difficulties emerge. Moreover, the form that my discussion takes is less one of direct argumentative engagement with the theory, and more one of trying to think about how it is supposed to work in practice; an approach that I take to be entirely appropriate, as Forst is clear that his is a critical theory and not simply a form of 'ideal theory', in the Rawlsian sense.

Much of the weight of Forst's argument depends upon his principle of the right to justification and the robustness of the associated distinction between the ethical and the moral. This, in one form or another, is fairly well trodden ground as the distinction between the moral and the ethical is very roughly the Habermasian analogue of the Rawlsian distinctions between the right and the good, as in *A Theory of Justice*, and political and comprehensive doctrines, as in *Political Liberalism*. And, although Forst makes clear that there are significant differences between his views and Rawls's, what is likely to strike those coming from outside this debate is the structural similarity between the theories, rather than the differences of detail. The distinction is clearly fundamental for Forst, for not only does his account of the normative basis of toleration rest on it, so, too, does much else in his political philosophy.[27] It is an area, therefore, in which Forst cannot afford to give much ground. Nor, given the largeness of the issues, can I be expected to do much more than chip away at it and gesture towards some more general concerns.

However, although a distinction between reasons that are general and shareable, on the one hand, and those that are not, on the other, is frequently invoked in contemporary political philosophy, and has indeed become the lingua franca of an increasingly popular discourse of public reason and in most forms of deliberative democracy, it remains, I believe, more deeply problematic than most of its adherents (including Forst) acknowledge, however it is precisely set up. I agree that such a distinction does have some force in restricting the political relevance of, for example, a rather naive form of religious argument. Thus, if the *only* reason a person can advance for favouring some law or policy is that God or some holy book demands it, then in a modern pluralistic society that person cannot really expect this to cut much ice in persuading those who either believe in some other God or holy book, or believe in neither. Such an appeal may not be entirely pointless – for instance, if what is at stake between this naive believer and a non-believer is of no real importance to the non-believer, then the non-believer might be moved to go along with the naive believer, but this would still not be because God or the holy book commanded it, but because the non-believer appreciates how much it means to the naive believer. However, any reasonable believer would, I think, have to accept – however much he or she thinks it *should* be otherwise – that just asserting something to be God's will or enjoined by a holy text is unlikely in most contexts to amount to anything more than preaching to the converted. However, for this very reason, it seems to me that this really does not take us very far – not nowhere, I should stress – in the context of current debates about toleration in societies like our own.

This is because, first, although such appeals are still to be heard in political contexts, they are rarely the only kind of arguments that are advanced by their advocates. Religious believers, or at least their representative spokespersons, are mostly sufficiently sophisticated to appreciate that direct appeal to the truth of their religion is not likely to be politically effective, and hence they typically also or instead invoke other or additional reasons. Thus, to take the case of the Rushdie affair, Muslims in Britain advocating censorship of *The Satanic Verses* rarely if ever appealed solely to the truth of the Koran or to religious teachings directly, but to considerations such as offence, respect for the beliefs of others, civility and protection of disadvantaged groups that do not invoke any esoteric or inaccessible reasons, and such reasons would, moreover, seem to be entirely consistent with the requirement of reciprocity. I shall return to this case, which is briefly discussed by Forst, later, but here I want only to make the simple point that exclusive reliance on non-public reasons of the sort that clearly would run foul of the requirements of generality and reciprocity are not as common as to be likely to eliminate very much from political discussion, at least in societies like ours.

The second reason why this requirement does not take us very far complements the first. This is that some kinds of reason, which certainly appear to meet the conditions of generality and reciprocity, could also be invoked to support the preferential treatment of particular ethical practices. For example, something as straightforward as an appeal to the will of the majority can be, or so it seems to me, a perfectly general and reciprocal second-order reason, which could quite properly be invoked to support non-neutral state policies. This is not to deny that there are contexts in which such an appeal may be problematic – for instance, where there is an entrenched and permanent majority view, particularly if this holds across a broad range of fundamental but disputed questions – but that does not mean that it will always fall foul of the generality and reciprocity conditions. As Forst accepts, there have to be some issues on which majority decision-making will be sufficient to decide the matter. Moreover, the force of the claim that majority decision-making is permissible only when fundamental rights are not at stake inevitably depends upon what those rights are taken to be.

We should also, though, at this point reflect further on the epistemological component of the right to justification. To recall: this holds that 'reason is not sufficient to provide us with the one and only, ultimate answer about the truth of the good life which would show that all other ethical beliefs are false'.[28] There are at least two observations to be made about this epistemological dimension to the distinction between the moral and the ethical. First, it seems to me, we do indeed have to be very optimistic to think that more than a few basic moral principles, and not least principles of political justice, will fare at all well when faced with such an extremely demanding epistemological standard; and, more importantly, and even more optimistically, to have well-grounded confidence that we are in any position to know what they are. Forst, it must immediately be noted, accepts that 'consensus is not to be expected' even about 'moral' matters, but then the question arises of how these differ from merely ethical beliefs, especially as it is often the case that views of justice are intertwined with broader beliefs about the good life. However, I shall return to this and some related questions in a moment.

For my second comment on the epistemological component, which pushes in the opposite direction, is that there can surely be better and worse reasons, and sometimes much better and much worse reasons, not just for moral principles, but also for favouring or rejecting some views of the good life, without being able to claim that we can demonstrate all contrary beliefs to be false. Most of us would very much doubt that a life lived mostly in an alcoholic stupor is a good or worthwhile life for human beings, and although we would probably be hard-pressed to prove it, many of us would nonetheless feel more confident about this than about the moral correctness of a good many specific principles of distributive justice, such as the difference principle. Does that mean, though, that the state cannot legitimately actively discourage what is widely believed to be excessive alcohol consumption and even impose a broad range of restrictions on it, simply on the grounds that it is generally bad for people to become intoxicated on a regular basis? (That is, without the state having to rely exclusively on sometimes all too convenient arguments about the costs to the health service or public order considerations and such like.) But perhaps this is unfair to Forst, as he tends to talk about ethical values as depending for their validity upon their affirmation by people in their ethical identity. My problem is that I am not entirely clear what this means. Does this, as it might appear, exclude our putative excessive consumer of alcohol? If it does, though, what then is the status of the values that the state in this case is actively trying to encourage? Suppose our regular drunk sees his fondness for the bottle as part of his attachment to a hedonistic or sybaritic lifestyle; does this amount to an ethical identity? And, if so, does this mean that after all the epistemological constraint should come into play? In short, once we focus less exclusively on matters like religious belief, the epistemological component may seem less persuasive. Thus, the general point I want to make here is that this epistemological component sets the bar for legitimate state action far too high. This is because if some such test is the appropriate one to be applied, then I strongly suspect that one consequence will be that there is very little state action that can be justified on this basis, including many welfare policies that liberal egalitarians would endorse.

The kind of arguments that I have just advanced are, of course, hardly novel, and Forst is probably wearisomely familiar with them. And, indeed, putative responses to most of them are easily found. But these responses, and I do not think that Forst is unusual in this regard, seem either to undermine the claim to be able to resolve practical disputes about toleration or are able to do so only by importing a good deal more by way of controversial substantive content into the argument than is admitted. An example of the first kind of response, in a context which picks up on earlier point and returns us to the Rushdie affair, is to be found in Forst's explanation that the 'shareable' character of moral reasons is not equivalent to agreement, and that generally consensus on moral principles is not to be expected.[29] However, he still thinks that 'with the help of the criteria of reciprocity and generality, we can plausibly identify better and worse arguments for generally valid norms in many cases, looking at the claims and the reasons given.'[30] And it is true that he then goes on to offer a sketch of an argument for this in the Rushdie case, but I have to say I do not find it very persuasive (even if my own preferred outcome in this example happens to be largely similar to his own). This is because, and admittedly I dramatise to make the point, there is nothing in the ideas of reciprocity and generality themselves that can tell us whether a society of untrammelled freedom of expression in which, say, people can ridicule and abuse the deepest convictions of others is preferable to one in which such expression is significantly circumscribed, although at some cost to freedom of speech, on grounds of offence, taste and civility. Nor is it clear how the ideas of reciprocity and generality might point to any particular compromise as the right balance of reasons. Forst may *claim* that the balance of reasons points clearly in one direction, but others honestly disagree: and there lie the problems, both theoretical and political.

As Glen Newey remarks: 'Forst seems to underestimate the justificatory problems posed by reasonable disagreement. It is hard to see how the conditions that make for reasonable disagreement can be kept from undercutting the basis on which others' judgements are held to be reasonable.'[31] The *theoretical* problem is what might be called the indeterminacy of reason, and unfortunately for Forst this infects the moral sphere as well as the ethical. Thus, moral/political principles, no less than ethical beliefs, are radically underdetermined by the criteria of reciprocity and generality. What we are dealing with here, I suggest, is a familiar Kantian illusion about the power of largely formal criteria to generate robust, substantive moral content. The *political* problem is what is to be done in the face of this kind of disagreement. In short, it is unclear what, if anything, follows from Forst or anyone else being convinced that the reasons point in one direction, when others disagree, for reasons that are not demonstrably false, irrelevant or confused (although it is important to acknowledge that purported reasons can be false, irrelevant or confused, and that the view I am articulating, therefore, is not one in which 'anything goes' or one reason is as good as any other).[32]

The only way that the under-determination of moral/political principles by the criteria of reciprocity and generality can be overcome is, I believe, by adopting the alternative response, and importing a good deal more by way of controversial substantive content into the argument than is explicitly admitted. This is sometimes what would seem to be going on when the application of the criteria of reciprocity and generality are allowed to be shaped by the weighing of specific values in a way that seems not to be determined by the criteria themselves, but by a particular political vision. It is only on this basis that, for example, a certain understanding of freedom of speech can be claimed to have near absolute primacy over almost all competing values. Forst's view of the relative merits of the arguments in the Rushdie affair seems to be an example of just such a process. It is not, and this point needs to be stressed, that Forst's position in relation to the Rushdie affair is either mistaken or unattractive. Rather, the point is that there is nothing so compelling about it that it need make those moderate Muslims, for instance, who favoured greater restriction give up their own views as clearly less persuasive than those of Forst. In the Rushdie case most parties to the disagreement did not even invoke different values; rather they attach different weights to values that they for the most part shared. Thus, for example, no serious contributor to the Rushdie controversy denied that freedom of speech and the right to criticise the views of other were valuable and important. And, a few First Amendment fundamentalists apart, nor did anyone think that there were no grounds for ever restricting freedom of speech. Rather, the disagreement was about how these values were to be interpreted, for instance what exactly is meant or implied by 'respect', and also how freedom of speech should be weighed against other important values, such as those of civility and religious freedom.

In short, it seems to me little more than an article of faith to believe that appeal to reciprocity and generality will be sufficient to resolve, or even significantly narrow the boundaries, with regard to most disputes about toleration.[33] In the Rushdie case, for instance, Glen Newey has shown that it is far from clear what the tolerant view actually is.[34] It would be better, I believe, simply to accept that all that may be possible in many cases is to engage in processes of negotiation and bargaining, with a view to trying to reach some sort of *modus vivendi* between the parties in conflict.[35] Such an outcome can still be tolerant, but it would be the coexistence, and under some conditions the permission, conception of toleration that would most likely be needed; although this would clearly be deficient from Forst's point of view. Whatever the merits of this particular suggestion, however, my principal claim is that the criteria of reciprocity and generality are insufficient in the Rushdie case and many others to show that only one interpretation of the requirements and boundaries of toleration is clearly preferable to another, unless one imports into these ideas either a lot more substantive philosophical and normative baggage. The consequence of doing that, though, is that any claims grounded in these concepts will also be a lot more controversial and contestable in ways that Forst's argument had sought to circumvent.

To make what I am here arguing more explicit in relation to toleration, consider another of Forst's examples, and an example that seems to me one of his strongest: the case of homosexual marriage in Germany. 'The question was', he says, 'whether toleration is the mere permission to be different, but not fully equal, or whether toleration requires equal respect of differences and therefore equal rights'.[36] And he answers that: 'Seen through the lens of the principle of justification … it seems that the argument for equal rights in questions of marriage is a claim that is hard to reject, if one-sided ethical and religious views are ruled out as a basis for decision.'[37] Now, I cannot pretend that my sympathies are other than with the view that Forst endorses, but let us try to consider what someone who thought differently but accepted something like the right to justification might say.

One thing that they might want to do is to distinguish equal legal rights from the particular institution of marriage, which could be regarded, and surely with some plausibility, as 'cultural'. It could be argued that while the state must ensure that there are equal legal rights for all citizens, this requirement could be met through the institution of civil partnerships, which have equal legal standing to marriage, but do not have the legal title of 'marriage'. Is there a compelling objection to such a policy, given the particular historical meaning of 'marriage' in Germany and other countries with a largely Christian heritage? At the very least, it is not obvious why civil partnerships with equal legal standing could not be regarded as a 'fair compromise' between the contending parties, perhaps until a majority has been persuaded of the case for same-sex marriages and/or cultural understandings change. Also, though, if we now treat homosexual marriage as in all respects on a par with heterosexual marriage, why should we be so conventional as to limit marriage, for example to dyadic relationships? Why not, for instance, polygamous and polyandrous relationships? Perhaps some will agree that those, too, should be accommodated within the institution of marriage? If so, then, why not, for example, simply give equal status to all contractual relationships of a quasi-marital kind, as long as there are the necessary protections against force and fraud? Again, some will have no problems with this. Would this, though, be the logical implication of the right to justification in this area? If it is, then some people might be rather less happy about embracing such a requirement than if they just thought it was about equal rights for same-sex couples. What lies behind this rather torturous, and undeniably highly tentative, line of reasoning is the thought that eventually we will often reach an ethical or cultural consideration that does seem to mark the limits of toleration, although of course we may still be tempted to try to dress it up in 'moral' terms.

Continuing to pursue the theme of how the respect conception of toleration is supposed to help us resolve practical disputes, let me move on to a different kind of context – one in which I am looking essentially for further clarification, but where I also suspect that any such clarification will also lead to further problems. The issue here concerns the implications of the respect conception of toleration for how groups should treat each other when they are not seeking to use state power to advance their own ethical beliefs and values. For instance, is it compatible with the respect conception for Catholics or Jews, say, to proselytise aggressively against the 'abomination' of homosexuality? I suggest that the respect conception faces a dilemma here. On the one hand, to adopt a latitudinarian position about civil society is likely to be problematic for the respect conception, because it seems hard to reconcile this with the kind of reciprocity and mutual respect that is integral to it, and the kind of civic or societal culture that may well be necessary to support it (although the latter is to a large degree an empirical question). On the other hand, however, if the respect conception does require that the expression of such open hostility towards the ways of life of others must be significantly restricted, then it at least raises the question of how much toleration is really being extended to those who hold such views. It would appear that the objection component in such views becomes effaced or effectively neutered. It may also be that this will tend to push in the direction of the esteem conception, of which Forst is rightly, in my view, critical. I just do not see how the right to justification, the distinction between the moral and the ethical or the invocation of the values of reciprocity and generality will settle such questions about the scope or limits of toleration.

By way of bringing this discussion to a conclusion, let me try to bring together what I take to be at least one of the implications of this rather heterogeneous series of reflections. For one important question that captures many of my worries, and which I therefore want to press on Forst, would run something like the following: is there any space within his account for a state/government ever legitimately to have a view, more specifically, to disapprove of some practice or behaviour, and also tolerate it legally (on anything other than narrowly prudential grounds)? What I infer from his account, although I am not entirely sure if I am right to do so, is that when matters are in normatively good order, the state or government will only take a view of behaviour or practices if they are immoral, rather than merely unethical, in which case they will be intolerable, and the state or government should not, at least ideally, extend toleration to them. On the other hand, if something is a matter of ethics, rather than of morality, then the state or government would appear to have no business taking a view about the merits or otherwise of such activities, as its role in such cases is limited to ensuring that toleration is practised by its citizens. Thus, the only legitimate policies for the state or government (ideally) are: promote toleration in the sphere of the ethical and practice intolerance towards the immoral. My question is not so much concerned with the now familiar debate, which is principally conceptual, about whether such a state or government can properly be called tolerant at all.[38] Rather, my question is the normative one of whether there is any legitimate space for, or whether it is necessarily wrong for, a state or government to actively show its disapproval of some activities while still tolerating them in the sense of not legally forbidding them or acting in any other way the intention of which is essentially prohibitive? If Forst sees no problem with such a scenario, then I fail to see how such a relaxed response is consistent with his theory. On the other hand, if his answer to this question is negative, as I think his theory must require it to be, then in my view there is something wrong with his theory, in that it effectively excludes an important sphere of toleration.[39]

At the risk that I am barking up the wrong tree, let me say a little more about why I think that a normative theory of toleration should allow space for a state or government to be tolerant in something like the permission sense. There are in short, it seems to me, many things on which it is legitimate for a government to have a normative view that are not matters of morality, in Forst's sense, but which involve on his view only matters of ethical disagreement.[40] Let me list just a few of them: health (including sex) education, the built environment, which things that should be taxed and at what levels, what should be subsidised and to what extent, public iconography and much else. I also believe that questions of toleration can importantly extend to practices within groups that in some respects conflict with values such as gender equality. In such cases a form of toleration that one might think of as 'discouragement without prohibition' may be the most appropriate response, and not just on prudential grounds (although in politics I think we always do well not to belittle such grounds). It seems Procrustean to say that such gender attitudes are either a matter of ethics, and therefore the state should in no way interfere, or they are matters of morality, in which case the state is actually required to intervene. Surely the state may sometimes legitimately encourage or discourage, especially through essentially non-coercive means such as advertising campaigns, expressing public approbation or disapproval, or by supplying or withholding some forms of institutional support and so on?

The fundamental problem is that I see no single or sharp distinction here between the moral and the ethical, and hence no single, unique perspective from which an authoritative judgement can be made about what should or should not be tolerated with respect to the many disputed cases that arise within modern pluralistic societies. For sure, toleration depends upon people accepting that their own beliefs or opinions cannot always be a sufficient basis for interfering coercively with the behaviour of those who disagree with them. Thus, there has to be an acceptance that there will be lines between where coercive interference is justified and where it is not, but what I have not yet seen convincingly shown, by Forst or anyone else, is that there are compelling reasons to believe that generally there is only one, normatively correct place in which such lines are to be drawn. Does this then mean that disagreements about the limits of toleration only mimic the conflicts about values that it was supposed to defuse or pacify, thereby rendering toleration otiose? This does not follow: there is no reason to think that this must be the case. What it does imply is that toleration does not stand altogether outside of conflicts of value, and that *theory* cannot necessarily be expected to supply us with answers to questions that have to be addressed *practically* and *politically*.

As should be clear from my account of it, Forst's normative theory of toleration is ambitious and challenging. Moreover, nothing I have argued, and this point needs to be emphasised, has been intended to show that there is no place for the respect conception of toleration. Rather, I have sought to express some doubts principally with regard to two features of his story. First, I have argued that the respect conception, because of its reliance on the right to justification and the distinction between the moral and the ethical, is a good deal more problematic and fuzzier than Forst's account of it acknowledges. In this respect I have been engaged in an exercise that has been aptly described as muddying the waters.[41] Secondly, and connectedly, I want to suggest that there is still a significant place for the permissive and coexistence conceptions of toleration, which is not explicable solely in terms of their being a stepping stone to the respect conception. Toleration remains, therefore a complex and multifaceted value that is, as Forst rightly argues, normatively dependent; but where we differ is that, unlike him, I do not see it as uniquely tied to or validated by one normative perspective. Thus it is often indeterminate in its application, which can be controversial, disputed and subject to negotiation. This does not make toleration practically useless, quite the contrary, but it does mean that its openended character eludes capture even by Forst's immensely sophisticated and in many respects highly attractive theory of it; as it has also escaped capture by political liberalism, value pluralism and other theories that have aimed to offer a comprehensive normative account of it.[42]

Notes

1 The fullest account of Forst's views on toleration is to be found in his monumental and seminal work, *Toleranz im Konflikt: Geschichte, Gehalt und Gegenwart eines umstrittenen Begriffs* (Frankfurt/M: Suhrkamp, 2003). As a non-reader of German I have not been able to consult this edition, but a somewhat abbreviated edition has more recently been published in English as *Toleration in Conflict*. Forst himself says that the English-language version 'contains everything essential' (Forst, *TiC*, p. xiii), I assume that nothing serious is lost through this limitation. Moreover, he has published numerous articles on toleration in English which I draw on – 'Toleration, Justice and Reason', in C. McKinnon and D. Castiglione (eds), *The Culture of Toleration in Diverse Societies* (Manchester: Manchester University Press, 2003); 'The Limits of Toleration', *Constellations*, 11:3 (2004), 312–325; 'A Critical Theory of Multicultural Toleration', in A.S. Laden and D. Owen (eds),

Multiculturalism and Political Theory (Cambridge: Cambridge University Press, 2007); 'Toleration', *Stanford Encyclopedia of Philosophy*, 2007; 'Two Stories about Toleration', *RECON Online Working Paper*, 2010/15, as well as an interesting exchange with Wendy Brown – see W. Brown and R. Forst, *The Power of Tolerance: A Debate* (New York: Columbia University Press, 2004).

2 I can hardly forbear from sheepishly noting that I have sometimes been guilty of purveying something rather too close for comfort to this somewhat blinkered story myself – Horton, 'Toleration', in D. Miller (ed.), *The Blackwell Encyclopaedia of Political Thought* (Oxford: Basil Blackwell, 1986). It also seems to play a role in shaping Susan Mendus's account in *Toleration and the Limits of Liberalism* (London: Macmillan, 1989).

3 In Forst's view, it is Bayle who makes the crucial move that enables the emergence of the respect conception of toleration that Forst himself champions. It is Bayle who connects 'the normative thesis involved in the non-religious principle that actions which affect the freedom of others are in need of reciprocal justification with the epistemological thesis of the finitude of reason in religious questions, which are thus matters of reasonable disagreements. It is these two components of practical and theoretical reason which ground the central insight into the *non-justifiability of religious coercion*, and hence the duty of toleration' (*TiC*, p. 264). Locke, by contrast, only moved beyond the more limited permission conception of toleration, reluctantly and hesitantly, in his later *Letters*, when under pressure from his indefatigable interrogator, Jonas Proast; a change which meant that, according to Forst, he had to 'abandon the main argument of his first *Letter*' (*TiC*, p. 231).

4 Forst, 'The Limits of Toleration', 313.

5 Forst, 'Toleration, Justice and Reason'; 'Toleration' and 'Two Stories about Toleration'.

6 *TiC*, pp. 20–21.

7 Forst, 'Toleration', 2.

8 *Ibid.*

9 *Ibid.*, 3.

10 *TiC*, p. 27.

11 *Ibid.*, p. 28.

12 *Ibid.*, pp. 28–29.

13 *Ibid.*, p. 29.
14 *Ibid.*, pp. 29–30.
15 Forst, 'Toleration', 5.
16 *Ibid.*
17 *TiC*, p. 31.
18 Forst, 'Two Stories about Toleration', 1.
19 W. Brown, *Regulating Aversion: Tolerance in the Age of Identity and Empire* (Princeton: Princeton University Press, 2006).
20 Forst, 'Two Stories about Toleration', 10.
21 For the full account of the right to justification, see Forst's *RtJ*.
22 Forst, 'A Critical Theory of Multicultural Toleration', 303.
23 Forst, 'Two Stories about Toleration', 10.
24 Forst, 'Toleration, Justice and Reason', 77.
25 *TiC*, p. 455.
26 *Ibid.*, p. 455.
27 See Forst's *RtJ*.
28 Forst, 'A Critical Theory of Multicultural Toleration', 303.
29 Forst, 'Two Stories about Toleration', 10.
30 *Ibid.*
31 G. Newey, *Toleration in Political Conflict* (Cambridge: Cambridge University Press, 2013), p. 95.
32 There may still of course be a political problem of how to respond to those who hold silly or deeply confused reasons for a belief, if they refuse to modify such beliefs and those beliefs have socially significant implications; but that is a different problem from the one with which I am concerned.
33 In fairness, it should be noted that Forst concedes that there can be a few grey areas and difficult cases, such as abortion.
34 G. Newey, 'Fatwa and Fiction: Censorship and Toleration', in J. Horton (ed.), *Liberalism, Multiculturalism and Toleration* (London: Macmillan, 1993).
35 See J. Horton, 'Modus Vivendi and Religious Accommodation', in M. Mookherjee (ed.), *Democracy, Religious Pluralism and the Liberal Dilemma of Accommodation* (Dordrecht: Springer, 2010).
36 Forst, 'A Critical Theory of Multicultural Toleration', 306.
37 *Ibid.*

38 See P. Jones, 'Making Sense of Political Toleration', *British Journal of Political Science*, 37:3 (2007), 383–402, and 'Political Toleration: A Reply to Newey', *British Journal of Political Science*, 41:2 (2010), 445–447; Newey, 'Political Toleration: A Reply to Jones', *British Journal of Political Science*, 41:1 (2010), 223–227; P. Balint, 'Not Yet Making Sense of Political Toleration', *Res Public*, 18:3 (2012), 259–264.

39 See J. Horton, 'Why the Traditional Conception of Toleration Still Matters', *Critical Review of International Social and Political Philosophy*, 14:3 (2011), 289–305.

40 It may be that some of what I go on to say would be regarded by Forst as relating to issues that are not 'fundamental' and therefore a matter of democratic discretion. However, given the nature of at least some of these issues and the range of examples that Forst himself discusses, I think that this could at best be a partial response.

41 I owe this characterisation to Andy Mason.

42 An earlier version of this chapter was presented at a conference on Rainer Forst's work organised by David Owen and Matt Matravers at the University of York in June 2011. I am very grateful to them for the invitation to present the paper and also for the extensive and helpful discussion the paper received on that occasion. Not least, I am especially grateful to Rainer Forst for his characteristically generous and searching comments on the paper and for his courteous but vigorous defence of his own position, which has led to revisions in the way that I have formulated the argument here, although I am sure that it will no more persuade him now than it did then.

5

Overcoming toleration?

Daniel Weinstock

There has been a lot of talk in recent years of the difference between ideal and non-ideal political theory, and of the appropriate place that both of them should play in political theory.[1] Those who would give greater pride of place to ideal theory argue that normative theory is rudderless if is not guided by the kinds of ideals that are produced independently of all consideration of human frailty and moral mediocrity. Those who argue, on the contrary, for shifting theoretical emphasis over to the non-ideal side of the ledger have held that an emphasis on ideal theory does not so much prepare us to deal normatively with non-ideal circumstances as it does set us on the wrong track.[2]

It could be that there is no definitive answer to the ideal/non-ideal theory debate. It could be, for example, that the best strategy depends on the kind of concept or argument one is trying to understand. Take the concept of democracy, for example. Bracket all of the aspects of the real world that seem to militate for non-ideal theory – the moral turpitude of human agents, their epistemic limitations, and the like – and we would still need to understand how best to arrive at a scheme for collective decision-making in the face of reasonable disagreement, unless of course one assumes that disagreement is *itself* a manifestation of the non-ideal, in which case one has most likely run together the non-ideal with the non-human. Some concepts may just naturally have their natural habitats in non-ideal, and others in (more close to) ideal contexts.

On the face of it, it would seem that if any political concept reflects the non-ideal political circumstances in which humans find themselves, it is that of toleration. The need for toleration, and for an understanding both of the need for – and the limitations of – practices of toleration, is born after all in a context in which people not only disagree about how their common lives should be organised, but are willing to coerce others into seeing things their way, or at least into acting as if they did. Some of our most important theoretical treatments of toleration were born in contexts where philosophers were not just observing vigorous disagreement about justice or about the good life, but also the willingness on the part of some to commit acts of extreme violence in the name of their construals of these concepts. Toleration was born in contexts in which people were convinced that their conceptions of the good, and the conceptions of the right that they associate with them, are so clearly superior that they warrant being forcibly imposed upon others, often for those others' own good. We may not have come up with the concept of toleration, had human agents not shown themselves more than willing to act in these ways. This would seem to call for an account of toleration that tilts towards the non-ideal.

Rainer Forst's *Toleration in Conflict* is one of the most learned and profound accounts we possess of both the theory and practice of toleration. It provides us both with a challenging set of arguments about how best to think about toleration, and with an historical contextualisation of arguments about toleration that is of impressive erudition. I want however to argue in the context of the present chapter that Forst's argument ends up being not so much an account of toleration, as it is an argument for the need, from an ethical point of view, for the overcoming of the sets of non-ideal circumstances that have through history tended to make it necessary, at least according to one of its (non-ideal) construals. Now, one could argue that it is actually true that humans would be better off were they not inclined to impose their views on one another by coercive means (or perhaps also, to hold the kinds of views and engage in the kinds of practices that might in some circumstances invite a justified *ceteris paribus* inclination to intervene). The problem I want to outline in the present chapter is however this: in ideal circumstances people would still disagree with one another and would in the face of disagreement evince attitudes and modes of behaviour that might look like toleration. But to the degree that one sees, as I will argue one must, the inclination not just to disagree but to limit the freedom of those with whom one disagrees as central to the circumstances within which the felt need for toleration emerges in the first place, the concept Forst defends ends up placing us beyond toleration, rather than in its natural element. Now, this would not be a problem were in not for the fact that he also views his conception of toleration as normative for all others. This, I will argue, is a mistake, one that Forst is moreover at least implicitly aware of, as is evinced by a number of key passages in the book.

I will proceed as follows. First, I will provide a (necessarily sketchy) account of Forst's overall argument that highlights the main structural elements of the view he defends. Second, I will identify a puzzling feature in that account, one that facilitates the conflation of non-ideal and ideal toleration, but that Forst himself tacitly rejects at various points in the text. In the third and fourth sections of the chapter, I will describe two families of reasons that might underpin a non-ideal conception of toleration, one that is more attuned than Forst's is to self-restraint as a constitutive ingredient of the structural account of toleration. The first of these families of reasons is consequentialist in nature, while the second emphasises the fallibilism of the kind of human judgement that is central to Forst's own way of thinking about toleration. Finally, I will offer some considerations for thinking that these two conceptions of toleration ought to be thought of as distinct, rather than, as Forst thinks, of the non-ideal kind drawing its normative justification from its approximation of the ideal kind.

I

Forst's book is long and theoretically very rich, and it thus defies any attempt at brief summary. The following attempt will, perforce, leave many things out. I hope that none of what is omitted involves mischaracterising the arguments in Forst's work that are relevant to the present chapter.

The first important aspect of Forst's theory is the structural account he provides of toleration. Toleration involves three coordinated 'components' that Forst labels 'objection', 'acceptance' and 'rejection'. To begin with the 'objection component', to tolerate means that there are in one's social circumstances some 'convictions and practices' that one regards as 'false or condemned'.[3] These should be of sufficient importance to warrant a normative (though not necessarily a moral) condemnation. Second, Forst holds that toleration involves an 'acceptance component'. To tolerate involves to condemn, but also in some sense to accept. To tolerate means that though one condemns, one's condemnation does not involve the claim that the practice or conviction one is considering lies so far beyond the normative pale as to warrant an 'all things considered' condemnation. Citing Forst: 'The important point here is that the positive reasons do not cancel out the negative reasons but are set against them in such a way that, although they trump the negative reasons ... and are in this sense higher-order reasons, the objection nevertheless retains its force.'[4] Finally, toleration involves a 'rejection component'. Some practices and convictions do actually lie beyond the normative pale, and in their case 'the rejection can no longer be offset by reasons for acceptance'.[5]

The second important feature of Forst's account for present purposes is his claim that toleration, as it has just been spelled out in terms of these three structural features, is a normatively dependent concept, in the sense that it is not in and of itself a value, nor does it designate practices that are necessarily valuable just in virtue of presenting these three structural features. As Forst puts it, 'toleration is a positive attitude or practice when it subserves something good, that is, when it is required for the sake of realizing higher-level principles or values and is justified accordingly'.[6]

Why must the principles that justify be 'higher-order'? That is, why must they be distinct from, and normatively more binding than, the ethical outlooks that would in their absence underpin the various attitudes of objections, acceptance and rejection that moral agents of morally and culturally diverse societies would form towards one another? Forst's answer is that otherwise, the concept of toleration would end up mired in the 'paradoxes' that have characterised many accounts of toleration. For example, any account of toleration that ended up drawing lines between practices and convictions that, though objects of disagreement and objection, do not fall beyond the moral pale, and those that do on the basis of a particular 'conception of the good' would end up tolerating on sectarian grounds, that is, it would end up drawing such distinctions on the basis of normative resources with no greater warrant than those among which it was making distinctions. Forst speaks here of the 'paradox of drawing the limits'.[7] The account also places moral agents in a seemingly contradictory position, normatively speaking, both allowing them to endorse their own normative viewpoints through their opposition to certain practices and convictions, and seemingly requiring that they distance themselves from those very viewpoints through their acceptance of the practices and convictions they oppose. This is the 'paradox of the relativisation of truth'.[8]

These and other paradoxes[9] dissolve in Forst's view when we distinguish between two normative perspectives that moral agents inhabit simultaneously. On the one hand, they adhere to thick, 'ethical' conceptions of the good that provide them with norms and guidance as to what is of ultimate value in life, on what it means to lead a worthwhile life, and so on. On the other hand, they are answerable before thinner but normatively more weighty moral norms that specify the sphere of what agents owe to one another, independently of their thick conceptions of the good. In a manner that is reminiscent of many Kantian theories, Forst believes that as agents that demand justification from one another for the ways in which their actions impinge upon one another, moral agents must ultimately recognise the moral value inherent in the very ideal of justification, one that is already inchoately implicit in demands for justification that rest upon particular contestable conceptions of the good.[10]

Such a distinction dissolves the paradoxes we have just briefly outlined, as well as many others besides. The moral perspective provides us with a non-question-begging way in which to distinguish between practices and convictions that, though they can be (ethically) objected to and condemned, should nonetheless be (morally) accepted, and ones that fail both the sectarian ethical and the inescapable moral tests, thus doing away with the 'paradox of drawing the limits'. Moral agents can moreover be rescued from the paradox of the relativisation of truth through the realisation that they are occupying different moral perspectives when they simultaneously ethically condemn or object to some practice or conviction that is part of another ethical framework and recognise it as acceptable from a moral standpoint. Thus, in Forst's view, 'no other values or norms except the *principle of justification itself* can provide the foundation of the higher-level, generally justified and itself tolerant theory of toleration'.[11]

Thus, Forstian toleration involves condemning views and practices that emanate from other ethical frameworks when they come into opposition with our own, but accepting them to the degree that there is no moral reason that we can come up with that might justify limiting the freedom of those who hold these views and engage in these practices (for, as Forst points out in the Introduction of his book, 'toleration turns essentially on the justifying reasons for specific freedoms or restrictions on freedom',[12] and rejecting them when such reasons do exist). Toleration, as a normatively dependent concept, acquires value on Forst's view when the various attitudes of objection, acceptance and rejection that constitute it are grounded in the right kinds of reasons.

II

It is interesting to note something that is *not* part of Forst's account. Many standard accounts have indeed argued that the main structural features of any account of toleration involve not just objection, but the disposition to place obstacles, and at the limit to prohibit, the offending convictions and practices on the basis of that objection, combined with the decision not to succumb to that inclination, on the part of those who are actually in a position effectively to act on this disposition. The tolerant person or the tolerant institution is inclined, all things equal, to prohibit, but decides for whatever reason, to prescind from prohibiting. Implicit in this standard account is that it is part of the ordinary language analysis of toleration that it is a virtue or practice that is undertaken by agents who have the *power* to place such obstacles in the way of the realisation of the offending practices and views of others. According to this view, one of the difficulties of toleration lies in the fact that it requires a degree of self-overcoming on the part of those who disapprove and who have the power to act on their disapproval.[13]

Forst objects to the inclusion of the power to prohibit as a necessary structural feature of toleration. He writes that 'to conclude that the tolerating party must be in a position of power from which it could effectively prevent the practices in question is unfounded. For a minority which is not equipped with such power can also adopt an attitude of tolerance and be of the (uncoerced) conviction that were it to have sufficient means of power at its disposal, it would not use them to the disadvantage of others'.[14]

I want to say a number of things to about this passage, all of which go towards suggesting that it does not amount to a sufficient reason to remove what one might refer to as 'self-restraint on the part of the powerful' from the structural features of toleration. First, it arguably establishes the opposite of what Forst takes it to establish, in that it suggests that it is only by projecting itself into a position in which it has power to pose obstacles in the carrying out of a practice or the expression of a conviction with which it disagrees that the members of a powerless minority can determine whether or not they would be tolerant, were they to be powerful.

Second the claim that the inclusion of power among the structural ingredients of toleration is 'groundless' seems to me to be itself groundless unless it can be adequately backed up. Normative concepts do not denote natural kinds. We decide how to carve out normative space on the basis of the degree to which the concepts we employ allow us to develop normative perspicuity, which I define as our capacity to 'pick out', with the use of distinct concepts, normative realities and situations that are best thought of as distinct. In my view, we must combat against the temptation to include too many normative considerations under the same concept. Take the debates that have dominated political philosophy for decades now as to the 'best' way in which to think of liberty.[15] Is liberty 'really' about the absence of external obstacles, is it 'really' about internal self-determination, or is it 'really' about the absence of arbitrary interference? Clearly all three of these options pick out normatively relevant facts about human agents and the situations that they find themselves in in trying to exercise their wills. It is better for them, all things considered, that they not be faced with obstacles in the realisation of their wills. It is better if they are self-directed, rather than impelled by neuroses, compulsions and obsessions. It is better if they do not have to be subjected to the arbitrary will of others. It is sterile to argue that one or the other 'really' captures the 'essence' of freedom. We need more concepts rather than fewer in this context, to capture the fact that talk of 'freedom' often conflates what are in fact quite different normative considerations.

Now, this is not to deny that there can sometimes be groundless conceptual distinctions. It would, for example, be normatively uninteresting to have distinct concepts for interferences with agents' freedoms that emanate from blonde and from dark-haired persons. Whether it is groundless to draw the contours of a normative concept one way or another must be determined on a case by case basis.

Thus, it would be 'groundless' to include 'self-restraint' among the structural characteristics of the concept of toleration if distinguishing a conception that included it from one that did not was more like distinguishing between obstacles to freedom that are caused by blonde and by dark-haired persons than it is like distinguishing between the kinds of 'internal' obstacles that positive freedom denotes and the more external ones that negative freedom alters us to. But I don't think that it is. The moral stakes that are involved in situations in which ethical disagreement is couched in a context of significant power differentials, and in a context where, moreover, there is a presumption on the part of the powerful that ethical difference justifies the limitation of the rights of those who have less power, are more urgent than are contexts in which this is not the case.

There is ample evidence throughout the book that Forst realises this. In a passage I have already quoted, from the Introduction to the book, he writes after all 'toleration turns essentially on the justifying reasons for specific freedoms or restrictions on freedom'.[16] In the case studies with which he ends the book, moreover, Forst deals with cases in which the question of power is central, to wit, the power of a majority and of the political institutions that represent it to impose their wills upon religious minorities, in the area of religious signage and in that of compulsory schooling.[17] A conception of toleration that is centrally concerned with working out how the holders of different 'thick' ethical conceptions should distinguish between which of the alternative conceptions with which they disagree should be accepted and which should be rejected is on the face of it different from one in which what hangs on this distinction is the limitation of the freedom of (relatively) powerless minorities or individuals. There would seem to be a difference between a conception of toleration that focuses on reasons to accept and to reject and one that focuses on reasons to act or not to act on one's *prima facie* inclination to limit the freedom of those with whom one disagrees. Making the kinds of distinctions that are central to the first conception of freedom does not settle the issue of whether one should or should not limit the freedom of those with whom one disagrees. There are reasons for powerful groups and institutions to tolerate even where (a) they consider that a group's convictions and practices are beyond the moral pale, and (b) they are antecedently inclined to intervene in order to put an end to the practices in question, or to prohibit the expression of the impugned convictions. It is to the elucidation of these kinds of reasons, and of the kinds of situations in which they arise, that I will devote the next section. As I will try to make plain, there are reasons to prescind from placing obstacles in the path of those whose views one rejects that cannot be reduced to reasons that one might have to accept (in the Forstian sense) views that one opposes.

III

Consider, first, a group whose practices or convictions uncontroversially lie beyond the moral pale. One may be justifiably convinced that these practices are morally odious, and still consider that it would be a mistake to act so as to limit or eliminate the freedom of this group to engage in it. One might for example come to the conclusion that more harm than good would come from prohibition. This conclusion might be reached for a number of reasons. One might for example think that one lacks the enforcement mechanisms with which effectively to put an end to the practice in question. One might think for example that by trying to prohibit and failing one would in effect be driving the impugned practice underground, thus making those who are subjected to it more vulnerable than they would be in a situation in which the practice was not prohibited.[18] In the area of speech, one might think that the prohibition even of racist speech would be counter-productive, as it would end up making 'speech martyrs' of those whose freedom of speech had been abridged. One might, second, fear on valid socio-psychological grounds that the attempt to prohibit might lead to a reaction on the part of the group whose liberties were under attack to radicalise and to push to an extreme those aspects of its practices or convictions that had led the groups holding the reins of power to feel that it was morally (and not just ethically) justified in prohibiting in the first place. In the domain of cultural practices, Ayelet Shachar has for example written of the dangers of 'reactive culturalism'.[19] One might, third, fear on Lockean grounds that prohibition would only change the behaviour of groups whose practices and convictions were being condemned, but that it would not affect their inclination to engage in the behaviour in question, and that the transformation of behaviour unaccompanied by the satisfaction of an 'endorsement' condition is of far less value and satisfaction than transformation accompanied by endorsement would be.[20] One might, fourth, worry about the moral problems inherent upon providing majoritarian or even counter-majoritarian judicial institutions with the power with which to police behaviour in a manner that might generate a significant proportion of 'false positives', that is, of cases in which prohibitions are enacted on the basis of morally erroneous judgements (I will say more about this below).

Thus, it would seem from this (incomplete) enumeration that there are reasons that powerful groups should consider in deciding whether or not to use their control over institutions that persist even after the question of whether the impugned practices and convictions of a group or individual have been categorised in the minds of those holding power as ones that ought to be rejected (rather than merely opposed). This suggests that a conception of toleration that incorporates self-restraint among the core structural features is distinct from one that does not. Reasons to reject, and reasons to exercise self-restraint even after having rejected, belong to different families of normative considerations.

To this it might be responded that the reasons mooted here to abstain from acting so as to limit the freedom of groups whose practices and convictions have been deemed immoral are merely instrumental and consequentialist in nature, and that they should not go into determining the core conceptual architecture of the concept of toleration, but instead should merely be seen as having to do with the conditions of its application to real-world situations. The question of toleration would on this view be entirely conceptually exhausted by the considerations that are to be brought to bear in determining whether to accept-while-opposing or to reject.

This response would be inadequate. It would in particular beg the question against consequentialist conceptions of morality. The positions I am considering here are all premised upon the moral rejection of the practices and convictions in question, but wonder whether the best way in which to do away with these practices and convictions is to act against them, or whether in certain circumstances tolerating, in the sense of not intervening, is not the best way in which to give rise to long-term, sustainable transformations of attitudes and behaviours. They are not instrumental in a manner that excludes morality, but rather in a manner that is premised upon the fact that one can at times have a consequentialist attitude with respect to the realisation of moral values.[21]

I want now to highlight one of the reasons to prescind from acting to prohibit on the basis of a negative moral judgement which strikes me as particularly important in the present context because it is one that Forst himself explicitly acknowledges at various points, but to which he does not in my view ascribe sufficient importance. It has to do with the fallibilism that should be inscribed in the DNA of any liberal democratic coercive institutions with respect to its ability to exercise its powers on the basis of the distinctions that Forst puts in place as definitional of what he views as 'correct' toleration.

IV

Recall that on Forst's view, toleration requires that one distinguish between the practices and convictions that one opposes ethically but accepts morally, and those that one rejects both ethically and morally. The former ought, on Forst's view, to be tolerated, while the latter ought to be met by (morally justified) intolerance.

One might question Forst's argument for justified toleration by questioning the ethics/morality distinction upon which it is constructed. This would involve engaging in an iteration of the endless philosophical conflict between Hegelian and Kantian views of the normative domain. On a Hegelian view, thin, universalistic morality grows out of the thick ethical life of particular ethical forms of life, whereas a Kantian view will view moral principles as implicit in practical reason, or in the conditions of successful communicative action, or (as in Forst's view) the demand for justification.

I do not in the present context want to pursue this line of critique, which would constitute a strong argument against the view of toleration defended in the book. I want to explore a weaker, epistemic argument, one that Forst acknowledges, but to which he does not in my view ascribe enough weight. According to the weaker argument, whatever one thinks about the philosophical pedigree of the morality/ethics distinction upon which Forst's view is built, actual moral agents have a very hard time recognising and applying it correctly. They often decide whether or not to tolerate, and whether or not to act on the basis of that judgement, on the basis of considerations that they believe to be moral, but that are actually ethical. Human agents often judge one another on the basis of considerations internal to their thick ethical perspectives, that they falsely believe to be part of the content of a universalistic (and thus enforceable) morality.

Consider an example. There has in recent years been a spate of criticisms of the Muslim practice of veiling. Many Western feminists have seen veiling as betokening a patriarchal practice seeking to 'invisiblise' women and to control the conditions in which they can occupy public space.[22] Many partisans of a strict separation of religion from the public sphere have argued that allowing veiled women to wear highly visible religious signs, especially in formally public institutions such as courts, schools and the like, violates the principle of the separation of Church and state in ways that smaller, less visible religious signs do not.[23] Finally, many nationalists have argued that Muslim immigrants to countries whose religious traditions are not Muslim should conform to the norms and practices of the places to which they have chosen to migrate, a requirement that for some involves an abandonment of the Muslim veil.[24]

Notice a distinction between the first two motives for the rejection of the veil from at least some social contexts on the one hand, and the third on the other. The nationalist requiring of Muslim immigrants that they conform sartorially is not claiming to be making a moral claim. They are not claiming that it is wrong to wear headscarves in public, but rather that the prevailing ethos in non-Muslim countries does not support the practice, and that it is the responsibility of migrants that they conform to the ethical practices of the places to which they migrate.

The first two grounds for the criticism of veiling practices, by contrast, purport to transcend thick ethical frameworks. They are claiming that (for the feminist critic) gender equality and (for the *laïciste*) the separation of Church and state are abstract principles of public morality, and that veiling violates these principles.

The holder of the what I have here called the nationalist position is clearly intolerant according to the view of toleration defended by Forst. But he would contest this principle by refusing the claim that there is some set of 'moral' principles that are independent of 'ethical' ones, that ought to have normative priority over the latter. His is an 'ethical' critique of veiling, one that confronts one set of ethical standards to another.

Those who defend the second and third lines of arguments would, by contrast, not see themselves as intolerant. On the contrary, they would view themselves as espousing the Forstian distinction between morality and ethics and would claim to be rejecting and limiting the freedom of veiled women on behalf of a principle drawn from the former, rather than the latter, set of normative principles. The problem is that, arguably,[25] they are *wrong*, because they fail to realise the degree to which their application of moral principles is shot through with unexamined assumptions drawn from their own ethical framework. Thus, though the feminist principle of gender equality is undoubtedly correct, the assumption that veiled women necessarily fall foul of it assumes a particular way in which to realise the principle. Similarly, the view according to which some religious symbols are 'prominent' or 'ostentatious' whereas others are not tends to be grounded in the recognisable majoritarian tendency to see its own symbols and practices as constituting a kind of morally neutral default.

This kind of error in judgement, one in which moral agents think that they have transcended their ethical viewpoints and succeeded in making judgements on the basis of moral principles is, I would argue, ubiquitous. The reason for this is not that people are morally in error (in the sense that they are applying mistaken moral principles), but rather that they are epistemically mistaken, in that they have not managed to rid themselves of parochial ethical contents in making moral judgements. The kind of 'decentring' required by a view such as Forst's is very difficult for moral agents to achieve. What's worse, many people find themselves in the position described with the example above in which they *think* they have achieved it (and thus that they have reached the point of view required by toleration) but have in fact fallen short of it.

Far from thinking that the perspective that toleration requires is easily accessible, Forst acknowledges that it requires a kind of epistemic excellence. He writes that 'tolerant persons are ... "context virtuosi". They have to be able not only to differentiate between different contexts of justification but also to accord priority to moral imperatives in the case of ethical disagreement'.[26] He recognises, however, that human agents can be lacking in their ability to make the relevant distinctions between ethical and moral contexts in a reliable manner. They will tend to disagree, as in the example I developed in this section, as to how to apply relevant moral principles so as to determine whether a set of practices or convictions is or is not to be rejected. Writes Forst: '[T]hose involved should be aware of their own fallibility in these questions. Then, in cases in which the criteria of justification are not clearly violated, being tolerant means living with such differences and seeking the best possible solution.'[27]

The recognition by Forst that ordinary moral agents might not be very good at making use of the distinctions that are central to the account of toleration he provides – that such a conception requires a kind of moral epistemic 'virtuosity' – should give us pause. Even Kant believed that we could not move straight from a deduction of rational moral principles to conclusions about the kind of morality that is right for humans, given their constitutive finitude. Forst himself recognises that the 'right' conception of toleration for a social situation is not something that can be established in an absolute sense, but that there must be context-sensitivity in the determination. Speaking of his preferred, respect-based conception of toleration, he writes that though 'the conception and justification of mutual respect is a precept of practical reason, yet the other conceptions and justifications of toleration preserve their value in situations where it is not possible to establish a respect conception in the preferred sense'.[28] Now, Forst is here clearly thinking that there are properties of social circumstances that may make certain contexts inappropriate to think of toleration as requiring the kind of distinction between morality and ethics that is central to his theory, nor the kind of morality-based respect that flows from it. But it is not much of a stretch to suggest that the same kind of context-sensitivity may require sensitivity as to the epistemic particularities of human beings, particularities that make it the case that they may simply not be very good at making and applying this kind of distinction reliably. Just as a respect-based conception of toleration may not be appropriate to certain kinds of social situations (for example, ones that are shot through with deep ethno-cultural or religious cleavages), so it may not be appropriate to the kinds of beings possessed with the finite moral epistemological capacities that are those of humans.

Return to the example with which I began this section. Given the human tendency to mis-apply moral principles by exaggerating the degree to which the practices and convictions of those who are culturally different fall foul of them, and by underestimating the degree to which their own practices and convictions may sometimes pose problems, and given the fact that the distribution of political power, and thus of the capacity to effectively enact limitations on freedom often tracks divisions between cultural minorities and majorities, it seems sensible not to overtax the motivational and epistemic capacities of those who will be called upon to be tolerant. In such circumstances, it might be more appropriate to exploit reasons for toleration such as the ones with which I began the previous section, as well as others, that do not require the kind of decentring and making of fine contextual distinctions that Forst's does, and that emphasises, among other things, the costs that might accompany a majority acting on its judgements as to the moral acceptability of the practices and convictions of minorities, even from the point of view of the ends pursued by the majority.

V

Let us take stock. I pointed out in the first section of the chapter that the context of toleration includes not just in situations in which people reject practices and convictions to which they might well object, but which they ought also to accept, but also situations in which people who possess the power to get in the way of the realisation of those practices or the expression of those convictions are inclined to make use of their power. Forst oddly omits self-restraint from among the core structural features of toleration, and in so doing occludes many of the (non-ideal) settings in which it is called for, and in which the reasons for self-restraint might be quite different from the reasons that are considered in deciding whether to accept or reject a practice or a set of convictions on moral grounds. There may be reasons to tolerate even that which one rejects, either because more harm than good would come from acting on one's judgement of rejection, or because one might want to prescind from acting on what one might feel to be legitimate reasons for rejection out of a healthy scepticism about one's own capacity correctly to distinguish between judgements of other practices and convictions that stem from a pure moral standpoint, and those that, though they appear to be grounded in a moral standpoint, are nonetheless tinged in sometimes fateful ways with parochial ethical elements.

Now, Forst does not deny that there are different 'routes' to toleration. Much of the book is indeed made up of historical explorations through which some of these routes are explored. The claim is made throughout the book however that his view is the correct one, that it 'trumps' all of the other conceptions that may result from adopting one of the routes made up by other sets of reasons than the ones around which he builds his conception. Other conceptions are normatively lacking with respect to it, and gain what normative validity they have from the fact that they approximate or somehow prefigure the 'correct' view.

Why does Forst feel that he is on firm footing making this claim as to the dependency of other conceptions upon the preferred one, and as to the superiority of the latter relative to the former? Remember the paradoxes to which Forst claims other conceptions of toleration give rise. A conception that does not ground itself in the distinction between morality and ethics does face the difficulty of having to say that there is something to be said for the intolerant person who illegitimately rejects a practice but prescinds from getting in its way for one or the other of the various reasons I have given a partial list of. We may have to say of the person whose judgements are intolerant that her actions evince toleration. Such a paradoxical situation is in Forst's view an affront to reason. 'The "space of normative reasons"', Forst writes, 'is extensive and complex and the essential task of practical reason is to systematize it, a task which must reckon with deep-seated conflicts, for example between ethical ties and moral duties'.[29] Now, there are many ways in which to understand the requirement of systematicity that Forst gives voice to in this passage. On a modest reading of what 'system' requires of practical reason, the demand would be that the space of reasons be depicted theoretically with as much precision as possible. Systematicity would here mean (to use a photographical metaphor) high resolution. But systematicity might also mean simplification, in the sense of making the tensions and conflicts among the elements that make up normative space disappear, of revealing the deeper unity that lies beneath them.

There is a danger that attends the task of systematicity as simplification. It is that the real complexity of the normative domain is sacrificed at the altar of theoretical elegance and simplicity. Normative theories should have just as much theoretical simplicity as their object domains will allow. What may at the end of the day distinguish my view of toleration from Forst's is our different views of what the real level of irreducible complexity of the normative domain really is.

In closing I would like to at least sketch an argument for the importance of maintaining a clear separation between toleration as Forst understands it, and the non-ideal conception that I have sketched. I want in order to do so to mine a linguistic intuition that comes from reflecting upon the distinction that emerges, at least in the languages with which I am familiar, between the verb and the adjective associated with toleration. When we refer to a tolerant person, we think of someone whose dispositions and traits of character incline them to refrain from the kinds of censorious attitudes one associates with the *in*tolerant. A person who expresses or harbours negative judgements about persons or groups, but who nonetheless visibly struggles either to repress these judgements or to refrain from acting on their basis to limit the freedom of those with whose views or practices she opposes would not be labelled 'tolerant', though we would naturally say of her that she 'tolerates'. Indeed, we would find it odd to say of a person that she 'tolerates' were she not at some level moved *not* to tolerate. A person who no longer held intolerant attitudes would be a tolerant person, but in virtue of her tolerance would have placed herself in a position in which she no longer had to make any effort, or to do anything special, in order to tolerate. Toleration would, as it were, flow naturally from her character.

The noun 'toleration' is ambiguous between these two senses. It seems to fit both the person or group naturally disposed to seek pacific relations with those people or groups with which it disagrees, and those who are antecedently inclined to intervene or act to limit the freedom of those with whom it disagrees, but who exercise self-restraint, that is, to prescind from acting on this inclination, not because one has extinguished the inclination to do so, but in virtue of some other set of reasons, that may have to do with the consequences that one envisages might flow from acting on one's intolerant attitudes, or with the prospect that one may, after all, be wrong in one's judgements (which is not the same as to claim that one on moral grounds *accepts* the view that one has decided to tolerate).

For Forst, the 'correct' view of toleration is that of the person who has come to the understanding that there is a big difference between disagreeing with someone and coming to the conclusion that their position is to be rejected. The tolerant person is, to repair to a term used by Forst and that I have already cited, a normative virtuoso capable of placing herself in the appropriate normative context depending on the nature of the practices or convictions with which she is confronted. Such a person would be, according to the distinction that I have tried to extract from my linguistic intuitions, tolerant, rather than someone who tolerates. She would, at least in one sense, have placed herself beyond toleration by ridding herself of the normative confusion as between that which one opposes and that which one rejects upon which *in*tolerance – the tendency to see as rejectable those practices, traits, beliefs that one merely opposes – is grounded.

Clearly, we are not all moral virtuosi. Many people view their ethical beliefs as providing them with warrant to reject. And many who have understood the distinction between the ethical and the moral standpoints that Forst makes central to his account are just not very good at keeping that distinction clear. That is, they smuggle ethical contents into what they in good faith believe to be moral judgements.

In such a non-ideal context, it is important that we keep in mind the reasons that there might be to tolerate, reasons that are independent of the kinds of grounds that lead people over time to develop the disposition to be tolerant. It is important, in other words, that (as paradoxical as it may sound) we keep a place open for a concept of toleration fit for the intolerant, or for the imperfectly tolerant.

Now, Forst at various points concedes that regimes of toleration may start off in an 'imperfect' way, with groups either permitting others to carry on with their practices on the condition that they not question the pre-eminent status of those doing the permitting, or coexisting without the respect born of a moral perspective (in conditions where no group is in a position to lord it over any other). He suggests, however, that what value there is in these states of affairs rests in their being way stations in the direction of a more respect-based practice of toleration (in much the same way as Rawls is in *Political Liberalism* prepared to concede some value to *modus vivendi* arrangements).[30]

It could very well be the case that, empirically, situations in which people decide to tolerate lay the foundations for their becoming tolerant. Forst writes that a 'coexistence' conception of toleration 'could lead to an increase in trust that makes more extensive toleration possible'.[31] This is, of course, possible. That is, it is possible that the extended peace that *modus vivendi* afford can lead people from exercising toleration to being tolerant. It might be a better state of affairs in which people no longer need to revert to the range of reasons that might lead them to exercising self-restraint, in circumstances in which they possess an antecedent disposition to act on their disapprovals. But this does not mean that the concept of toleration that is built around these reasons it itself confused or inferior to the conception of toleration that is appropriate to persons who are tolerant. On the contrary, such a concept may be the correct one to apply to the radically non-ideal sets of circumstances which are the ones that most call for the practice of toleration.

Notes

1 Successive versions of this chapter have been presented at the University of North Carolina at Chapel Hill, the University of York and the University of Minho. Thanks to audiences at all of these talks for comments that have immeasurably improved the argument.
2 The second part of G.A. Cohen's *Rescuing Justice and Equality* (Cambridge, MA.: Harvard University Press, 2008) is about as rigorous and thoroughgoing a defence of ideal theory as we possess. For a vigorous defence of the claims of non-ideal theory, see Jacob Levy, 'There Is No Such Thing as Ideal Theory', *Social Philosophy and Policy*, 33:1–2 (2016), 312–333.
3 *TiC*, p. 18.
4 *Ibid.*, pp. 20–21.
5 *Ibid.*, p. 23.
6 *Ibid.*, p. 33.
7 *Ibid.*, p. 403.

8 *Ibid.*, p. 480.
9 I am not sure that any of the 'paradoxes' that Forst points to as pointing to the limitations of traditional conceptions of toleration are, technically, paradoxes at all. For a philosophical discussion of paradoxes, see M. Sainsbury, *Paradoxes*, 3rd edn (Cambridge: Cambridge University Press, 2009). For scepticism about the paradoxes associated with toleration, see John Horton, 'Three (Apparent) Paradoxes of Toleration', *Synthesis Philosophica*, 9:1 (1994), 7–20.
10 Forst has developed this view at length in his *RtJ*.
11 *TiC*, p. 400.
12 *Ibid.*, p. 8.
13 See for example C. Mackinnon, *Toleration: A Critical Introduction* (Abingdon: Routledge, 2007), p. 14.
14 *TiC*, pp. 25–26.
15 Here I briefly summarise the argument I developed in my 'Berlin's Methodological Parsimony', *San Diego Law Review*, 46 (2009), 839–858.
16 *TiC*, p. 8.
17 *Ibid.*, pp. 544–571.
18 This is the reasoning to which physicians in Seattle arrived at in arriving what has come to be known as the 'Seattle compromise' with respect to female genital cutting.
19 A. Shachar, *Multicultural Jurisdictions* (Cambridge: Cambridge University Press, 2001).
20 See W. Kymlicka, *Multicultural Citizenship* (Oxford: Oxford University Press, 1995).
21 Philip Pettit has made this point in a number of writings, including 'The Consequentialist Perspective', in M. Baron, P. Pettit and M. Slote, *Three Methods on Ethics* (London: Routledge, 1997).
22 Susan Okin's book *Is Multiculturalism Bad for Women?* (Princeton: Princeton University Press, 1999) has been an important font for this kind of thinking.
23 On this issue see J. Bowen, *Why the French Don't Like Headscarves* (Princeton: Princeton University Press, 2008).
24 In France, this kind of conservative nationalist position has been held among others by the controversial essayist Éric Zemmour. See his *Le suicide français* (Paris: Albin Michel, 2014).

25 M. Brown, 'Multiple Meanings of the *Hijab* in Contemporary France', in W. Keenan (ed.), *Dressed to Impress: Looking the Part* (London: Bloomsbury, 2001).
26 *TiC*, p. 505.
27 *Ibid.*, p. 465.
28 *Ibid.*, p. 401.
29 *Ibid.*, p. 464.
30 J. Rawls, *Political Liberalism* (New York: Columbia University Press, 1994).
31 *TiC*, p. 468.

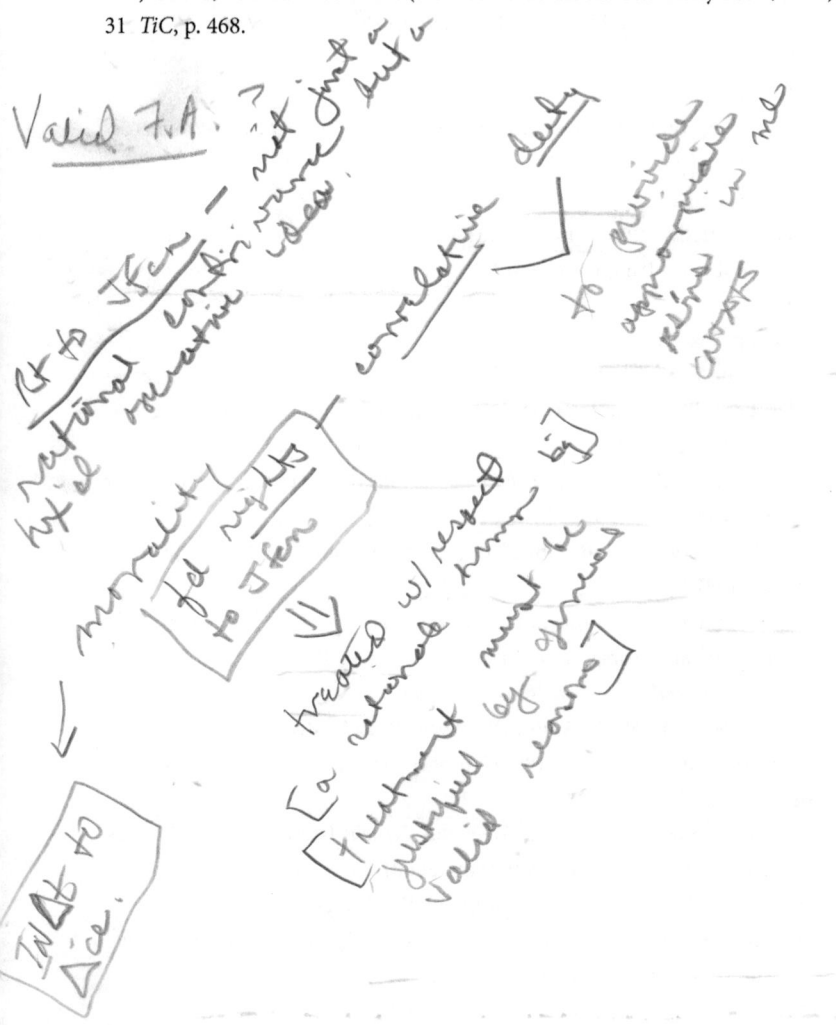

6

On turning away from justification

Melissa S. Williams

I The practice of justification

Rainer Forst's constructivist theory of justice offers a compelling account of what it means to act morally. At the heart of human morality, he argues, is the commitment to demonstrate our respect for other persons as rational beings who are also finite and vulnerable. Respect for others' rational nature demands that we act towards them only in a manner that could be justified by generally valid reasons. Responsiveness to others' vulnerability – which is always particular, unique to each individual – demands that we engage in a reciprocal exchange of reasons with those whom our actions affect, reasons that *they* in particular can recognise as valid. Forst distils this core of morality to the recognition of the fundamental 'right to justification' of every human being, and the correlative duty to provide appropriate reasons in moral contexts.[1]

The Kantian insight that morality must begin from an attitude of respect for other human beings as 'ends in themselves' is unassailable, and Forst's constructivist approach is an important advance in grounding that insight in an analysis of human relationships – rather than in an appeal to natural, transcendental or other foundationalist or metaphysical truth-claims. Among the many virtues of Forst's approach is the complexity and nuance of his constructivism, which draws insights from formal-pragmatic reconstruction (like Habermas's discourse ethics) and political constructivism (aimed at clarifying the conditions under which members of a collective can autonomously generate the order of rules and norms that bind them), but is also informed by his past practice of historical reconstruction in his magisterial study of the history of toleration.[2] Historical reconstruction, in its most fully developed form, 'would show that in all concrete legitimations of given social relations that are and have been provided, questioned, revised, or rejected, demanding the right to justification – and the corresponding normative status of persons – represents a kind of deep normative grammar of justice'.[3] Forst's historical and empirical study of toleration, like his more recent studies of debates over multiculturalism, he argues, shows that 'the right to justification is not just a rationalistic contrivance but a historically operative idea'.[4]

My purpose in this chapter is to interrogate Forst's account of morality by means of this third mode of reconstruction, namely, the empirical and historical analysis of the actions by which human agents establish moral and just relations between themselves. I agree wholeheartedly with Forst that such relations must be motivated by and must express an attitude of respect towards others' agency as moral and rational beings and must be structured by practices of egalitarian reciprocity. I further agree that the practice of justification – demanding, offering and responding to reasons from a stance of mutual respect – is a paradigmatic exemplar of the actions through which human beings establish moral and just relations.[5] I am less convinced, however, by Forst's view that justification is *the* (unique) modality of practice by which moral and just human relations are established, as he sometimes claims.[6] Nor do I believe all moral practices of reciprocal respect can be reduced to or reinterpreted as practices of justification, or that they fully count as moral practices only once they have been redeemed through a practice of justification.

Justification is *one* of the practices by which we establish moral relations, and perhaps in grand historical perspective it will prove to be the most important one. But the practice of justification, like all human practices, can only be carried out by finite and embodied human beings operating in real space and time and in particular and situated social relationships. It is a linguistic performance, mediated by social hierarchies, cultural norms and the discourses that are circulating in a particular context at a particular moment in time. In some contexts, in some times, agents who are striving to establish moral and just relations between themselves consciously and deliberately turn away from practices of justification to engage in other, non-linguistic practices of egalitarian and reciprocal respect. Analysing and reconstructing the 'normative grammar' that is at work in these moments, I believe, preserves the moral core of Forst's theory – the duty to treat others with respect for their autonomy and concern for their vulnerability – while unsettling the conclusion that the 'right to justification' exhaustively expresses that moral core.

II The cure for the ills of justification

Before turning to the sorts of non-linguistic practices of reciprocity that I have in mind, let me first acknowledge Forst's response to a line of criticism that, like mine, flows from the observation that the practice of justification, as a linguistic practice, plays out in contexts that are (*inter alia*) suffused by power inequalities, and the process of justification may (unjustifiably) reinforce and reproduce these inequalities. Like earlier critiques of other theorists of discourse ethics, deliberative democracy and public reason,[7] Forst's critics draw attention to 'the subordinating power of justification, that is, to the ways in which certain conceptions of practical reason and practices of justification can and do serve to entrench, rationalize and legitimate relations of domination'.[8] As Kevin Olson argues, the danger of reinforcing social hierarchies through our theoretical constructions is endemic to the 'linguistic turn' in normative theory, since the intellectuals who generate such theories are at risk of 'falsely universaliz[ing] those skills and activities' – particularly skills of language use – at which they are adept. 'Thus well-intentioned ideas such as recognizing the humanity of others through the public use of language can rationalize a political system that privileges some while framing others as less competent' and 'establish a seemingly neutral domain of politics that is differentiated along pre-existing lines of group privilege.'[9]

Forst's response is that this line of criticism mistakes the critical and empirical analysis of social relations with the theoretical ('conceptual and criterial') apparatus that makes such analysis possible.[10] Citing his work on toleration, he points out that people who have been subjected to domination have often been radically innovative in generating new discourses and practices of resistance that, over time, can transform social relations of justification such that the dominated come to be recognised as justificatory equals:

> [T]he structure of asking for better justifications and ultimately for ones that could gain assent by all as free and equal is an essential part of every such struggle if it is a struggle for emancipation. It is a 'deep grammar' of social conflict and emancipatory aims – and as such, it 'belongs' to no particular culture, history or life form. The language of emancipation and of no longer wanting to be denied one's right to be a participatory equal is a universal language spoken in many tongues.[11]

What is necessary to protect against the danger of false universalisation that Olson points out, on Forst's view, is a self-consciously *critical* theory of justification that acknowledges that 'reason-giving comes in a myriad of forms, and when critique goes well, it shows that some forms of justification fail and exclude certain voices'. Critique itself may take a myriad of forms, some of which are non-linguistic performances ('holding up … pictures of missing persons in a public square'), but it too must proceed in accordance with the 'deep grammar' of justification.[12]

Forst's critical theory of justification thus takes a *longue durée* view of history. In a different response to different critics, and again drawing on his historical study of toleration, he notes that the *logic* of a right to justification emerged even before the *discourse* of rights had formed. The progressive development of the right to justification is neither linear nor inevitable, but

On turning away from justification   121

once this dynamic is set into motion, there is hardly a stopping-point … [T]he 'right' to ask for better justifications is in principle boundless and generates more and more criticism. Eventually, the superior kind of justification for norms of toleration and justice will be the one which *reflexively* uses the principle of justification itself.[13]

We get a clearer view of what Forst has in mind by a critical and reflexive practice of justification when we turn to his concept of the 'basic structure of justification' as the ultimate object of justificatory practice. Drawing on Rawls's notion of the basic structure of society as the subject of justice, Forst distinguishes two aspects of justice as it pertains to the basic structure. The first, which corresponds quite closely to Rawls's sense, is what Forst refers to as 'full justice', the state of social relations that would obtain if the actually existing basic structure of society (its core institutions and the relationship between them) were fully justified to all who are subjected to the relations of power that it institutionalises.

But it is the second aspect of justice in the basic structure that highlights the reflexive quality of Forst's conception: what he calls 'fundamental justice'. Fundamental justice, on Forst's view, pertains less to the material structures of a social order – core economic institutions, such as markets and relations of production and consumption; core social institutions, such as the system of education by which individual subjectivity and social opportunity are shaped – than to the institutionalised practices through which these material structures are justified (or fail to be justified). This re-reading of the concept of the 'basic structure' draws our attention more sharply to the 'structure of justification' as constitutive of the basic structure of social relations than does Rawls, and amplifies the importance of critical reflexivity not only with regard to the reasons we offer one another in justifying or criticising existing practices, but also to the practices of reason-giving themselves. Forst's idea of fundamental justice thus goes even deeper than Rawlsian or Habermasian ideas of procedural justice; it is 'a substantive starting point of procedural justice'. It expresses the ideal that '[b]ased on a moral right to justification, arguments are presented for a basic structure in which individual members have real opportunities to codetermine the institutions of this structure in a reciprocal and general manner'.[14]

For Forst, the need for a 'basic structure of justification' arises from co-existence under a shared order of rule.[15] The idea of fundamental justice generates potent resources for the critique of existing structures of justification – and, as in the case of many transnational relations of domination, of the absence of such structures. If the greatest challenge for transnational justice is to institute relations of justification where they do not currently exist and to open up systems of transnational power and domination to both state and substate actors that are subject to them,[16] the greatest challenge within established social practices of justification is to continuously subject them to critique, uncovering the ways in they may conceal relations of domination. Once again, we see that a truly *critical* theory of relations of justification must be alive to 'the injustice of justice', the possibility that criteria we use for what counts as a reason or an argument in practices of justification may themselves function as vehicles of dominating agents, silencing the dominated by ruling their reasons, their experiences and their arguments out of court.[17] In this way, Forst reconciles his Kantian view of the moral respect owed to persons as justificatory equals with the contextualised critique of social power such as we find in Foucault or Bourdieu:

> In critical theory, it is important ... to always be aware of the different worlds one is a part of and thus to use at least two different versions of normativity: the normativity of the (noumenal) power structures that surround us and fix and 'normalize' identities and that determine what can be said and what not; and the normativity of critique directed against such reifications, essentially claiming a right to justification and the right to construct a normative order on the basis of (more) acceptable reasons. These two normativities are always intertwined, but we must not lose track of their conceptual distinction.[18]

On Forst's view, then, we make advances along the path towards justice by engaging in the practice of justification. When practices of justification are themselves imbued by unjust relations of power, they must become critically self-reflexive; we must try to find the practices of justification that can themselves be justified to those who are affected by them. 'I do not see', Forst states, why such circumstances 'would call for anything but a *better practice of justification*, applying the criteria of generality and reciprocity in the right way'.[19]

Jane Addams and John Dewey both invoked (though not uncritically) the familiar idea that 'the cure for the ills of democracy is more democracy'.[20] Similarly, we can read Forst as arguing that the cure for the ills of justification is more justification, qualified in much the same way that Dewey qualified his endorsement of the claim about democracy. That claim, Dewey wrote, 'is not apt if it means that the evils may be remedied by introducing more of the same machinery of the same kind as that which already exists, or by refining and perfecting that machinery. But the phrase may indicate the need of returning to the idea itself, of clarifying and deepening our apprehension of it, and of employing our sense of its meaning to criticize and re-make its political manifestations'.[21] Forst's critical and reflexive view of the 'basic structure of justification' – justification's machinery, if you will – strikes me as very much in keeping with this Deweyan spirit. It is a view towards which I am deeply sympathetic.

And yet (there had to be an 'and yet'): I am not wholly persuaded that the 'right to justification' is an adequate account of the fundamental character of morality or justice. To explain why, I now turn to 'prefigurative' practices that establish moral and political relationship but are not best understood as practices of justification. Like practices of justification, these practices' moral core lies in the duty of reciprocal respect between human beings as moral equals. The practice of justification, I will argue, is but one instantiation of the moral commitment to reciprocal respect, even if – especially in complex social relations that are subject to established norms and power relations – reflexively critical practices of justification should hold a privileged position in our understanding of what justice demands. To show this, I look to cases in which agents arrive at the judgement that the cure for the ills of justification is not more justification. In these cases, agents turn away from justification in order to enact moral relationship.[22]

III Turning away from justification: the normative grammar of prefigurative practice

The term 'prefigurative practice' denotes forms of social cooperation that are constructed as islands of just and moral relationship within larger contexts of social, political or economic domination. Prefigurative practice both emerges from and instantiates a critique of domination in the larger context, and yet it is not reducible to its function in resisting domination as a social structure. In addition to this, and as a free-standing goal, prefigurative practice is a method by which (a) individual agents retrain the internalised habits of mind and action that they have acquired as participants in a system of domination, and (b) collectives establish modes of living-together based on a shared moral commitment to mutual respect and egalitarian reciprocity. A characteristic feature of prefigurative politics is its refusal to separate ends from means in the pursuit of just social relations: the only means by which such relations can be established are those that are compatible with the end of egalitarian respect.

There are numerous historical examples of prefigurative politics.[23] Carl Boggs, the political scientist who is credited with coining the term, traces the phenomenon to early anarchist and syndicalist reactions to early industrialisation, through the Paris Commune of 1871, and on into the council movements and soviets of revolutionary movements across Europe.[24] The worker control and participatory democracy movements of the 1960s provide further examples, as do the more recent practices of the democratic movements, including but not only Occupy, that emerged in the wake of the 2008–9 global financial crisis.[25]

In all of these examples, inclusive and egalitarian practices of justification – varieties of deliberative democracy – were central and defining features of the prefigurative practice of establishing just relations. For that reason, they tend to reinforce Forst's claim that justification is constitutive of moral relationship as such. For the sake of analytic clarity, in what follows I will focus on two examples of prefigurative practice in which practices of justification are not doing the primary work in establishing moral relationship: Gandhi's *satyagraha* ('truth-struggle' or 'truth-force') movement and the contemporary movement of Indigenous resurgence in North America.

Gandhi is often (mis)quoted as the source of the leading slogan for prefigurative politics: 'Be the change you wish to see in the world.' What he actually said is more nuanced:

> We but mirror the world. All the tendencies present in the outer world are to be found in the world of our body. If we could change ourselves, the tendencies in the world would also change. As a man changes his own nature, so does the attitude of the world change towards him.[26]

For Gandhi, prefigurative practice was first and foremost a matter of individual self-discipline and experimentation in living in accordance with one's own (evolving) judgements of moral conduct.[27] But it was often simultaneously a collective and self-consciously political undertaking, which Gandhi led in many different modalities of action.

In some cases, the forms of collective action that Gandhi led functioned as discursive contributions to a politics of justification in relation to British colonial authorities, asserting a clear 'no' in response to colonial policies. Consider, first, Gandhi's promotion of the *khadi* (homespun) movement, which became central to his own public self-presentation when he abandoned Western-style suits in favour of the *dhoti* (loincloth) and spent long hours spinning cotton on the simple spinning wheel that became the symbol for the anti-colonial struggle. A pillar of the *swadeshi* movement for economic self-sufficiency, the *khadi* movement was conjoined to the boycott of British imports, particularly of machine-woven fabric made of Indian cotton, as a protest against the partnership of colonialism and capitalism in producing the economic dependency of the colonised people on the economic system that exploited them.[28] Or consider the Salt March, in which Gandhi led *satyagrahi* to the coast to make salt in defiance of the colonial assertion of monopoly control over salt production.[29]

In other cases, however, Gandhi's experimentation in collective forms of prefigurative practice cannot easily be read as a 'no' addressed to colonial powers. This is clearest in the case of his utopian experiments in communal living, including the Tolstoy Farm in South Africa (1910–1913) and a succession of ashrams in India.[30] Whereas the Gandhian politics of resistance and civil disobedience said 'no' to colonial domination through practices of non-violent non-cooperation, the ashrams said 'yes' to the ideal of egalitarian reciprocity as a daily practice of cooperative living-together. Membership in the ashrams was entirely voluntary and open to any person who was prepared to commit to this ideal and willing to serve the other members of the community by sharing equally in the work necessary to sustain it, without regard to gender, religion, ethnicity, class or caste. This equal sharing of work was an especially strenuous form of retraining internalised habits for upper-caste *satyagrahi*, for whom performing the labour associated with Dalits or other low-status groups (cleaning latrines, spinning cotton) was deeply revulsive. In cultivating and deepening within each of its members the ethos of service to the other in practical social relations of egalitarian reciprocity, the ashrams were conceived as ends in themselves. But they also served as a training ground for the moral powers that made the difference between justifiable and unjustifiable practices of resistance to colonial domination through non-violent non-cooperation. Within the 'no' addressed to colonial powers was embedded an ongoing 'yes' to cooperative relationship based on reciprocal concern and respect, addressed to other *satyagrahi* who had joined the struggle.

We find a similar logic in the contemporary political resurgence of Indigenous peoples, in which, as Dene political theorist Glen Coulthard writes, 'the methods of decolonization prefigure its aims'.[31]

For Coulthard, the prefigurative politics of Indigenous resurgence is grounded in an ethic of reciprocal responsibility not only in relation to other human beings, but also in relation to the land. The mode of domination characteristic of settler colonialism, he argues, has not been that of exploitation and proletarianisation but rather of the dispossession of Indigenous land and the transformation of land into alienable property to be used instrumentally for economic production. Not only did colonial dispossession wrest away from Indigenous peoples the material conditions for their economic self-sufficiency and generate relations of dependence on the colonial state for mere survival, but it also disrupted the lifeworld in which Indigenous relational ethics was practicable. Consequently, 'Indigenous anticolonialism … is … a struggle not only *for* land in the material sense, but also deeply *informed* by what the land *as a system of reciprocal relations and obligations* can teach us about living our lives in relation to one another and the natural world in non-dominating and nonexploitative terms'.[32] More concretely, Indigenous resurgence entails the iterated embodied performance of reconnecting 'with lands and land-based practices', from traditional harvesting and cultural production (carving, hide-tanning) to 'walking the land' in order to reawaken the spatial imaginaries embedded in oral tradition, to relearning Indigenous languages and ceremonies.[33]

A common feature of all prefigurative practice is that it entails a deliberate and self-conscious *turning away* from a politics of justification and critique addressed to the dominating agent, and a *turning towards* those whose solidarity one seeks in constructing and enacting an alternative ethical form of life based on relationships of egalitarian reciprocity.[34] As noted earlier, in some forms of prefigurative practice, practices of mutual justification play a central and defining role in establishing relations of egalitarian respect. But I have highlighted the Gandhian and Indigenous modes of prefiguration because here we do not find practices of justification playing this foundational role; rather, non-discursive practices that are understood by agents as performances of (or, in Gandhi's terms, experiments in) reciprocity and respect are doing the normative work.

IV Justification and interruption

Why turn away from the 'game of giving and receiving reasons'[35] in favour of non-discursive modes of reciprocal concern and respect? I believe that what is going on in the modes of prefiguration that give priority to non-discursive practices of reciprocity is a three-fold interruption of existing relations of justification.

The first interruption is a response to relations of domination in the larger context, relations that suffuse the existing and available structure of justification. The critique of and active resistance to dominating agents is first expressed *within* the justification game as a refusal of the reasons offered in defence of that power. This is the initial 'no', which may be performed initially through discursive actions (such as written and spoken critiques of the injustice of the Salt Act, or the assertion of Aboriginal title against the one-sided imposition of extractive economic development on Indigenous lands) and repeated through the embodied performance of direct actions of resistance and non-cooperation (civil disobedience in the form of the Salt March, or the physical occupation of lands targeted for extractive development). This 'no' disrupts the justification game as it has been constructed by and for the advantage of the dominating agent. It is, in Forst's terms, a demand for *better* justifications than the ones now on offer. This 'no' interrupts the justification game as it is now being played by challenging the existing rules of the game but does not abandon the game itself. Rather, it demands that the 'basic structure of justification' be rendered more just through a reform to the rules of the justification game. I think Forst is correct that even in its nonverbal and embodied forms, this 'no' is at root a discursive move in the justification game.

This first interruption of the practice of justification does not trouble Forst's theory. To the contrary, it is a constitutive moment in his account of justification as a critical and reflexive practice by which the 'basic structure of justification' can progress in the direction of 'fundamental justice'.

The second interruption of prefigurative practice – the 'turning away' from the dominating agent – is a response to the failure of the dominating agent adequately to respond to the initial 'no'. Its communicative content in relation to the dominating agent reiterates the initial 'no' to signal that the existing structure of justification is not acceptable, but takes the further step of signalling that because the dominating agent's failure to recognise the dominated as equal subjects of justification, the dominated withdraw their recognition of the dominating agent as a partner in intersubjective communication. The logic of this move is well captured in Hegel's master-slave dialectic in the moment when the slave turns away from the master in order to do the work through which his agency will be reflected back to him in the form of its finished product. This is an emancipatory moment because it liberates the slave from dependence upon recognition by the master and activates his capacity for *self*-recognition as sufficient affirmation of his agency.[36] In prefigurative political practice, the cultivation of self-recognition through *praxis* is a collective and intersubjective undertaking, but one which bypasses dominating agents' granting or withholding of recognition as lacking salience for dominated subjects' agency and worth.

In contrast to the first interruption of the practice of justification, this second interruption is not constitutive of Forst's idea of the progressive development of the basic structure of justification, but neither does it pose serious challenges for that account. 'Turning away' from practices of justification that engage the dominating agent is morally unproblematic, as the duty to recognise that agent as a moral subject has already been met through antecedent actions, including the discursive 'no'. 'Turning toward' those with whom one stands in solidarity against domination and interacting with them as moral equals does not repudiate the moral character of the context one shares with the dominating agent, but redirects one's agency from the fruitless effort to wrest moral recognition from that recalcitrant agent, and focusing instead on the constructive work of constituting an *ethical* community through shared practices rooted in egalitarian respect. Forst would likely agree with prefigurative practitioners that the constitution of such

130　　　　　　　　　　*Responses*

ethical communities, where it does not conflict with the moral duty to treat all human beings as equal subjects, is an intrinsic good. And he might go further to note that this work can sometimes be empowering for dominated agents in the larger moral context, when through this intersubjective practice they deepen and refine their own reflexive and critical understandings of the structures of domination, and re-engage dominating agents from this strengthened position. On this reading, prefigurative communities function in a manner similar to 'subaltern counterpublics', which stand in a contestatory relation to the larger public sphere.[37]

These first two forms of interruption are common to all prefigurative political practice, discursive and non-discursive. The third interruption, however, is distinctive to those forms of prefiguration that eschew discursive practices of justification and critique in favour of the embodied performance of egalitarian reciprocity in relation to others. Here, there is not only a turning away from the dominating agent, but a turning away from the practice of justification – of reason-giving and reason-demanding – itself. This (always partial) renunciation of the practice of justification is not based on a rejection of reason or a denial of humans' rational nature. Rather, it begins from (but is not exhausted by) the understanding that practices of reason, and especially social practices of reason-giving and reason-demanding, and of recognising others as rational subjects, are never innocent of power relations. As Glen Coulthard puts it, 'the issue of recognition is obviously a tricky one because it usually plays out in a way that, in order to be recognized you have to make yourself like the power structure that is recognizing you – in this case it's not so much an identity but the structure of a program … Recognition … has a kind of assimilative pull to it'.[38] Gandhi directed his critique towards rationalism as a form of ideology: 'Rationalists are admirable beings, [but] rationalism is a hideous monster when it claims for itself omnipotence … I plead not for the suppression of reason, but for a due recognition of that in us which sanctifies reason itself'.[39]

It makes sense to read these critiques of recognition and rationalism as similar in spirit to the critiques of Enlightenment reason that we find in Foucault's analysis of the power/knowledge that produces 'docile bodies', or Bourdieu's analysis of 'symbolic violence'.[40] And as we have seen, Forst has a ready response when this line of criticism is advanced his theory: that one must not flinch from acknowledging the role of power (specifically: 'noumenal power')[41] in constituting the subjects who are capable of recognising one another as equal agents of justification, nor from the fact that that power is sometimes a form of domination, and hence unjustifiable. Rather, the power-suffused character of justification demands that we continuously subject its practices and social structure to critique and demand that those structures be reformed when we find that they are distorted by relations of domination.

This is fair enough, but it leaves unanswered the question of what agents are doing when they interrupt discursive practices of justification not by subjecting those practices to rational critique, but instead by substituting non-discursive performances of egalitarian respect within cooperative relationship. Why do they regard the embodied performance of these practices – cleaning latrines, spinning cotton, tanning hides, tapping trees for sap – as emancipatory?

We can find a partial answer, I believe, by understanding these practices as a mode of resistance to social hierarchies in the larger social order. Where socially necessary tasks are culturally associated with dominated or stigmatised groups, even by members of the prefigurative community, their performance by people who enjoy higher status within the larger social context has a status-levelling effect and taking turns at work also expresses a commitment to distributive fairness. In contrast, as noted above, the practice of justification often reinscribes power inequalities insofar as it privileges those whose greater skill in reasoned argumentation reflects their higher status in a social hierarchy. Thus, displacing practices of justification with practices of service to community does double duty in generating greater status equality in prefigurative communities.

Other practices, particularly those associated with pre-capitalist modes of cultural and material production, serve a different function of revalorisation, having less to do with status hierarchies among persons and more to do with modernist views of economic and social development that identify pre-modern economic practices with 'backwardness' and 'underdevelopment'. Relearning these practices is simultaneously a critique of the relations of domination endemic to capitalist modes of production (a strong theme in both Gandhian and Indigenous critiques of modernity) and an affirmation of the forms of knowledge that are disvalued and erased by modern conceptions of scientific and technological progress. They also express an ecological ethic of sustainable human relationships with nature as against modernity's instrumental and anthropocentric stance towards the earth and its non-human inhabitants. In contrast to non-discursive practices that level status hierarchies within the cooperative community, there is no essential tension between prefigurative practices of production and the practices of justification and critique. Indeed, critique is a necessary complement to practices of prefigurative production, both because those practices are being reclaimed from cultural traditions that were likely structured by their own forms of domination, including gender-based domination, and because modern modes of domination have shaped the attitudes and habits of contemporary practitioners.[42]

Yet even where critique and justification are its antecedent and complement, non-discursive prefigurative practice interrupts ('turns away' from) practices of justification in at least three ways. First, since both discursive and non-discursive forms of egalitarian practice are performed in real time, they present an opportunity cost for each other; we can't do them both simultaneously. Second, the justification of practices entails that we stand at a distance from them, represent them in linguistic and ideational terms, and then subject them to critical assessment. In the moment when we treat our practices as objects of critical reason and argumentation, we are necessarily alienated from them; we are not wholly immersed in them. We must be prepared to abandon them if our reason so dictates. When the justification of a practice begins, the practice itself must cease – unless it is already the practice of justification that we are engaged in. In other words, just as the practice of justification interrupts embodied social practices and subjects them to critical evaluation, engaging in non-discursive practices of egalitarian reciprocity, particularly those whose performance demands our full attention and care, requires an interruption of the practice of justification.

Third, and most importantly for my argument here, non-discursive prefigurative practices of egalitarian reciprocity interrupt practices of justification by asserting that justification as such is not necessary to redeem the moral core of these activities, that they enact relations of mutual respect. When a person spins cotton as a contribution to a project of economic self-sufficiency, cleans latrines in a cooperative community of equals, or taps a tree for sap as part of a collective project of revitalising Indigenous culture, she is already conducting herself in a moral way, not only as a contributor to the 'deep grammar' of morality over history's *longue durée*, but right here, right now.

Forst might respond that we only know she is acting morally by attending to the justifications she has for performing these practices and confirming that her practice really does treat all affected others as moral equals. For human practices are always already 'bound up with justifications; no matter what we think or do, we place upon ourselves (and others) the demand for reasons, whether they are made explicit or remain implicit (at least initially).'[43] Now, I would agree with Forst that to count as moral the practices would have to be motivated by an intention to treat others with respect (and that intention would also have to be fulfilled by the practice). In other words, I agree that moral reasons must underlie the practice. But acting from moral reasons does not entail that those reasons are made explicit. Even if the moral reasons remain implicit, the action they underwrite retains its moral character. Justification is the practice of making reasons explicit and hence available for critical examination. It is the practice by which we come to hold our reasons reflexively. If we are to take Forst literally when he writes that 'morality is a relation … established by justification,'[44] then no person can act morally if she conducts herself unreflexively, for reasons that remain implicit. I think that is incorrect. What makes a relation moral is that it is sustained by practices that treat each person with equal concern (for her finitude and vulnerability) and respect (for her autonomy). Giving and demanding reasons is one practice by which we treat others morally, and it is also the indispensable means by which we attain critical reflexivity in our moral judgements and cultivate our capacity to correct our practices when they prove to be unjust. The practice of justification is a practice of morality, to be sure, but it does not exhaust the universe of moral practices.

Notes

1 *RtJ*, pp. 20–21 – on finitude and vulnerability see especially pp. 38–41. I will not unpack the phrase 'in moral contexts' here, except to note that Forst distinguishes among different contexts of justification which shape the *kinds* of reasons we owe to one another and the criteria for distinguishing valid from invalid reasons. Of particular importance is his distinction between ethical contexts (human communities oriented towards shared understandings of the good, in which relevant reasons are relative to that community), moral contexts (generated simply by the fact that one's actions affect another, where reasons must meet universal and unconditioned validity criteria of generality and reciprocity), and political contexts (or contexts of justice) (in which the object of justification is a shared order of binding rules and norms). See *RtJ*, ch. 3, for a thorough explication of the distinction between ethical and moral contexts, and ch. 4 for Forst's account of justification in contexts of justice; see also, generally, his *CoJ*.
2 Forst, *TiC*.
3 *RtJ*, p. 3.
4 *Ibid.*
5 'Insofar as the practice of justification is the basic form of reasonable human practice, practical reason yearns for a theory of just relations of justification'. *RtJ*, p. 8.
6 'Morality is a relation between us, and it is established by way of justification' as Forst puts it in 'Justifying Justification', in *JDRJ*, p. 176.

7 E.g. Iris M. Young, 'Communication and the Other: Beyond Deliberative Democracy', in S. Benhabib (ed.), *Democracy and Difference: Contesting the Boundaries of the Political* (Princeton: Princeton University Press, 1996), pp. 120–135; L. Sanders, 'Against Deliberation', *Political Theory*, 25:3 (1997), 347–376.
8 A. Allen, 'The Power of Justification', in *JDRJ*, p. 80.
9 K. Olson, 'Complexities of Political Discourse: Class, Power and the Linguistic Turn', in *JDRJ*, pp. 97, 98.
10 Forst, 'Justifying Justification', in *JDRJ*, p. 181.
11 *Ibid.*, p. 184.
12 *Ibid.*, p. 190.
13 R. Forst, 'The Right to Justification: Moral and Political, Transcendental and Historical', *Political Theory*, 43:6 (2015), 834, emphasis added.
14 R. Forst, 'Transnational Justice and Non-Domination: A Discourse-Theoretical Approach', in B. Buckinx, J. Trejo-Mathys and T. Waligore (eds), *Domination and Global Political Justice: Conceptual, Historical and Institutional Perspectives* (New York: Routledge, 2015), p. 92; see also *RtJ*, pp. 119–124.
15 See Forst, 'Transnational Justice and Non-Domination', p. 91: 'A moral context is one where others are affected by my actions in a relevant way, whereas a context of justice is one where we are participants in an order of rule and/or domination – in other words, one where we are subjected to a social normative order.'
16 *Ibid.*, p. 103.
17 *RtJ*, p. 8; see also Forst, 'The Injustice of Justice: Normative Dialectics According to Ibsen, Cavell, and Adorno', in Forst, *J&C*, pp. 151–164.
18 Forst, 'Justifying Justification', p. 191.
19 Forst, 'The Right to Justification', 826, emphasis added.
20 J. Addams, *Democracy and Social Ethics* (New York: Macmillan, 1902), pp. 11–12; John Dewey, *The Public and Its Problems* (Denver: Swallow Press, [1927] 1954), p. 144.
21 Dewey, *The Public and Its Problems*, p. 144.
22 I am indebted to Toby Rollo and James Tully for spurring me to reflect on prefigurative practice over the years, both in conversation and through engagement with their work. The word 'enact' enters my vocabulary here especially because of my interactions with Rollo. A partial explication of his

views on the 'enactive' (as contrasted with 'discursive') dimension of human agency can be found in T. Rollo, 'Everyday Deeds: Enactive Protest, Exit, and Silence in Deliberative Systems', *Political Theory*, 45:5 (2016), 587–609. Also in the background of my thinking here is James Tully's analysis of practices of 'civic freedom', particularly those of Indigenous peoples, in J. Tully, *Public Philosophy in a New Key*, vols. I and II (Cambridge: Cambridge University Press, 2008).

23 For an overview of the topic, see D.K. Leach, 'Prefigurative Politics', in D.A. Snow, D. Della Porta, B. Klandemans and D. McAdam (eds), *Wiley-Blackwell Encyclopedia of Social and Political Movements* (Malden, MA: Wiley-Blackwell, 2013).

24 C. Boggs, 'Marxism, Prefigurative Communism, and the Problem of Workers' Control', *Radical America*, 11:5 (Winter 1977), 99–122. Boggs's definition of the term is as follows: 'By "prefigurative", I mean the embodiment, within the ongoing political practice of a movement, of those forms of social relations, decision-making, culture, and human experience that are the ultimate goal.' *Ibid.*, 100.

25 See, e.g., M. van de Sande, 'The Prefigurative Politics of Tahrir Square: An Alternative Perspective on the 2011 Revolutions', *Res Publica*, 19:3 (2013), 223–239.

26 'Accidents: Snake-Bite', *Indian Opinion*, 9 August (1913), in Ministry of Information and Broadcasting (ed.), *Collected Works of Mahatma Gandhi* (New Delhi: Publication Division, 1995), vol. 13, p. 241.

27 M.K. Gandhi, *An Autobiography: The Story of My Experiments with Truth* (Boston: Beacon Press, 1993).

28 See C. Bayly, 'The Origins of Swadeshi (Home Industry): Cloth and Indian Society (1700–1930)', in A. Appadurai (ed.), *The Social Life of Things: Commodities in Cultural Perspective* (Cambridge: Cambridge University Press, 1986), pp. 285–321.

29 See D. Dalton, *Mahatma Gandhi: Nonviolent Power in Action* (New York: Columbia University Press, 2012), ch. 4.

30 See M. Thomson, *Gandhi and His Ashrams* (Bombay: Popolar Prakashan, 1993); A. Skaria, 'Gandhi's Politics: Liberalism and the Question of the Ashram', *South Atlantic Quarterly*, 101:4 (2002), 955–986; Susanne and Lloyd Rudolph, 'The Coffee House and the Ashram: Gandhi, Civil Society,

and Public Spheres', in S.O. Wolf et al. (eds), *Politics in South Asia* (Basel: Springer, 2015), pp. 157–168.
31 G. Coulthard, *Red Skin, White Masks: Rejecting the Colonial Politics of Recognition* (Minneapolis: University of Minnesota Press, 2014), Kindle edition, loc. 3374.
32 *Ibid.*, loc. 389.
33 *Ibid.*, loc. 3594.
34 *Ibid.*, *passim*; see also, e.g., T. Alfred, *Wasáse: Indigenous Pathways of Action and Freedom* (Peterborough, ON: Broadview Press, 2005), p. 19: 'We [must] choose to *turn away* from the legacies of colonialism and take on the challenge of creating a new reality for ourselves and for our people.'
35 *RtJ*, p. 14 (quoting Robert Brandom, *Making It Explicit* (Cambridge, MA: Harvard University Press, 1994), pp. 158f. and *passim*).
36 'Now, however, he ... posits *himself* as a negative in the permanent order of things, and thereby becomes *for himself*, someone existing on his own account.' G.W.F. Hegel, *Phenomenology of Spirit*, trans. A.V. Miller (Oxford: Oxford University Press, 1977), p. 118.
37 N. Fraser, 'Rethinking the Public Sphere: A Contribution to the Critique of Actually Existing Democracy', *Social Text*, 25/26 (1990), 56–80.
38 E. Ritses, 'Leanne Simpson and Glen Coulthard on Dechinta Bush University, Indigenous Land-Based Education, and Embodied Resurgence', *Decolonization: Indigeneity, Education & Society*, 26 (2014), accessed 26 November 2016 (https://decolonization.wordpress.com/2014/11/26/leanne-simpson-and-glen-coulthard-on-dechinta-bush-university-indigenous-land-based-education-and-embodied-resurgence).
39 M. Gandhi, 'Tyranny of Words' (14 October 1926), in Ministry of Information and Broadcasting (ed.), *Collected Works of Mahatma Gandhi* (New Delhi: Publication Division, 1994), vol. 36, p. 401.
40 M. Foucault, *Discipline and Punish*, trans. A. Sheridan (New York: Vintage, 1977); P. Bourdieu, *Outline of a Theory of Practice*, trans. R. Nice (Cambridge: Cambridge University Press, 1977).
41 R. Forst, 'Noumenal Power', *Journal of Political Philosophy*, 23:2 (2015), 111–127.
42 See, e.g., Anishinaabe scholar-activist Leanne Simpson's critique of the role of masculinist norms in Indigenous political practice in 'Queering

Resurgence: Taking on Heteropatriarchy in Indigenous Nation-Building', *Mamawipawin: Indigenous Governance and Community Based Research Space*, 1 June (2012), accessed 26 November 2016 (http://leannesimpson.ca/queering-resurgence-taking-on-heteropatriarchy-in-indigenous-nation-building).
43 *RtJ*, p. 1.
44 Forst, 'Justifying Justification', p. 176.

7

Power, attention and the tasks of critical theory

Patchen Markell

I am not the first reader of Rainer Forst's political philosophy to observe that there is a certain relentlessness and single-mindedness in his commitment to the practice of rational justification as the engine of social criticism and moral progress.[1] Seyla Benhabib, for example, has observed that Forst elevates the right to justification to the status of the 'supreme principle of practical reason'. For Benhabib, this results in the 'overmoralization' of ethical and political life, overlooking both the dependence of the 'universalistic moral point of view' on 'institutions, social practices, and ethical contexts to sustain and nourish it', as well as the fact that our collective life can 'never become fully transparent to the logic of justification'.[2] Likewise, Amy Allen has charged that Forst's account of justice as the right to justification, even as it acknowledges that 'particular justifications may be problematic or ideological or may serve the interests of those in power', does not allow for the possibility that 'our ideal of justification itself' may rest on exclusion and domination, or that the 'space of reasons' in which justifications are offered and critiqued may itself be constituted through the operation of 'the very [imperialist and neo-colonial] power relations that critical theory aims to critique'.[3]

Both Benhabib and Allen are worried, for different though overlapping reasons, about the *narrowness* of Forst's commitment to the idea of human beings as 'justifying, reason-giving beings';[4] and this is my worry, too, though I will press the concern in yet a third way. But I want to begin by affirming – as I imagine Benhabib and Allen would, too – that there is also something powerful, indeed something pleasing, in Forst's unyielding inhabitation of the register of justification. In other hands, the impulse to construct an overarching account of critical theory in which everything centres in the end upon the right to justification might come across not just as narrow, but as narrow-minded. In Forst's case, by contrast, this impulse gives his writing and thinking focus, drive and fire. Indeed, it can make Forst sound, in his own way, like those fierce 'pioneers of emancipation' he rightly admires, such as Pierre Bayle or the radical Levellers, who, as he puts it, persisted in their critiques despite being seen as 'immoral' or even 'crazy' by the standards of their own age.[5] I mean this as a compliment: the willingness to think and say what seems unthinkable or crazy, and to cleave to those ideas in the face of strong, sometimes overwhelming hostility, is an indispensable task of critical theory. Yet I also want to suggest that a more capacious sense of critical theory's modes of engagement with the world would not dilute this project or distract from this focus; to the contrary, it could help propel Forst, and the rest of us, even further in this direction.

In what follows, I will spell out this intuition by focusing on Forst's well-known exposition of the idea of 'noumenal power', along with some of his recent writing on the idea of critical theory and its relationship to the notion of justification.[6] Picking up on some of Forst's own remarks, I'll begin by briefly staking out a claim about Hannah Arendt's conception of power – not for the sake of staging an interpretive dispute with Forst about Arendt's work, nor to show that this is the 'right' way to use the word 'power' (whatever that could mean), but simply because I think that doing this will foreground a certain vital political phenomenon that seems to me to go missing in Forst's own analysis. If Forst conceives of power in terms of the effects people have upon each other *within* the space of reasons, and if Allen emphasises that power relations have always already constituted the space of reasons and set the 'condition of possibility for entering the space of reasons in the first place',[7] I want to stress that the space of reasons is also necessarily dependent on a prior sense of what there *is* in the world to be reasoned *about* – that is, a sense of the occasions for and objects of justification. There is no space of reasons, we might say, adapting a phrase of Arendt's, without a space of *appearance*. But understanding and transforming the constitution of *this* space, I'll propose, demands a mode of analysis and a style of intervention irreducible to, though not necessarily opposed to, the reconstruction and criticism of explicit or tacit justifications, one that deserves to be treated as a central part of the repertoire of critical theory – not least because it is indispensable to the task of thinking the unthinkable or the crazy.

Forst's conception of 'noumenal power' is easily misunderstood. To call power 'noumenal', for Forst, is not to say that it is purely ideational *as opposed* to material or sensible, but simply to say that it operates in and through the 'space of reasons'.[8] Power is a capacity to get someone to think or do something they would not otherwise have done by giving them or causing them to have a reason – that is, something that, descriptively, counts for them as a reason – to do it. Thus Forst says that the application of brute force to bring about a state of affairs in a way that completely bypasses your agency is not power – the policeman exercises power when he threatens you, but when he pulls you out of your car and throws you onto the ground, that is not power but force. This, Forst indicates, represents a point of convergence between his understanding of power and Hannah Arendt's claim that 'rule by sheer violence comes into play where power is being lost'.[9] More generally, though, he distances his conception of power from Arendt's on the grounds that power on *his* view is a normatively neutral concept, while hers is a 'one-sided' and 'purely positive' conception of power as a non-violent capacity exercised by people 'acting in concert' on the basis of 'free and equal consent'.[10]

Forst is right that there is at least a strand of this in Arendt's work, and much has been made of it by interpreters who wish to see in the very idea of power as she uses it a bottom-up, democratic, antihierarchical alternative to domination or 'power-over'. But Arendt's use of power was stranger and more complex than this. As I have argued elsewhere at greater length, at least sometimes, Arendt used the term 'power' to draw attention to a phenomenon that is irreducible to the general idea of a capacity to do something, whether that is specified as a capacity to get someone else to do something (of which Forst's conception is one variety), or as the capacity to achieve something new by acting in concert (the view Arendt is usually thought to hold). While both of those senses of 'power' are forward-looking – they refer to a capacity that precedes and is subsequently expressed or realized in an action – some of the central invocations of power in Arendt's *The Human Condition* do not have this anticipatory character. Rather than precede and explain action, in these uses, power survives or outlasts action. It becomes, as Arendt says in one crucial passage, 'what keeps people together *after the fleeting moment of action has passed*'.[11]

Power in this sense is not an agentic capacity waiting to spring forth. It's more like the sort of power we have in mind when we talk about the power of an image or a phrase or a scene to hold people's attention even once it has faded or receded. Sometimes we ascribe power in this sense to situations, as when we refer to situations as being 'charged': people have gathered, something has happened, and in the minutes or hours or weeks during which people remain engaged with each other and with the force of this event, we say things like the situation is tense or taut or fraught or crackling with possibility. (To be sure, this is forward-looking and anticipatory too, but it is not as tightly connected to any *particular* future action as is the more familiar idea of power as a capacity: its relation to the future is more like a stage-setting.) Or we might talk about actions or events themselves being 'powerful', in something like the same way that we talk about a work of art as being 'powerful': we mean that it holds us in its presence, that it commands our attention – which is not yet to *demand* anything in particular from us. Or, again, since events don't simply appear to us in an unmediated way, we might also ascribe power in this sense to those things – institutions, features of the physical world, aspects of the built environment – that organize our attention and let events and actions get a grip on us. It is the configuration of power in *this* sense that gives us occasions to speak to each other and interact with each other, that orients us within a world of objects, issues and concerns – or that lets us disperse or disengage into mutual indifference. As Arendt puts it, 'power is what keeps the public realm, the potential space of appearance between acting and speaking men, in existence'.[12]

As I indicated earlier, my aim isn't to criticise Forst for misreading Arendt, or even to claim that this appropriation of her ideas somehow represents the best specification of the concept of 'power'. So what bearing does this idea have on Forst's conception of power? For Forst, power is not just a simple dyadic relation between one agent and another: there is also such a thing as an 'order of power', which is also an 'order of justification'; it involves the patterning of relations among persons in a society by virtue of the widespread acceptance of certain 'narratives of justification', and this can include patterns of domination and subordination, supported by narratives of justification that 'could not be shared by free and equal justificatory agents in a practice of justification free from such asymmetry'.[13] One of the central tasks of critical theory, Forst rightly says, is to identify, analyse and criticise such situations: situations in which power has been configured as domination. Part of this analysis involves understanding how the orders of power in such situations are reproduced and sustained; that is, understanding how reflexive demands for justification or for transformation are shut down or foreclosed. And for Forst, since even these relatively stable orders of power are also orders of justification, and operate in and through the space of reasons, they must be understood, *pace* Habermas, not in terms of the congealment of norm-free sociality, but in terms of the tacit acceptance of a justificatory narrative that has come to seem natural or unavoidable, or, as Forst puts it, 'justification through everyday practice and socialization into a certain frame of mind'.[14] The aim of critical theory thus becomes to make these orders of power less stable, to draw out the tacit, sedimented justifications that sustain them, and to expose them to criticism.

This is where Allen's critique comes in. This kind of potentially ideological and dominating 'socialization', Allen argues, is not just a way of reproducing the acceptance of specific problematic social relationships.

It is also part of the very process of subject-formation by which people 'are given entry to the space of reasons', i.e. are recognised as bearers of practical reason with the authority to demand, receive, give, accept or reject justifications.[15] And this, in turn, means that practices of justification themselves may be implicated in relations of domination – not because justification as such is the monopoly of any particular group, but because the very idea of 'justification as such' is an abstraction from the concrete, historically specific, power-laden social practices in which the activity of justification inevitably takes place, and whose norms about what counts as a reason or who counts as a reasoner can therefore entrench as well as undermine oppression.[16] But while Allen focuses on the question of *who* gets to participate in the practice of justification and on what terms, Arendt's reflections on power raise the complementary question of *what* those practices of justification are *about* – that is, they draw attention to the constitution of the field of objects with which the subjects of practical reason engage.

For while Forst is right that the criticism and transformation of social relations can be foreclosed by people being socialised into a kind of tacit belief in the justified character of those relations (even if belief in their justified character just amounts to thinking there is no alternative to them), that foreclosure can *also* happen in ways other than through the mediation of beliefs or reasons, whether explicit or tacit. It can happen when the institutions and practices that make up the world are so configured that this or that aspect of the social world does not show up to us – all of us, or some of us – as an object of attention and practical concern. It does not appear, or it appears only asymmetrically, in the space of reasons. It's not that we accept these features of the world because we have been socialised into a tacit belief in their justifiability, or because we think there is no alternative: we – all of us, or some of us – simply do not think much about them at all. This un- or non-thinking might be motivated; that is, we might have an *investment* in the avoidance of such thought, in which case attention to the dynamics of desire and disavowal becomes an important critical resource, and one that is not reducible to the analysis of tacit or explicit beliefs and reasons.[17] (Here, the analysis of the constitution of the field of objects that appear in the space of reasons would re-join Allen's analysis of the formation of reasoning subjects.) But it may also be that something about the configuration of the world itself – of what Arendt called the 'human artifice' – fails to provoke or occasion such thought, or even inhibits it. Both of these sorts of configuration of attention and inattention, irreducible to the sedimentation of beliefs and reasons, not only run alongside the dynamics of everyday practice and socialisation that Forst describes, through which certain structures of justification come to be taken for granted; they are actually prior to and more fundamental than them, insofar as they help determine what aspects of the world appear to us as objects of justification in the first place.

Let me try to make this concrete. In the contemporary United States, such phenomena as residential racial and class segregation, mass incarceration and the racialised practices of policing that go along with both of these are among the most important examples of social orders sustained by a potent mixture of sedimented (bad) reasons, disavowal and the sheer inattention of many people whose lives – whose educational and occupational trajectories, whose patterns of interaction with government agencies, whose daily movements through social space – do not occasion much thought at all about white supremacy or carceral institutions. The demand for justification is, of course, an important part of the critique of these phenomena – but in many cases that demand must be accompanied or even preceded by a struggle to reconfigure the space of appearance, to bring these phenomena to attention or to alter the terms of their public representation. Such struggles are by definition disorienting, and they are likely to be inconvenient and upsetting: they represent attempts to induce changes in people's habits of perception and attention by conspicuously disrupting ordinary life and sense. Powerful people and institutions often respond to these challenges by borrowing norms of reasonability and civility familiar from the 'space of reasons' and using them to police struggles over the terms of our orientation in the space of appearance. To be clear, I am not proposing that Forst himself is engaged in that kind of policing; but one reason for critical theorists to avoid assimilating such struggles to the register of justification is to avoid inadvertently abetting attempts to foreclose radical challenges to political common sense.

Yet critical theory's task here is not only negative: it can also be, indeed it ought to be, a *source* of such challenges. This seems to me to follow precisely from Forst's own account of the enterprise of critical theory. On this account, a 'critical' theory has to do two things at once: it has to inquire into 'the rational form of a historically possible and normatively required social order that is generally justifiable', and it has to ask 'why the power relations that exist within a society (or beyond it)' have 'prevented the emergence of such an order'.[18] But if this second task of critical theory necessarily includes noticing and drawing attention to features or constellations of features of the world about which we do not merely have false or ideological beliefs, but about which we – some of us, or all of us – do not now think much at all, then this second task may also entail a third, one that I take to have been implied by Horkheimer's classic distinction between traditional and critical theory, too, but which is not explicitly thematised in Forst's account: reflection on the social location of critical theory itself, on the material, institutional and ideational conditions of its own practice, and on the blind spots and forms of non-thought that these enabling conditions also produce *as* they enable.[19]

The philosopher Brady Heiner, to give just one example, has recently published a striking essay that begins with a recollection of the prominence of tables and desks in the philosophical writings of philosophers from Marx to Husserl to Merleau-Ponty. Heiner proceeds with an account of his own office work-world at a public university in California, observing that 'this desk, at which I now sit as I write', along with 'every other item of furniture in my office', was manufactured by the labour of prisoners employed by a semi-private 'Prison Industry Authority' from which a variety of state agencies are *required* to purchase not just office furniture but a whole raft of other products. He then moves from the resulting examination of contemporary mass incarceration in California to a philosophical and political study of slavery, imprisonment and 'social death'.[20] (Heiner's essay was published in a volume that includes essays by prisoners as well as by non-imprisoned academics and which makes no genre distinction between them: the prisoners do not just appear as objects of concern or as voices of unmediated experience for philosophers to interpret, but as thinkers in their own right.) It's not that Heiner does not participate in the register of justification: he does. But his essay, and the book to which it belongs, are also interventions in the configuration of attention; they are gripping – they are powerful – not only because of the arguments they offer but also because of the way they reshape their readers' sense of what there is to be argued about.

This brings me back to Forst's invocation of the example of those historical figures who had the courage to pursue the critique of existing orders even when, as he puts it, this took them to places 'unheard of', leading them to be labelled 'immoral' or 'crazy' or accused of 'heresy'.[21] Of these descriptions, 'immoral' seems to me too weak to capture what Forst really means: the unheard of, the heretical and the crazy are not just things that, given the terms of an existing order, deserve to be condemned: rather, their very appearance as objects of attention and discourse tends to call into question an existing sense of what there is to be thought about and considered. (Heretical challenges to segregation, mass incarceration and racialised policing have been voiced for decades, both outside and inside academia, but they have been and often still are treated as crazy, particularly when they propose things like prison or police abolition rather than reform: Angela Davis may be one of the Pierre Bayles of this century).[22] Perhaps the best place to conclude these remarks – which have, after all, been dedicated to the idea that not everything is a question of justification – is not with a critique *of* Forst, but with an invitation *to* him – an invitation to say more about what heresies, what impossibilities, he thinks are rendered visible or invisible, speakable or unspeakable, by virtue of the various institutional locations of the practice of critical theory today. What does it mean for critical theory to be institutionalised in the increasingly neoliberalised university? From what other places does he think radical critics of contemporary society are speaking 'crazily' with admirable relentlessness? What politically productive relationships might be established across and among these various locations? And what phenomena and what possibilities for social transformation does Forst himself wish us to attend to and take seriously, even though doing so today might seem 'unheard of'?

Notes

1 An earlier version of these comments was prepared for a workshop on Rainer Forst's *Normativität und Macht* held at Rice University on 6 November 2015, organised by Christian Emden and Don Morrison; I am grateful to them, and to David Owen, Jana Sawicki and Rainer Forst, for the opportunity to participate and for the stimulating conversation.
2 S. Benhabib, 'The Uses and Abuses of Kantian Rigorism. On Rainer Forst's Moral and Political Philosophy', *Political Theory*, 43:6 (2015), 778, 784, 789.
3 A. Allen, *The End of Progress: Decolonizing the Normative Foundations of Critical Theory* (New York: Columbia University Press, 2016), pp. 156, 125.
4 *RtJ*, p. 13.
5 *N&P*, p. 7.
6 R. Forst, 'Noumenal Power', *Journal of Political Philosophy*, 23:2 (2015), 111–127; *N&P*, especially the introduction and ch. 1.
7 Allen, *The End of Progress*, p. 143.
8 Forst, 'Noumenal Power', 112.
9 *Ibid.*, 126 n. 48; Forst is quoting here from H. Arendt, *Crises of the Republic* (New York: Harcourt, Brace and Co., 1972), p. 152.
10 Forst, 'Noumenal Power', 114.
11 H. Arendt, *The Human Condition* (Chicago: University of Chicago Press, 1958), p. 201, emphasis added. This and the following paragraph draw on P. Markell, 'The Moment Has Passed: Power After Arendt', in R. Coles, M. Reinhardt and G. Shulman (eds.), *Radical Future Pasts: Untimely Political Theory* (Lexington: University Press of Kentucky, 2014).
12 Arendt, *The Human Condition*, p. 200.
13 Forst, 'Noumenal Power', 117.

14 *Ibid.*, 120.
15 Allen, *The End of Progress*, p. 150.
16 *Ibid.*, pp. 157–158.
17 On more and less productive ways of deploying the idea of disavowal as part of a political critique of power, see G. Shulman, 'Acknowledgment and Disavowal as an Idiom for Theorizing Politics', *Theory & Event*, 14:1 (2011).
18 *N&P*, p. 1.
19 This is the task of critical theory that Allen's project of 'decolonizing' brings into the foreground; see *The End of Progress*, p. xiii.
20 B. Heiner, 'Excavating the Sedimentations of Slavery: The Unfinished Project of American Abolition', in G. Adelsberg, L. Guenther and S. Zeman (eds), *Death and Other Penalties: Philosophy in a Time of Mass Incarceration* (New York: Fordham University Press, 2015), pp. 18f. The workshop at which I originally delivered a version of these comments was held in the Founder's Room in Lovett Hall at Rice University, around an enormous maple and cherry veneer table that, we were told, had been specially constructed for the G7 Summit held there in 1990.
21 *N&P*, p. 7.
22 See e.g. A.Y. Davis, *Are Prisons Obsolete?* (New York: Seven Stories Press, 2003).

8

Power, justification and vindication

David Owen

The first question of justice, Rainer Forst argues, is the question of power. Because the focus of justice is the relations in which we stand to one another, it tracks relations of power conceived as the ability '*to influence, use, determine, occupy, or even seal off the space of reasons for others*'.[1] Justice does not require the absence of power, rather it requires that persons stand in relations of equality with respect to the exercise of power – something that Forst marks with the idea of a right to justification. Thus, in any scheme of rule, what matters is that those subject to power have the power to contest and shape the relations of rule to which they are subject by demanding justifications that they can, considered collectively and severally, endorse. It is for this reason that Forst identifies 'the first demand of justice of those subjected to a normative order' thus: 'to have standing as equal normative authorities within such an order'.[2] More fully specified:

> The first task of justice is to create structures of justification in which arbitrary rule is banished, even against national and international lines of force – structures in which those who are subjected to rule or domination, whether of an economic, political, or legal kind, can bring 'the force of the better argument' to bear against those who exercise such rule or domination.[3]

Forst refers to this task as the construction of *fundamental* justice, that is, a basic structure of justification, which he distinguishes from *full* justice, that is, a justified basic structure. Notably, Forst continues

'Democracy as a practice of justice acquires special importance in this context ... Democratic rule is a discursively justified form of rule, which means a form in which structures of justification exist that are adequate to the scope of the rule exercised'.[4] Hence, in contexts of (in)justice, what is required in some institutionalised form or other are forms of democratic rule appropriate to the relations of power in question.

So justice, power and especially justification are the central pivots around which Forst's account turns and that I will come back to the issues raised by the preceding sketch later. But in order to come back to these issues in the appropriately critical spirit, I want to begin with Forst's reflections on morality.

Let's begin with Forst's commitment to the grounding of morality in a second-order practical insight:

> The type of moral perception in question can be understood, with Wittgenstein, such that the perceptual 'seeing' of a human being at the same time corresponds to a practical attitude towards him, an 'attitude towards a soul' ... With regard to Wittgenstein's discussion of 'seeing aspects' which as an understanding form of 'visual experience' is a form of practical cognition in that a reactive and reflexive 'attitude' corresponds to what one 'sees', one could say, moreover, that perceptually recognizing the nature of a human being as being a moral person is an essential aspect of 'seeing' human beings and that 'aspect blindness' in this respect (Stanley Cavell speaks here of 'soul-blindness') means having lost the capacity to perceive human as humans and, accordingly, to treat them humanely. Thus the fundamental form of moral recognition of other human beings as moral persons with a right to justification corresponds to a specific capacity for moral perception, the capacity to perceive and understand oneself and others as 'humans'.[5]

Now while I share Forst's sense of the importance of Wittgenstein and Cavell on moral perception here,[6] it should be noted Forst is moving rather rapidly over a considerable range of material and I want to slow things down a bit by focusing on the issue of soul-blindness.

In *The Claim of Reason*, Cavell remarks:

> It is sometimes imperative to say that women or children or black people or criminals are human beings. This is a call for justice. For justice to be done, a change of perception, a modification of seeing, may be called for. But does it follow that those whose perceptions, or whose natural reactions, must suffer change have until that time been seeing women or children or black people or criminals as something other than human beings?[7]

To explore this question, one example that Cavell considers is that of slavery. Cavell imagines the slave-owner saying of the slaves that they are 'not human beings' and ask what he could mean by this, given that '[e]verything in his relation to his slaves shows that he treats them as more or less human':

> When he wants to be served at table by a black hand, he would not be satisfied to be served by a black paw. When he rapes a slave or takes her as a concubine, he does not feel that he has, by that fact itself, embraced sodomy. When he tips a black taxi driver (something he never does with a white driver) it does not occur to him that he might have more appropriately patted the creature fondly on the side of the neck.[8]

Cavell's response is that the slave-owner 'means, and can mean, nothing definite':

> This is a definite state of mind. He means, indefinitely, that they are not *purely* human. He means, indefinitely, that there are *kinds* of humans ... He means, indefinitely, that slaves are different, primarily different from him, secondarily perhaps different from you and me ... In the end he will appeal to history, to a form, or rather to a way, of life: this is what he does ... It could be said that what he denies is that the slave is 'other', i.e., other to his one. They are, as it were, *merely* other; not simply separate, but different. It could also be said that he takes himself to be private with respect to them, in the end unknowable by them.[9]

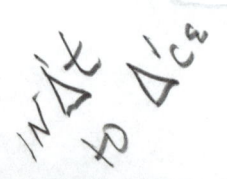

Cavell's charge is that the slave-owner is thus 'missing something about himself, or rather something about his connection with these people, his internal relations with them, so to speak'.[10] What the slave-owner cannot see and thereby denies, as Raimond Gaita puts it, is 'that the slave has his kind (the slave-owner's kind) of individuality – the kind of individuality that shows itself in our revulsion in being numbered rather than called by name and that gives human beings the power to haunt those who have wronged them, in remorse'.[11] It may be helpful here to introduce briefly a further example explored by Gaita concerning James Isdell, Protector of Aborigines in Western Australia in the 1930s, who administered a programme in which children of mixed blood were (typically forcibly) removed from the Aboriginal mothers 'and placed in circumstances in which (it was hoped) most of them would have children with lower class whites':

> Responding to the question, how did he feel taking children from their mothers, Isdell answered that he 'would not hesitate from a moment to separate any half-caste from its Aboriginal mother, no matter how frantic her momentary grief might be at the time'. They 'soon forget their offspring', he explained.[12]

As Gaita remarks, these words, coming from Isdell, 'marked his sense of the kind of gulf that existed between "them" and "us". "Our" children are irreplaceable; "theirs" are not'. Isdell was not ignorant of the facts concerning the victims of his actions; rather 'he suffered a kind of blindness to the meaning of what they did and suffered':

> Although the grief of the women who had lost their children was visible and audible to him, he did not see in the women's faces or hear in their voices grief that could lacerate their souls and mark them for the rest of their days. It was literally unintelligible to … Isdell that sexuality, death and the fact that at any moment we may lose all that gives sense to our lives could mean to 'them' what it does to 'us'.[13]

Isdell could not see that 'their' loves, griefs, joys and desires go deep in 'them' and have depth in the same way that they do for 'us'. It is not that Isdell necessarily lacks sympathy, it is rather that he cannot see the suffering of these Aboriginal women as having the same kind of claim on his sympathy as the suffering of, for example, White Australians.

I have dwelt on these examples to underscore my agreement with Forst that 'the fundamental form of moral recognition of other human beings as moral persons … corresponds to a specific capacity for moral perception, the capacity to perceive and understand oneself and others as "humans"',[14] to clarify the concept of seeing others as humans in play, and to note that the scope of such moral recognition can be less than universal, or rather than it takes itself to be universal with respect to the relevant 'kind' of human being but can be – and has been – practically compatible with sortal distinctions between kinds of human being. As Cavell observes, it is 'to deny just this that Marx, adapting Feuerbach's theology, speaks of man as a species-being. To be human is to be one of humankind, to bear an internal relation to all others'.[15] Forst is, of course, a follower of Marx in this respect, but this leaves open the question for critical theory of the relation of power and moral perception, a question posed not least by Kant's own demonstration of racist attitudes.

My reason for introducing this digression on Cavell is two-fold. First, as already stressed, it is to draw attention to that soul-blindness can be specific rather than general. The slave-owner is not soul blind with respect to other slave-owners, only in relation to slaves. Inadvertently Forst's summary of this discussion may make it appear that seeing another biological human being as human in the sense of equal moral standing means seeing all other biological human beings as humans in that sense – and Cavell's and Gaita's example help to ward off this possible misunderstanding. The second point is that overcoming soul-blindness is not a matter of being provided with additional facts or normative reasons but of 'soul-dawning', of coming to notice or see an aspect that one could not see before. It may contingently be the case that being offered a new fact or justifying reason provides the occasion for soul-dawning, but it could just as well be reading a novel or looking at an artwork that initiates aspect-dawning in this form – and the practical work on the self that this new form of receptivity demands. This point matters for two reasons.

The first is that it makes clear that while it *may* be the case that anyone anywhere could, in principle, be struck by the second-order moral insight that leads them to see *all* others as moral persons; in practice, cultivating this form of moral perception as a form of universal moral perception is interwoven with the formation of an specific kind of ethical culture (in the broad sense of this term) and hence also with the political institutions and practices through which we shape and govern our moral and ethical conduct. It is plausible that a society in which social practices are regulated by a deep commitment to human rights is considerably more likely to cultivate the salient form of moral perception than one that lacks such norms. (I'll come back to this point.)

The second pertains to Forst's understanding of power in which I think there is a certain degree of ambiguity or, perhaps, ambivalence around this point. Consider the following passage:

> Power is not only exercised by and over free agents; it is also the word for what is going on when someone acts for certain reasons for which others are responsible – that is, for reasons that he or she would not otherwise have had and that still characterize him or her as an agent for whom alternatives of action remain open … To be a subject of power is to be moved by reasons that others have given me and that motivate me to think or act in a certain way intended by the reason-giver. Hence, while in political philosophy we usually inquire into the justification of power, in what follows I am interested in the *power of justifications*.[16]

The first part of this passage would be consistent with the dawning of an aspect as an exercise of power in the sense that aspect-dawning or aspect-change reconfigures some area (perhaps all) of the space of reasons of the agent. For example, if soul-dawning occurs the slave-owner now has, and recognises himself as having, a range of reasons for acting, and not acting, in various ways towards the slave that he (or she) did not have before. (A nice illustration of this point is the way that religious conversion changes the space of reasons that the convert inhabits.) The final two sentences of the passage point, however, to a narrower view in which it is giving particular reasons (justifications) rather than the aspectival reshaping of the space of reasons that marks out power. This ambivalence also comes into the foreground with Forst's discussion of structures. He writes:

> structures that rest on and reproduce noumenal power have a certain *influence* over persons that appears to be a form of power. Within a patriarchal structure, for example, women may conform to patriarchal roles even when the patriarch leaves things implicit or is absent, or no longer tries to dominate. That means that the noumenal power structure that supports social power relations is still in place, with the result that a certain order of action is upheld. It is, however, more appropriate to speak of 'influence' rather than 'power' in cases where power is not intentionally exercised by persons over others. Structures do not 'exercise' power as persons do; rather they rely on and provide opportunities for exercising it.[17]

This is, it seems to me, a little awkward. First, Forst has already identified influence as a mode of power. Recall that power refers to the ability 'to influence, use, determine, occupy, or even seal off the space of reasons for others'. Second, structures, such as patriarchal structures, can be seen as an order of continuous aspect perception (what Rancière would call a 'police order' and what Honneth would call a 'recognitive order') that work by configuring the general space of reasons of the agents whose conduct produces and reproduces such structures and the '*patterned asymmetries in the social capacity to act*' to which they give rise.[18] This is a form of power and it is somewhat unclear why we should not speak of it as such; not least since if structural power works through an order of continuous aspect perception, it is not different in kind to exercises of power by individuals (for example the charismatic prophet or political demagogue) that work through bringing about aspect-dawning or aspect-change. Indeed, the latter are integral to the human capacity to contest and transform structures as normative orders. It would seem that Forst's resistance to speaking of structural power, even as he effectively acknowledges it, points to an ambivalence between the wider and narrower views. It is only on the latter view that justificatory reasons are the normative medium though which power is exercised – and it is this, I think, that pushes Forst in this direction. The issue raised by cases of aspect-change is whether they can be adequately captured in terms of the language of justification.

Take, for example, the case of liberalism's historical victory over the ancien regime, Bernard Williams comments:

> If we ask why we use some concepts of this [ethical and political] kind rather than others – rather than, say, those current in an earlier time – we may deploy arguments which claim to justify our ideas against those others: ideas of equality and equal rights, for instance, against ideas of hierarchy. Alternatively we may reflect on an historical story, of how these concepts rather than the others came to be ours: a story (simply to give it a label) of how the modern world and its special expectations came to replace the *ancien regime*. But then we reflect on the relation of this story to the arguments that we deploy against the earlier conceptions, and we realise that the story is the history of those forms of argument themselves: the forms of argument, call them liberal forms of argument, are a central part of the outlook that we accept.
>
> If we consider how these forms of argument came to prevail, we can indeed see them as having won, but not necessarily as having won an argument. For liberal ideas to have won an argument, the representatives of the *ancien regime* would have had to have shared with the nascent liberals a conception of something that the argument was about, and not just in the obvious sense that it was about the way to live or the way to order society. They would have had to agree that there was some aim, or reason or freedom or whatever, which liberal ideas served better or of which they were a better expression, and there is not much reason, with a change as radical as this, to think that they did agree about this, at least until very late in the process. The relevant ideas of freedom, reason, and so on were themselves involved in the change.[19]

I admit to sharing Williams's scepticism concerning the usefulness of appeals to justification in this context. Rather to address these kinds of cases, I think we need to introduce the concept of 'vindication' to mark a reconfiguration of the space of reasons that the relevant agents do not have reasons, all things considered, to regret even though the reconfiguration was not one for which justificatory reasons could be given independently and in advance of the aspect-change itself.

This last point directs us to the wider import of the concept of vindication – and the distinction between justification and vindication – beyond issues of aspect-change in stressing that the concept of vindication comes into play when justificatory reasons cannot be given independently and in advance of the action or outlook in question. So we might consider Williams's famous example of a fictionalised Gauguin who abandons his wife and small children to go to Tahiti to pursue what he takes to be his true vocation as a painter. Williams's argues that Gauguin's actions cannot be rationally justified because, at the point of deliberating of whether to leave, he cannot know if he will be successful or even what success would amount to in this context; rather Williams proposes that in the light of Gauguin's success that his action is retrospectively justified. But this seems wrong. Gauguin's actions remain rationally (and morally) unjustified; it is rather that his conduct is vindicated, despite the moral costs to his family, by the value of the gift of his art to the world. Both Gauguin and the audience that has inherited his artworks have reason, all things considered, not to regret his choice.

Let us now return to our opening concern with the founding of basic structures of justification, perhaps especially in contexts of transnational power (although the point also applies to state contexts). Given that fundamental justice is already a substantively demanding basis for procedural justice and that the founding of a transnational basic structure of justification is not a simple political task, this requirement fairly naturally raises the question of what norms should guide the political task of constructing such a basic structure of justification.

Here we may say (with Machiavelli) that the questions of power and, indeed, of political violence enter the frame. Forst argues, following Arendt and Foucault, that violence is to be distinguished from power because 'power over' is about seeking to conduct the conduct (in Foucault's felicitous phrase) of self or others in various ways, that is, to shape the space of reasons (reflective or habitual) that they inhabit, whereas the exercise of violence or force on a subject is what happens when someone is treated as a thing (for example, when torture is not about seeking an admission but just about inflicting pain for its own sake). This is a reasonable distinction in a two-party context but, as Forst acknowledges, it does not help us with the notion of political violence since this is also a communicative act directed at an audience and at shaping the space of reasons of that audience. But this is to get ahead of ourselves, let us step back to confront the initial question concerning founding a basic transnational structure of justification in a context marked by (often multiple forms of) domination. We can note, further, that the stakes are, in one sense, higher than merely those involved in establishing a basic transnational structure of justification because, as noted above, we have good reason to think that such a structure will also support the spread of forms of moral (and, for that matter, ethical) perception that help stabilise the commitment to a basic structure of justification. This gives further edge to the question of what norms govern the political action of bringing about such a basic structure. Forst is well aware of complex and often violent history of political struggles for rights and statuses on the part of varied social groups but, as far as I am aware, has not addressed directly the issue of what range of action is justified in pursuit of establishing the right to justification, that is, a basic structure of justification – or to put the point another ways, what limits there are on such political activity. Forst may, of course, reply that this is a contextual question – what the appropriate limits are in any given case may relate to the form and extent of resistance by power-holders to the transformation of social and political relationships. This raises the question of whether there are any limits that are not context-relative (for example, those marked by basic human rights – e.g. not to be tortured) – and it would be surprising, as a Kantian, if Forst did not hold that there were moral limits to justified political action.

Now suppose that a political movement aiming to establish a basic transnational structure of justification breaches some of whatever the moral limits on justifiable action are and yet thereby successfully establishes such a basic structure. Their act is unjustified, but it may still be vindicated (I say 'may' because I do not think that the mere fact of success by itself necessarily vindicates the conduct in question). We might call this 'the Machiavelli question' since it is precisely the kind of issue addressed by Machiavelli in respect of the founding or re-founding of a republic, namely that the performance of morally unjustified actions may be necessary for the establishment of good ends. Whereas justification is always in the present tense of practical deliberation and hence prospective, vindication is always retrospective. Moreover, the acts of (re)founding may fail – in which case nothing redeems the unjustified actions in question – but even if they succeed they do not 'retrospectively justify' (as Williams's reflections on moral luck would have it); on the contrary, the actions in question remain unjustified, it is simply that justification is not the only relevant normative game in town. In Machiavelli, the criteria for vindication are tied to the question of whether the republic established is a well-functioning stable republic that endures and the future generations of citizens living a free civil life cannot, all things considered, regret its establishment despite the moral costs this involved. This may have had claim to be reasonable response in Machiavelli's period but would not suffice today since, for example, a republic established on the basis of ethnic genocide could potentially meet this standard. Rather the question for us would be whether the cosmopolitan community of humanity would have reason, all things considered, not to regret the establishment of such a basic structure despite the moral costs involved. This does not amount to a full account of vindication but it will suffice for current purposes, namely, to indicate an account of normativity and power in relation to political action does *prima facie* need to consider the role of vindication as well as that of justification.

We might notice that the introduction of the concept of vindication and its distinction from justification helps to make sense of a common and fairly basic reaction we can have to political actors when we recognise their hands are dirty, but are glad that they (and not us) did what they turn out to have done.

The above remarks are obviously sketchy and rather more work would need to be done to work out a fully satisfactory account of vindication. However the role of these remarks here is simply to propose the thought that, in relation to both outlooks and actions, the category of justification is not sufficient to account for the relationship of normativity and power in human affairs and the concept of vindication points to a dimension of this relationship that Forst may wish – and need – to consider.

Let me end with a tentative thought drawing on a distinction to which Foucault draws attention between two orders of problems for democratic rule that he specifies in terms of the notions of *politeia* and *dunasteia*. Problems of *politeia* pertain to 'the constitution, the framework, which defines the status of citizens, their rights, how decisions are taken, how leaders are chosen, and so on', where these problems 'have their own form, they imply a certain type of analysis, and they have given rise, they are at the point of origin of a whole form of reflection on the nature of law, the organization of society, and what the State should be'.[20] Problems of *dunasteia* address 'the problem of the political game, of its rules and instruments, and the individual who engages in it', where these problems 'are political problems in the strict sense ... of the practice of the political game, and of the political game as a field of experience with its own rules and normativity'.[21] The thought here, I take it, is that political theory typically either focuses on questions concerning the form of a just constitution or free state or equal society – or on questions pertaining to the practice of politics. Think of Rawls and Machiavelli as theorists who are more oriented respectively to the former and the latter. To the extent that this distinction can be sustained it seems to me that Forst's focus has been on problems of *politeia* rather than *dunasteia* – and the question of the relationship between the two is an issue not only for him but for all of us doing political theory today. Or as we might put it, we need to move forward to a 'Forst-Machiavelli' programme.[22]

Notes

1 *N&P*, p. 42.
2 *Ibid.*, p. 43.
3 *Ibid.*, p. 167.
4 *Ibid.*, pp. 167f.
5 *RtJ*, pp. 41f.
6 See, for example, D. Owen, 'Cultural Diversity and the Conversation of Justice', *Political Theory*, 27:5 (1999), 579–596; 'Perfectionism, Parrhesia and Care of the Self: Cavell and Foucault on Ethics and Politics', in A. Norris (ed.), *Stanley Cavell and Political Philosophy* (Stanford: Stanford University Press 2006), pp. 128–55; D. Owen and C. Woodford, 'Foucault, Cavell & the Government of Self and Others', *Iride*, 25:2 (2012), 299–316.
7 S. Cavell, *The Claim of Reason: Wittgenstein, Scepticism, Morality, and Tragedy*, new paperback edn (New York and Oxford: Oxford University Press, 1999), p. 372.
8 *Ibid.*, p. 376.
9 *Ibid.*, pp. 376f.
10 *Ibid.*, p. 376.
11 R. Gaita, *Good and Evil: An Absolute Conception*, second edn (Abingdon: Routledge, 2004), p. 156.
12 *Ibid.*, p. 333.
13 *Ibid.*, pp. 333f.
14 *RtJ*, pp. 41f.
15 Cavell, *The Claim of Reason*, p. 376.
16 *N&P*, p. 38.
17 *Ibid.*, p. 45.
18 C. Hayward and S. Lukes, 'Nobody to Shoot? Power, Structure, and Agency: A Dialogue', *Journal of Power*, 1:1 (2008), 5–20.
19 B. Williams, 'Philosophy as a Humanistic Discipline', in Williams, *Philosophy as a Humanistic Discipline* (Princeton: Princeton University Press, 2006), p. 190.

20 M. Foucault, *The Government of Self and Others. Lectures at the Collège de France 1982–83*, ed. F. Gros, trans. G. Burchell (Basingstoke: Palgrave Macmillan, 2010), pp. 185f.
21 *Ibid.*
22 I am grateful to Professor Don Morrison, Director of the Boniuk Institute for the Study and Advancement of Religious Tolerance, and his colleague Professor Christian Emden for the invitation to participate in this workshop at Rice University in Houston on the work of Rainer Forst and for all their hospitality, intellectual and otherwise, during this event. I would also like to thank the other participants, Patchen Markell, Jana Sawicki and, especially my old friend and sparring partner, Rainer Forst for helping to make it such an enjoyable event.

Part III

Reply

The dialectics of toleration and the power of reason(s): Reply to my critics

Rainer Forst
(Translated by Ciaran Cronin)

Philosophers – even Kantians – have dreams. And one of them is to have a group of great minds discuss your work and force you to surpass your previous philosophical attempts. With the chapters collected in this volume, the first part of that dream has come true; whether the second part has also come true is for the reader to judge. I will forever be indebted to the friends and colleagues who did me the honour of delving deeply into my ideas and pointing out their possible shortcomings to me. In one way or another, all of them take issue with the rationalism of my view, which they find excessive or one-sided. The challenges they pose are major ones and require us to reflect together about the very nature of political philosophy.

I The power of arguments (reply to Teresa Bejan)

It is a great pleasure and honour to be the subject of Teresa Bejan's criticisms, since she is one of the foremost political theorists and intellectual historians of toleration. Her book *Mere Civility*[1] masterfully reconstructs and interprets the discourses on toleration in seventeenth-century England (including its American colonies) emphasising the importance of the social virtue called civility. Her brilliant style brings the thinkers she discusses and the contexts in which they developed their ideas back to life, and it shows how much power their thinking retains.

Bejan is an exemplary close reader and she exhibits a superb grasp of my project in general and of *Toleration in Conflict* in particular. She rightly points out that my historical narrative is primarily intended to be a history of arguments rather than a history of ideas which are explained exhaustively with reference to their historical contexts.[2] I believe that there is great merit in a detailed history of ideas, and I confess that my attempts to situate the authors I discuss in their historical contexts and networks often fail to measure up to the standards of historical experts, as Bejan indicates (TB 33)[3] when she reminds us of the many aspects of the biographies of Locke or Bayle which must be taken into account when we try to understand the development of their thought. But I cannot accept her criticism that I neglect the practical experiences of the thinkers I discuss and reduce their context to 'high-altitude snapshots of state laws and policies' (TB 34). With regard to Bayle, for example, I go to considerable lengths to demonstrate how his experiences of persecution in France and the harassment he suffered at the hands of his fellow Huguenots in the *refuge* community of Rotterdam shaped his thought and how this treatment was a reaction to his works. I am convinced that we cannot understand a theorist of toleration if we do not understand the social struggles and conflicts in which his or her thought was formed.

Nevertheless, there is a deeper issue at work here. Apart from doubts about whether a historian of past centuries can ever claim to have shown 'how it really was' – *wie es eigentlich gewesen ist*, to cite the words of Ranke which Bejan (TB 31) uses – what I have in mind is the question of what it means to take a past thinker seriously *as a thinker*, as a philosopher. For we may treat him or her as an object of historical study and paint a detailed picture of all of his or her experiences, readings, networks and so on – in other words, we may try to draft a complete social-noumenal map of an author's formation. But – and here I follow Gadamer's hermeneutics – I think that we will fail to understand a philosopher if we do not relate to his or her works as works of philosophy, as raising truth claims whose genesis can be partly, but never fully, explained by their social context, since we can never completely reconstruct a noumenal map of a philosophical mind in a genealogical mode. But however perfect (or imperfect) our understanding of the genesis and context of an idea or a body of thought may be, we do not understand a philosopher in the sense of *Verstehen* (in contrast to *Erklären*)[4] if we do not relate to the validity claims raised by his or her work as truth claims *for us*. These claims were addressed to his or her contemporaries, to be sure, but, more than that, they developed an argument that ought to be taken seriously and that may transcend its particular context, even though it can and should also be understood as part of that context. The point of my history of arguments must be understood in this sense: they are ideas in context, but they are also ideas beyond context – or at any rate their contexts are multiple, and one of them is the context of reasoning about what is right.

With respect to that perspective, Bejan objects to what she regards as the progressive narrative of my work that it is not surprising that the 'preferred foundation and its corresponding conception of toleration should emerge victorious in his historical account' (TB 38), because it follows a 'preordained trajectory of the respect conception' (TB 38). And she concludes: 'What is the use, we might ask, of doing history *or* genealogy, if we are not going to learn anything more from our encounter with the past than what we already knew already going in?' (TB 38). I would like to offer a few remarks in response to this challenging criticism. First, as I hope is clear from the book as well as the lead essay in this volume, I am far from regarding the history of toleration, whether understood as real history or as a history of moral reflection, as a history of progress *tout court*. In my dialectical history, there have been steps of regress as well as steps of progress, as well as many steps in between; the real social space of noumenal power never fully clears up in a rational way. All I claim is that, *when* progress has been made, it was a matter of overcoming false and one-sided justifications of toleration and establishing more reciprocal terms of toleration. But I make no general claim about the facts of such progress, past or present. So the respect conception is not 'victorious' in any historical, Hegelian or Whiggish sense. It is still contested and is often marginalised, while the permission conception is the dominant one, even in democratic societies. That is the implication of my critical theory of toleration.

But second, and even more importantly, I do hold that a Baylean – sometimes proto-Baylean, sometimes neo-Baylean – justification of the respect conception is superior to the others. And although I am not sure exactly how I did what I did looking back at the process of writing this long book, I don't think it was 'wishful thinking' (TB 38) to argue that one particular strand of the justification of toleration is more justifiable than others, namely one which does indeed connect Bayle and Rawls and which I radicalise by constructing a reflexive justification of toleration based on the principle of justification itself (something which Rawls never did). But even though I interpret Rawls in a (hopefully illuminating) Baylean light, I do not turn Bayle into a Rawlsian. And I am indebted to Teresa Bejan for pointing out to me (just recently, in January of 2019) that she found notes on Bayle in Rawls's papers, probably stemming from the early to mid 1960s.[5] That is highly interesting, similar to Rawls citing Bodin's *Colloquium heptaplomeres* approvingly in his reflections on religion and reasonable disagreement (a reference of which I was not aware when I made the connection between Rawls and Bodin).[6]

These are important findings in their own right. But my point is a rather different one in the space of philosophical reason(s) and does not depend on genealogy or history, because Bayle's (or Bodin's) arguments can be understood *better* in the light of Rawls's conception of 'reasonable disagreement', and Rawls can be understood *better* by reading him in the light of Bayle's normative and epistemological arguments for toleration, because exactly these two components appear in Rawls in a form that is similar in some respects and quite different in others. Does this mean that I fabricate a preordained history in which Bayle and Rawls are destined to emerge victorious? I don't think so. I merely reconstruct a set of powerful arguments as these emerged in very different contexts (in the one case, seventeenth-century Calvinist thought, in the other, twentieth-century Kantianism with a Protestant background) and reconstruct their philosophical implications and claims (as well as their similarities and differences). The truth that emerges is not one beyond context, for Bayle developed his thought in the conflictual situations of his time; but nevertheless the power of his arguments transcends this context and is applicable to other social times and places. If we disregard that argumentative power, we do not really understand what his philosophy is about (in the sense of *Verstehen*), because we have to read and interpret him in our own language, which is the only one available to us.

So I think I explored the history of arguments for toleration with a philosophical as well as a historical intention, but the philosophical one was primary. This is why I reconstructed and distilled twenty-five different justifications of toleration in a number of versions and forms. Some are more dated than others, but all of them still speak to us, not because we are contemporaries of Augustine or Montaigne, but because their thought has a certain enduring force and we had better have an eye and an ear for their messages.

I did not and could not foresee what I would find in the dense history into which I delved; but I admit that I was looking for something, namely the best possible reconstruction of the many arguments for toleration that I could find. And my aim was not to provide a historical protocol of these arguments but to try to take them seriously as arguments, with their strengths, weaknesses and dialectical failures. Along the way I encountered many surprises and (for me) unknown, interesting thinkers, so I don't think I only found what I already knew. Yet I admit that I cannot imagine how a historian of ideas could explore a field of thought and knowledge without any *Vorbegriff* of what can be found there. That pre-judgement can and must be corrected, if necessary; but I am not sure how different my way of doing history is from a theorist who finds the virtue of civility in the works of a number of seventeenth-century authors to be a response to the problem of intolerance. We find a lot of new and surprising things when we conduct historical research; but if we do not begin with some notion of what we are looking for, we will find nothing.

However, one thing one can learn, and I think I definitely did learn, even from less well-known thinkers, is modesty. For we often think, in some quarters of philosophy more than others, that we were the first to have a particular idea or develop a particular argument, so that we do not make much of an effort to look into the past of the discourse in which we are engaged to discover whether that idea existed previously and, if so, in what form and what counter-arguments were raised against it. That is a poverty of philosophy, which is often paired with immodesty, and historical knowledge helps us to overcome that poverty. I think that Bejan and I can agree on that (at least).

When it comes to what underlies our different conceptions of the virtue of tolerance, it appears to be a variant of the difference between the views of a Kantian moral philosopher and those of an empiricist-minded virtue ethicist. However, I think that the difference which Bejan discovers rests in large part on a misunderstanding – in fact, on two misunderstandings.

The first stems from a misreading of how I use the term 'respect'. While I, like any Kantian, distinguish between respect and esteem and stress that respect toleration means respecting others as equal *persons* even though one objects to their *views* as false, wrong, crazy or blasphemous, Bejan (like many other writers)[7] gets my position wrong when she assumes that my notion of respect is close to that of the UNESCO declaration, which states that 'tolerance *is* respect, acceptance and appreciation of the rich diversity of our world's cultures' (TB 39). Not only is that not what I mean by respect; it also articulates a view in which there is no room left for objection, so that, according to my analysis, it is not even a view of toleration. That is a conceptual mistake that I am at pains to avoid.

Second, in her book Bejan criticises an interpretation of toleration that she calls *reductio at respectum*, by which she means a reduction of the complex virtue of civility as toleration to 'a form of Neo-Kantian respect for persons'.[8] In a recent review article, she scolds me for such a reduction,[9] and this also seems to be at work in her criticism that my Kantian view, which asks persons to 'imaginatively adopt the perspective of self-legislator', may be 'one thought too many', as it were (TB 34), to use Bernard Williams's nice phrase.[10] Without that additional thought, tolerance appears as what it realistically is according to Bejan, namely 'the habitual forbearance, the mental (and physical) toughness, of "putting up" with it and not asking why' (TB 34). In her book, she stresses the plurality of motives for civility as tolerance, such as 'unreflective habits of good breeding, from respect not for others but for God or the social order, from a recognition of another's superior (or inferior) merit, from personal pride or chauvinism, or even from private intolerance and evangelical zeal'.[11] The reason why I think that this is a misreading of my view is that I consider the respect conception of toleration (based on a neo-Baylean justification) as only *one* among a considerable plurality of conceptions and stances of tolerance. It is a mistake not to recognise that, of course, I regard *all* versions of the other conceptions of toleration – permission, coexistence and esteem – based on all kinds of justifications and motives (religious, pragmatic, sceptical, epistemic, strategic and so on) as forms of toleration. So there is simply no such *reduction ad respectum*. That assumes that my *normative* argument for one particular justification and form of toleration constitutes the whole of my *analytic* and *reconstructive* argument. But if this was what I meant – namely that only that one conception and justification deserves to be called toleration – why would I write a book on four conceptions and twenty-five justifications of *toleration*? So when I am reminded of the many forms of toleration and its motivations assumed, I am eager to learn more; but I think I have an understanding of quite a few of these forms and motives. It is not part of my project to reduce this spectrum.

But Bejan might still think, as some of my other critics in this book do, that the respect conception based on a neo-Baylean and neo-Kantian perspective is not a plausible interpretation of tolerance at all because, let us say, it is too far removed from real life and what people really think – or thought. So even if Bejan agreed that the argument I make here is a normative one, she seems to think that it is based on one thought too many, because it is indeterminate (TB 36f.) or is an example of Lutheran dogmatism (TB 37) in a highly rationalistic fashion (and in that respect is quite un-Lutheran). Again, many of these arguments derive from a categorical conflation of the normative and the empirical. For I would never deny that the term 'respect' is interpreted in very different ways in different cultures; but that is not a reason for not developing a critical conception of respect that relates to such '*contingent* historical factors' (TB 37). Likewise, I do not see why we should not develop a critical, reflexive conception of toleration which can serve as a norm for evaluating the many other forms and justifications for toleration. The only reason for rejecting such an approach would be a thoroughly historicist scepticism concerning the possibility of making normative arguments at all that achieve a certain distance from social contexts, a distance created by (finite) reason. I suspect that this is what underlies the differences between us, and in that respect I must plead guilty: I believe that reason is a faculty that enables us to evaluate and distinguish better from worse arguments on the basis of principles. And I believe that this is neither one thought too many nor a rationalist dream, but instead just what we, as *participants* in social struggles, ought to do – namely reflect on the false justifications to which we are subject and may have adopted and question them. This is the most contextual, situated attitude of which critical minds like Bayle are exemplars. We can never be sure that we will not reproduce blind spots ourselves; but in a conflict in which both sides think that their killings are in accordance with God's will, we would hope with Bayle that there is a voice of practical reason that cuts through this cruel clash of worlds of interpretation. The history of toleration and intolerance that I reconstruct is a history of social criticism, and without rational standards, such criticism is doomed to fail. A historicism that leaves no room for such critique turns into an affirmative mode of thought.

II Toleration and the masochism of reason (reply to Chandran Kukathas)

It is always a great pleasure and challenge to engage with Chandran Kukathas's work. He is unrivalled in how he questions established ideas and arguments in political theory by analysing the ways in which they constrain the value and practice of liberty – or, as in this wonderful piece, toleration as a limitless, and in that sense libertarian, virtue of reason.[12] Like Bejan, Kukathas does not think that there is a thought missing in my work but rather that it contains one too many (CK 57), although this time it is not an overdose of Kantian rationality, as in Bejan's critique, but quite the opposite. Kukathas wants me to become more of a Kantian discourse theorist and to interpret toleration exclusively as a virtue of reason that heeds the forceless force of the better argument and not as a virtue of justice at all. But whereas he thinks that because of the way I make toleration dependent upon justice (in the respect conception only, I need to add), toleration ceases to exist and becomes an 'ex-concept' (CK 68, n. 29),[13] I believe that if we followed his interpretation of Bayle, not only would Bayle cease to be an inspiring thinker of toleration, but that three important concepts would be jettisoned, namely toleration, reason and justice. Let me explain.

Kukathas and I share an admiration for Bayle's genius.[14] We cherish Bayle for presenting a proto-Kantian argument that tries to develop principles of rational impartiality (see the initial quote on the first page of Kukathas's chapter) which can identify the errors of the persecutionists and are not just theoretical but also practical principles, conveying 'truths of morality' (CK 51). We agree that Bayle developed various arguments against the perceived legitimacy of persecution, some religious, some moral and some epistemological. But while I think that the argument for the absolute freedom of the erroneous conscience (which has deep roots in Christian discourse and found an outstanding champion in Abelard)[15] was an error that Bayle was quick to correct, Kukathas tries to develop that argument further and thinks that Bayle's main importance resides there. By contrast, I argue that Bayle realised that that argument led to the paradoxical conclusion that the 'conscientious persecutor' was to be tolerated,[16] and I believe that he found a way of resolving the problem, namely by reverting to the normative argument about the reciprocity of claims demanded by reason in combination with the idea of reasonable disagreement. Bayle did not believe that private conscience which was blind to the 'natural light' of reason ought to be tolerated, although he did not advocate forcing the unreasonable to change their ways as long as they did not act violently themselves. He explicitly states that 'a religion which forces conscience has no right to be tolerated'.[17] For otherwise, *religious* conscience, dictating persecution, would completely usurp the place of reason and morality in *moral* conscience and lead to all of the conflicts and crimes that Bayle toiled hard to overcome – and the natural light would be extinguished.

However, Kukathas's interpretation, contrary to his intention, does extinguish this light. According to him:

> The one mistake Bayle makes ... is to argue that it would be justifiable to use force to prevent the attempt by some to persecute others, even if it would not be justified to use force to change the minds of persecutors. If force cannot be justified by a claim to be in possession of the truth, it is hard to see how the use of force can be justified in any circumstances. (CK 54)

But here, I fear, it is not Bayle who makes a mistake but Kukathas. First, defining the realm and drawing the limits of toleration with the help of reason must be possible, for otherwise why write a treatise on toleration as a duty which all reasonable persons must accept? Second, to draw such limits does not mean that the exercise of force or violence is justified – for that, additional circumstances must exist. And third, if such force were exercised, it would not be exercised because one is 'in possession of truth' but in order to prevent intolerable crimes from being committed. And fourth, Bayle thinks that the natural light of reason, as a faculty of practical reason that would unite all human beings if only they consulted it properly, is essential for the very definition of such crimes as immoral acts. So the use of force is not justified by an arrogant claim to possess the truth in speculative matters, which would indeed, as Kukathas says, be authoritarian and at odds with Baylean and Kantian rationalism. However, it is justified by the 'truths of morality' (CK 51) which the natural light conveys and which Bayle is at pains to emphasise. He argues that while agreement is not to be expected about speculative truths, human reason can know 'moral laws without exception' which 'enlighten every man coming in to the world'.[18] This is what he means when he argues in the quotation with which Kukathas begins his chapter that impartial reasoning makes people understand the errors of colonising morality by religion and of declaring crimes to be good deeds.[19] In Kukathas's interpretation, this difference between religious truths and moral truths gets lost. But that difference, which I call a proto-Kantian *deontological difference*, is what matters to Bayle. Justice as reciprocity must set the limits to what religion asks or allows you to do towards others.

With respect to the rationalism Kukathas defends, it is one thing to say that one can never win an argument by the use of force, as every good Habermasian or Kantian or Baylean would have to say, but it is quite another to conclude that the 'use of violence could never be justified by appeal to reason' (CK 54), since in that case one would never have good reasons to stop a killer or a violent attacker. On the contrary, one even has a well-founded duty to do so – however not in order to win an argument, but in order to save a person from being killed or attacked. Otherwise, reason turns into a powerless masochistic device, because it would never be conclusive enough to lead to a practical judgement. It would have to tolerate its enemies and be willing to be persecuted or destroyed by them.

In my normative argument, and I think in Bayle's, too, reason and justice are connected, for the limits of toleration need to be drawn by considerations of reciprocal and general justice. Kukathas, however, regards this as a mistake. He lists various reasons for this. First, he believes that toleration is not a normatively dependent concept at all but an ideal in its own right. In response, I think that toleration *ought* to be a virtue of justice but not that it necessarily *is* (here, as above in the context of Bejan's critique, my normative and reconstructive arguments should not be confused). Furthermore, I do not think that Kukathas successfully defends the claim that toleration is an independent ideal, since he makes it completely *dependent* upon reason, arguing that for the right understanding of toleration 'a commitment to reason and reasoning is fundamental' (CK 60). So it is normatively dependent in his interpretation as well, since he refers to it as the 'moral stance which is most consistent with a respect for reason' (CK 63).

The main reason why Kukathas thinks that toleration has nothing (or very little) to do with justice and that we 'eviscerate toleration by subordinating it to justice' (CK 60), however, is an essential one, and it goes back to what I noted above, namely his scepticism concerning practical reason. He believes that if justice provides the grounds and limits of toleration, it implies that we need not and maybe must not tolerate what 'we define as unjust', which in his view is a 'pretty important class' (CK 64) of things we disagree about: 'Toleration cannot simply be a matter of justice because we actually disagree about what is justice.' And thus 'we should not seek to enforce our view of justice when we are powerful enough to do so' (CK 64). But here I beg to differ. First, I do not see how a political order of toleration could ever come about without at least a minimal agreement on fundamentals of justice. And in fact, Kukathas acknowledges this and admits that his view might not 'supply the foundation of any kind of political order' (CK 66). But if that is the case, I do not see how any order of toleration could come into existence in the first place, while arbitrariness and domination could arise and dominate the social order. Second, the fundamental agreement of justice that my view entails is an agreement to regard others as free and equal members of a community of justification to whom we owe reciprocally and generally acceptable reasons for the norms we live under. This rules out certain views that deny such equality, but that does not mean that such views are necessarily suppressed or penalised. They can still be tolerated for the sake of democratic inclusion; yet if they lead to violent attacks on others or on the general order of justification, the limits of toleration need to be drawn by force if necessary. Third, within the realm of basic justice, lots of reasonable disagreements about justice remain as legitimate objects of debate and democratic decision-making.[20] And fourth, the differences about the right forms of religious or ethical life that remain relevant within the realm of reciprocal justice are far from 'trivial', as Kukathas assumes, for debates about religious symbols in public, religious educational practices, same-sex marriage and so on are not trivial. They are debates about what it means to respect others as equal citizens. And in order to decide such questions, we had better have public standards of justification and justice in place. Otherwise, arbitrariness reigns, since no one knows any longer what basic justice means. Tolerating others because that is what justice demands does not imply that one no longer thinks what they do is wrong, for example wearing a burqa; it only means accepting that a general ban would violate democratic respect. That is why justice is needed: it opposes the religious impulse to ban or dominate what you find wrong, although the way in which it does so leaves the judgement of wrongness in place.

This, I think, is the essential point of contention between us. I believe that history teaches us that most of the time toleration is a question of the fair and just treatment of minorities and that scepticism about justice that places justice claims on the same normative and epistemological level as religious claims, which is what Kukathas in effect does, is exactly what Bayle was fighting against with the weapons of reason. So eliding that difference puts us back where Bayle began – to a defence of the categorical difference between moral versus religious truths and to the argument for an order of justice that protects minorities and regards them as normative equals (which Bayle demanded in moral, although not political, terms). I also think that it is a conceptual truth that toleration cannot be limitless, since, for example, a toleration based on reason cannot imply that the destruction of reason ought to be tolerated, which is what Kukathas paradoxically advocates. Otherwise, the ideal of toleration would be empty. And so would the idea of reason, for if reason could never speak with sufficient justification until a de facto 'complete agreement' (CK 66) exists, it would have no voice at all. It would cease to exist, just as would toleration and justice.[21]

III Toleration and the deontological difference (reply to John Horton)

It is especially gratifying to have John Horton comment on my reflections, since he is a true giant among toleration scholars. Without his work, stretching over decades, this field would be so much poorer and narrower.[22] And my own work would not have been possible, because his lucid analysis of the paradoxes of toleration in particular helped me enormously to think through the conceptual issues of toleration.[23] Thus any praise of my work by him is a wonderful recognition[24] – and his critique especially worrisome. As far as I can see, there are a number of issues I need to address given Horton's analysis, but they all go back to one major worry, which is similar to those of Bejan and Kukathas – namely the deontological difference between a notion of justice as framing the realm of the tolerable conceptions of the good and as limiting that realm. Can such a difference be drawn in the first place, is it necessary, and is it helpful?

Contrary to Kukathas, Horton agrees with my analysis that toleration is a normatively dependent concept, but he raises serious doubts about my – again: normative, not descriptive – suggestion that we should take the principle of reciprocal and general justification to be the right one for determining the space and limits of toleration.[25] Before I go into the details of Horton's challenging arguments, let me preface my comments with the following remark. I do indeed believe that if the history of toleration entails some learning processes, the most important among them is a process of rationalisation leading to the realisation that the deontological difference between *moral-political* norms to which no one can reasonably object (though a lot of people do object to them) and *ethical* values that can guide one in one's personal and communal life is the right response to the political wars and conflicts of religion. The main thought is quite simple: you can still regard a different religion or way of life as false while recognising that you do not have any reciprocal-general reasons to overpower or outlaw it. But you can still voice your criticism and objection. Yet to call this a learning process does not mean that I think that this insight has carried the day, that it is accepted by most people in democratic societies – or that it is always conclusive. So when Horton points out that my own approach needs to engage with substantive debates and that its conclusions will be contested and seen as partial, there is no disagreement. I know that they are, which is why my approach is one of critical theory. It goes against the grain of what many people think who advocate some version of the permission conception, sometimes in populist or ideological terms. But I think that philosophy should find ways to distinguish between more or less reasonable disagreements and contestations, and I do not see why the fact of contestation or resistance implies that those who disagree are right or that rightness cannot be ascertained. I think I am in agreement with Horton concerning this point, for such a radical sceptical realism would amount to giving up philosophy, and this is not his view. And I am willing to admit, as I will explain below, that the deontological difference might not always lead to one clear conclusion, although I will try to lend it sharper contours than Horton thinks it has.

Thus with respect to Horton's avowed scepticism concerning 'bright and optimistic stories' (JH 78), and in light of what I just said, I join him in that scepticism. My tale is not one of general progress; rather, it is a dialectical story which lists criteria of progress and historical achievements on the one hand and the rationalisation of power and domination on the other. But I make no general assessment concerning the victory of one or the other tale.[26] Taking up Kant's famous formulation, we still do not live in an enlightened society, maybe not even generally in an age of enlightenment, but at least in one in which some people fight for enlightenment. And their struggles are of interest to me as a critical theorist.

I also agree with Horton when he says that a view which focuses on ruling out religious reasons from the justificatory discourse about general norms does not get us very far. This is not only because, as he says, religious believers are 'sufficiently sophisticated' (JH 80) to rephrase their claims in a more general language, but also because I do not think that reified notions of 'public' versus 'private' or 'secular' versus 'religious' reasons help us when it comes to understanding and evaluating normative claims. That is why I focus on the reciprocity of claims and of reasons as criteria which are at the same time more concrete in evaluating competing claims and more general in reflecting on the moral quality of the reasons adduced to counter objections. But Horton is sceptical about these criteria and about my explanation of the work they can do in § 38 of *Toleration in Conflict* especially.

With regard to questions of blasphemy which so often lead to vicious and violent conflicts in Western and non-Western societies and which Horton discusses with reference to the so-called 'Rushdie affair', I recognise that those who want to ban works of art that they see as demeaning and intolerably insulting the founders of their religion often use a general language of civility, respect and toleration to ground their demands. And I also accept that some caricatures or other expressions of criticism are intended to insult certain religions and thus are expressions of intolerance.[27] This is an intolerance of which we can and should be critical in civil society, but it is not one that should be banned by law. So here is an important difference on which I should have placed greater stress in my work and about which Horton is right to enquire.[28] But contrary to Horton, I do not think that the call for a ban on blasphemous expressions can be 'entirely consistent with the requirement of reciprocity' (JH 80). For those who call for these bans do not want to leave the authority to determine what counts as 'blasphemy' with democratic law-makers or courts but want to reserve the definitional authority for themselves. Therefore it is not true that they are offering general and reciprocal reasons for their cause. If their views were to ground our common political and legal life, the door would be opened to a wild variety of arbitrary decisions about which kinds of speech or art have to be banned, since Muslim, Christian, Hindu and many other groups would define the limits of what can be tolerated according to their own lights. We would then be back to what Bayle saw as the main problem, namely that religious definitions of what counts as intolerable would determine how we have to live in a society marked by religious difference and disputes.

Again, this does not mean that state authorities can never outlaw certain insulting expressions, but that the threshold for determining what is intolerably insulting must be set very high and not be defined in partial terms. It must be based on clear moral judgements, such as a ban on denying the Holocaust. My claim is not that such a ban must be upheld generally or under particular circumstances, like the German case, but I want to leave the possibility open for arguments of such a kind which need to be placed in the right political context. And I do not want to rule out that vicious condemnations of particular religious groups could exceed a threshold above which such expressions amount to an intolerable denial of equal citizenship and basic rights. But again, the threshold of justification must be set very high for this and above it must clearly lie the realm of strict moral intolerability. So, yes, there is a certain 'indeterminacy of reason' when it comes to the application of the principle of reciprocal and general justification, as the Holocaust example shows. But I do not consider this to be a reason for general doubts about the principle itself, which is meant to single out such special cases of intolerable intolerance. There are many other cases of intolerance – say, of an anti-Muslim or an anti-Semitic nature – of which we should be critical; but here the limits of the tolerable must be a subject of discussion and action within civil society, not primarily of the legal state. Thus, to answer one of Horton's questions (JH 88), there are examples of expressions of which the state might be wary but which it cannot justifiably ban, because the result would be a political situation in which infringements of free speech would be a constant danger (I will return to this point).

Where I am somewhat more sceptical than Horton is when it comes to the idea that in such cases the coexistence conception is of much help, or that 'processes of negotiation and bargaining' (JH 85) will lead to practical conclusions which are more concrete and useful than applications of the respect and justification principle. For notoriously, both in the past and currently, such debates arise in the relation between majorities and minorities, so that the negotiation power is very unevenly distributed. Hence certain bans will most likely operate to the detriment and disadvantage of minorities rather than the other way around. I understand the relevance of discussion and deliberation, but we still need principled responses to such questions.

Horton also worries that my threshold of justification may be too high and restrictive for certain forms of normal, majoritarian lawmaking in various fields such as 'health (including sex) education, the built environment, which things should be taxed and at what levels, what should be subsidised and to what extent, public iconography and much else' (JH 88). One particular example he mentions is state policies that discourage people from excessive consumption of alcohol which, he believes, might fall under my rubric of the impermissible imposition of a certain notion of the good (JH 82). I understand these worries and agree that I need to say more about cases in which majority decisions are justifiable and cases in which they need to reach a higher threshold of strict reciprocity and generality.[29] In general, I believe that a democratic state has the task of educating young persons on health and issues relating to sexuality, but that it does not have the authority to impose a particular personal or sexual identity on them or to discriminate against their identities as they understand them. As I argue in *Toleration in Conflict*,[30] general citizenship education does not require students to be 'neutralized' in their dress but must take their religious identity into account and respect it; yet this does not mean that parents can take their children out of biology classes or prevent them from being taught about 'tolerance' in school, even though the school needs to reflect seriously on what that term means in pedagogical contexts. When it comes to issues of public aesthetics, I think majorities can decide, although they cannot ban mosques or minarets, even if a majority feels alienated by the sight of them. Here there is a clear line beyond which majority decisions are not justified, because they would overpower minorities without good reasons. Again, the implications of equal citizenship are what count.

When it comes to welfare policies, a democratic state must make sure that its citizens (and people in general) are protected against various forms of legal, political or social and economic domination and exploitation, and there is nothing paternalistic about such policies. Paternalistic policies that place restrictions on alcohol consumption can be justified in the case of young people, but they are justified for adults only when the latter endanger others through their drinking (by driving when drunk, for example). No state agency can justifiably punish people for being dependent upon alcohol by, for example, restricting their access to health care or work. This, of course, is not what Horton advocates; but if one thought that laws discouraging excessive alcohol consumption could be legitimate to the extent that they were based on certain ideas of the good life, as I take Horton to argue, the door would be opened to all kinds of paternalistic policies. Refraining from such legal sanctions does not mean that we respect the ethical identity of people who drink too much as part of a 'hedonistic or sybaritic lifestyle' (JH 82), but that we respect them as legal and political equals whom we have no sufficient reasons to re-educate through legal measures. As friends, for example, we ought to offer help or criticism, as may seem fit, but as citizens we need to abide by the respect principle and adhere to policies of social solidarity.

Another important example is same-sex marriage. Horton asks why the institution of civil partnerships with almost equal legal standing to married couples does not count as a fair compromise if a majority is against extending the traditional institution, and he asks furthermore where the extensions should stop, citing polygamy or other relationships (JH 86). In response, I think that the first solution, i.e. civil partnerships, is better than having no institution or rights at all; but I cannot see any good reasons for not granting full equal rights, since the 'Christian heritage' (JH 86) is not a sufficient reason for restrictions in a democratic state which is committed to equal citizenship. Consider how many restrictions of such rights could be justified on these grounds. Moreover, the extension argument, which generates slippery-slope concerns, must be taken seriously, but it cannot be used as an argument for restricting same-sex rights, an issue which needs to be addressed in its own right. If such arguments for extending the institution of marriage are taken seriously, one can reflect on the suggested justifications and the meaning of the institution. For example, one might raise concerns about the patriarchal implications of polygamy. I readily concede that this is a discussion in which the particular meanings of legal and cultural forms play a role.[31] Still, we cannot remain bound by this cultural particularity and the associated stereotypes and must enquire, sometimes radically, into what equal citizenship means. And the limits of what majorities are actually willing to tolerate must not define the limits of what should be tolerated.

But at this point political realists might raise a fundamental objection. They – and I am not saying that this is Horton's view, because he is not generally sceptical about better or worse normative reasons (see JH 83 where he rules out 'anything goes')[32] – might be of the opinion that toleration is essentially a *political* rather than a *moral* concept (a view which is closer to Glen Newey's).[33] And they might go on to infer that any justification of the realm and limits of toleration could depend so much on what (most) people are actually willing to tolerate that a principled approach like mine is doomed to remain a 'Kantian illusion' (JH 83). Underlying this objection, I take it, is essentially a disagreement over what political philosophy can and should do. The two extremes here are not useful, since the one fabricates a fantasy of beings who are nothing but perfectly programmed moral angels, while the other takes humans to be self-interested beings who can never be guided by normative reasons. Neither Horton nor I occupy either of these extremes, but we may be closer to one or the other end of the spectrum. I for one try to have my cake and eat it as well. For, as a sociological realist, I know where the limits of toleration lie for most people, but, as a normative theorist, I try to assess where they go wrong. A critical theorist needs to be both a sociological realist and a normative critic. But that orientation is not illusory. If there could never be a devout Catholic who hates the sight of mosques, or a devout Muslim who hates the sight of Catholic churches, in his or her town but who nevertheless understands that it is a duty of justice to allow them to be built, then my theory is a mere illusion and of only theoretical interest. But I doubt that this is the case.

To return from these declarations of faith to Horton's challenges, he rightly asks whether on my view a state can ever disapprove of some practice and behaviour and still tolerate it legally. Unlike the drinking example, this is not a case in which the state condemns a practice on ethical grounds (which it should not) but instead on moral grounds, but nevertheless tolerates it. Before answering I would like to highlight what I argued for above, and emphasise once again that this is an important aspect of my view that I did not sufficiently explain. As citizens and members of *civil society*, we can morally *condemn* certain expressions or practices without *outlawing* them; so here, as I see it, the political community has an important task in forming normative judgements below the legal level. Examples of this are certain patriarchal pedagogical practices, but also certain insults directed against particular groups.

Still, Horton's point is well taken. For I think that the state – or better, the citizens as law-makers – can justifiably raise moral objections against certain views and practices, say, of a racist nature, and nevertheless tolerate such views by not outlawing them. The reasons for this are in part prudential but there could also be some moral ones, such as refraining from creating a social climate of bans and restrictions on freedom of speech. There will be hard cases, such as Nazi symbols and speeches and demonstrations – or political parties. Here a state has to act prudently and, as I argue in *Toleration in Conflict*,[34] this is a point at which the logic of the permission conception enters into the respect conception. The main imperative of equal citizenship remains valid and it calls for a limit of *social* toleration of such immoral and undemocratic groups; but there may be prudent reasons for *legal* toleration. So I agree with Horton that the permission logic might reappear even in a democracy, but I would restrict this to cases such as these and do not think that it amounts to the classic authoritarian conception. Rather, it is based on equal respect.

In sum, I agree with Horton about the grey zones of justification and application but I do not think that this speaks against the use of and need for a principled, respect-based account. I also think that it can do much more work than Horton thinks it can. So I agree with him that all toleration answers must be 'addressed *practically* and *politically*' (JH 89); but unlike extreme realists I think that most of the time the factual political practice of toleration is wrong and leads either to open intolerance – as when majorities ban minarets by popular vote – or to intolerance veiled as tolerance, such as allowing same-sex marriage only if it is not called marriage. This is the sense in which my account is a critical realist one, and it implies the need for critical principles.

IV Toleration for earthlings (reply to Daniel Weinstock)

Among contemporary political philosophers, Daniel Weinstock is unrivalled when it comes to thinking through the theory as well as the practice of what constitutes a just, legitimate or practicable multi-ethnic or multi-national state.[35] As he makes clear, it matters whether it is justice that one is looking for, or legitimacy or stability; but whatever one is looking for, normative political theory must remain a theory for earthlings, to use a term of David Miller's – that is, its normative grounds and shape must be fit for human beings as they are or, better, as they could be given what they are.[36] These are deep waters to navigate through, and I am grateful to Weinstock for pressing me to do so.

Weinstock is absolutely right to remind us that the very term toleration applies to 'non-ideal political circumstances' (DW 94)[37] in which there is not only deep disagreement but also the (initial) willingness to restrict the liberty of those with whom you disagree. He believes, however, that I do not take sufficient account of the latter aspect and thus underestimate the importance of 'self-restraint as a constitutive ingredient of the structural account of toleration' (DW 96). I disagree with this as a critique, because I think that self-restraint is (conceptually) essential for any form of toleration. But Weinstock has a particular case in mind, namely that of reasons for tolerating what is immoral, and as I said above in the context of my exchange with John Horton, that is indeed a case I need to say more about.

Before going into this, let me say a word about the distinction between ideal and non-ideal theory and how I situate my reflections on toleration in relation to it. That Rawlsian distinction has come to mean many things to many people, and it is difficult to disentangle these many meanings.[38] In general, I try to avoid such reified distinctions and I do not work with idealised assumptions about persons or social circumstances. Rather, I try to combine sociological realism with principled normative argument, where the principles in question are for real people in real societies. I do not paint an ideal of a new society or any such thing; thus the respect conception that I normatively favour is not a mere ideal but rather a principled stance of all those who understand that they must not take their reasons for objecting as a basis for acting to the disadvantage of that to which they object if they do not have any good additional reasons for rejecting it. That holds as much for the French republican feminist who hates burqas but recognises that this is not a sufficient reason for banning them as it does for the devout Muslim who hates to see his daughter develop 'immoral' ideas about the good life but understands that he cannot stop her from following these ideas. This is just the stuff of normal, complicated life, no rationalist dream.

Why does Weinstock believe that my respect conception takes us beyond non-ideal circumstances of toleration? Because he believes that the toleration I normatively defend does not take sufficient account of the reality of social conflict and the 'inclination' (DW 96) of people in power to limit the freedom of those to whom they object. But I do not think that I make such a mistake. For before I distinguish the four conceptions of toleration and the twenty-five justifications for it, I distinguish the three components of any concept or stance of toleration. And the very first component, that of objection, entails that you find the views and practices of others bad or wrong. This implies that you would prefer that these views and practices should not exist or at least that they should be restricted, for otherwise you would not need any further components of toleration which matter in practice and curb your preferences. So as soon as the acceptance component comes in, self-restraint is part of the very definition of the attitude of toleration, since the reasons for accepting do not eliminate the negative reasons for objecting but only counterbalance them and keep them in check. They restrain their practical consequences but leave them basically intact.

So, in my view, Weinstock's 'tolerant person' (DW 112) who has ceased to have 'intolerant' attitudes and as a result no longer thinks that other people's views and practices are something that should be constrained, is not really a tolerant person. She may indeed be 'beyond toleration', as Weinstock suggests, since her objections do not matter much to her. She is on the verge of indifference, and if she is tolerant at all, then at most in the sense of the esteem conception. But this is not my picture of the 'moral virtuosi' (DW 113) of the respect conception, for their virtue consists precisely in curbing their inclinations to act on their objections. That is why it is a *virtue* of justice on a Kantian understanding: it controls the desire to act on your notions of the good, as I explain in *Toleration in Conflict*, where I call it the virtue of resisting 'the impulse to turn ethical reasons for objecting into moral reasons for rejecting',[39] which I believe is what Weinstock means (in some parts of his argument at least). Thus it is not the case that I neglect self-restraint as a component of toleration; I even use the term 'a certain self-overcoming'[40] that he finds lacking in my account (DW 100). Moreover, I use this idea when discussing both the personal virtue of toleration and the political one, where it is most important for members of majorities who need to accept that being in a majority is not a sufficient reason for pushing through intolerant policies.

According to my theory, the self-restraint conceptually implied by the core notion of toleration means different things if we consider the multiplicity of our conceptions and justifications of toleration, some of which are both pragmatic and strategic. And even though I admire the way in which Weinstock summarises my view, I think that in common with some of my other critics he neglects my analysis of *four* conceptions of toleration and my argument that, depending on the context, the respect conception might not be realisable, even though we need to look closely at why that is so (a point I will come back to).

In the permission conception as well as in the political version of the respect conception, tolerance is an attitude of the powerful in virtue of which they refrain from curbing the liberties of those with whom they disagree in the knowledge that they have the power to do otherwise. But they do so for different reasons, depending on which conception you use – only in the respect conception it is done out of respect for others as normative equals. I think that toleration must be freely motivated; but contrary to Weinstock I do not think that part of the very definition of being tolerant is that one actually has the power to constrain others. Minorities who do not have any such power can also have an attitude of tolerance in thinking that intolerance is wrong. They do not really need to have, or think of themselves as having, the power to prove this; and thus I do not think that my argument to the effect that they would not use their power for intolerant purposes if they were in a position to do so proves Weinstock's point that having power is an essential precondition for *being* tolerant (DW 100f.). It is not even essential for *acting* tolerantly in general, only for acting tolerantly as a political authority. To think otherwise would be to inject the permission conception into the very concept of toleration, a move often made in the literature on toleration.[41]

But, similar to Horton, Weinstock obviously has a point when he asks whether my account of the respect conception allows for reasons for tolerating not just those with whom we *ethically* disagree but also those whom we find – with good reasons – *immoral*. In *Toleration in Conflict*, I discuss this question with respect to anti-democratic fascist groups and parties, and it can be extended to racist groups generally.[42] There I list similar reasons to the ones Weinstock mentions for pragmatic or strategic toleration of what is in principle intolerable, and I admit that here the respect and the permission conception form a certain alliance. Clearly there are such cases, especially when it comes to the question of a legal ban, which should only be a measure of last resort (for example, a ban on a political party). But as I said above, social ways of drawing the limits of toleration through clear expressions of rejection in speech and non-violent action are also a way of drawing the limits of toleration vis-à-vis what is immoral. Still, cases like these mean that it may be morally permissible and in some cases even advisable to tolerate what is intolerable. I accept Weinstock's and Horton's point in this regard. But it does not speak against the respect conception; it simply spells out its implications more clearly with regard to such cases.

Weinstock is also right to point out people's epistemic tendencies to regard what is essentially an ethical objection as a moral rejection, as his excellent example of feminist, republican and nationalist criticisms of Muslim veils shows (DW 106). But as long as he calls this failure 'to realise the degree to which their application of moral principles is shot through with unexamined assumptions drawn from their own ethical framework' a mistake and 'wrong' (DW 107), we are not in disagreement. We disagree neither about what are the right principles to apply in such cases nor about how to apply them correctly, and we also agree that there is a constant tendency (or propensity, as Kantians would say) to interpret what is morally right in the light of one's ethical views. This is why the virtue of toleration (according to the respect conception) is the virtue of overcoming that inclination and why I favour a reflexive justification of toleration, since it entails the duty to check our own views as to whether we made such a mistake. The criteria of reciprocity and generality help in this regard, since it is in applying them that one should try to notice how much one uses ethical, traditional stereotypes in judging others and overlooks how one privileges one's own views, for example in arguing for republican public 'neutrality' which favours some symbolic identities over others. Weinstock's work is exemplary when analysing such deficiencies of even-handedness, as is Ayelet Shachar's.[43]

What I do not quite see, however, is how one can analyse and criticise such mistakes (knowing that we ourselves might commit them) and then argue that imperatives of respect-based toleration 'may not be appropriate to the kinds of beings possessed with the finite epistemological capacities that are those of humans' (DW 109). As I said above, I do not deny, descriptively speaking, that the respect conception is demanding and that the permission conception is most often the default position; but I do not agree that it is *too* demanding. It takes some work to accept that you do not have any good reasons to push through intolerant policies even if you happen to be part of a majority or are acting towards your children, for example, and I also accept what Weinstock calls 'the human tendency to mis-apply moral principles' (DW 109); but a mis-application remains a mistake, and reasonable people need to avoid mistakes. The virtues never come naturally, as Aristotle reminds us, but that is not a reason to water down the standards of virtue. Furthermore, I think it is a sign of mutual respect to remind each other (and ourselves) of these standards and not reduce them by regarding 'normal' people as incapable of living up to them. Nobody is 'overtaxed' by being required to understand that someone who wears a Muslim dress is your normative equal.

In sum, I agree with Weinstock that a theory of toleration, especially if it is a historical theory, and hence is descriptive as well as normative, should take the full range of non-ideal social circumstances into account. It should avoid oversimplifying things and sacrificing complexity 'at the altar of theoretical elegance and simplicity' (DW 111). I think that, given the multiplicity of conceptions and justifications of toleration I analyse, I avoid such pitfalls. But I believe that the task of a critical theory of toleration is not to look at things primarily from the perspective of majorities who feel over-encumbered by the claims of minorities but from the perspective of those who are not respected as equals and are dominated in various ways. That is what justice requires, in theory as well as in practice.

V Respect without justification
(reply to Melissa Williams)

This is a good moment to turn to Melissa Williams's chapter, since she continues and to some extent radicalises a line of argument pursued by Weinstock (and followed up on by Markell and Owen). Specifically, she enquires into the blind spots of the respect conception itself, or, more fundamentally, of the practice of justification – the practice of treating others as normative equals by respecting their right to justification – as the basic moral practice. Williams's work is in general an exemplar of dialectical reasoning,[44] and so too is her contribution to our debate.[45] While she upholds the perspective of moral egalitarianism, she reminds us through the historically informed and culturally situated form of thought that she has developed of alternative ways of practising mutual respect apart from, or even 'turning away from', justification. I welcome this as a great challenge to clarify my ideas, although I am not sure that I will be able to do so properly, since the issues Williams raises are complex and the examples she uses deal with contexts she knows much more about than I do.

Williams's basic critical claim is that my reconstruction of the practice of morality as a practice of justification is not false but one-sided, because it neglects other forms of moral practice that are not linguistically structured but expressive and performative in non-discursive ways. In what she calls 'prefigurative practices' (MW 123) that establish experiments of living as part of an attempt to resist and overcome forms of domination, communities cooperate in 'non-discursive practices of egalitarian reciprocity' (MW 133). In response, I recognise the importance of such prefigurative modes of action but am not quite convinced that they can or should be thought of apart from egalitarian forms of *discourse*, since I would like to consider these forms of cooperation as *democratic*, or as prefiguring egalitarian democracy, and in my view there can be no proper democracy without discourse. So I am not convinced by the strong distinction that Williams makes between discursive and non-discursive forms of cooperation. Prefigurative practices might suggest a different mode of communication and social cooperation, but not one which is beyond justification – though surely beyond colonial and oppressive justificatory practices.

Williams notes that my approach has been the subject of several criticisms by esteemed colleagues such as Amy Allen[46] and Kevin Olson[47] or Lois McNay[48] (and to some extent Catherine Lu[49]), who (rightly) point out that, from a critical perspective, normative orders as orders of justification have to be seen as orders of power and domination in which the terms and conditions of discourse imply a host of exclusions and power effects that disadvantage certain groups whose claims are either not heard or are silenced. I tried to reflect on this obvious truth in my theory of democracy in *Contexts of Justice* starting from feminist critiques of democracy.[50] Williams rightly points out that in my view a critical theory of justification has to critically assess the 'conditions of justification' within social orders in order to identify and overcome such power effects – with the help of discursive or non-discursive forms of criticism and protest, whereby the 'non-discursive' forms (like quiet protest or performances of resistance) also have to be seen in their discursive quality. We need not restrict the realm of justification in a society to explicit words. Furthermore, such critique can in principle never rest, since one can never be sure of the (e)quality of discourses that might falsely assume to have made progress. As I tried to show above, that is true of many advances in toleration.

Williams accepts my replies to such criticisms in general by affirming that 'the cure for the ills of justification is more justification' (MW 123), and yet she argues that this is only part of the story of emancipation, because sometimes the cure means turning away from justification. But what does 'justification' mean here? I think here her view is somewhat ambivalent, since there are several characteristics of the kind of order of justification that from her perspective rightly – shall I say: *justifiably?* – motivates a turn away from justification. I think I should indeed say justifiable, and thus argue (against Williams) that none of these moves escapes the general social question of justifiability, even if some of these emancipatory practices were correctly analysed as non-discursive.

In Williams's discussion, I see three ideal type candidates for the order of justification that prefigurative practices try to avoid. The first and most prominent ones are colonial or neo-colonial orders in which the terms of discourse are themselves of a colonising and oppressive nature. The second, more general kind of candidate are practices of justification which reproduce status hierarchies by privileging those who have 'greater skill in reasoned argumentation' (MW 131). And the third, even more general, type are practices in which moral respect can be expressed only by explicit moral reason-giving and not by implicit moral action, possibly in an 'unreflexive' (MW 133) mode. I will discuss these three types in turn.

As examples for the prefigurative practices which create 'islands of just and moral relationship within larger contexts of social, political and economic domination' (MW 124) of colonial and neo-colonial rule, Williams cites Gandhi's *satyagraha* ('struggle for truth') movement and Indigenous movements in North America. As she explains, such movements entail a 'no' to dominating forms of rule and a 'yes' to alternative forms of social life (MW 126). In Gandhi's case, such forms of life included forms of sharing hard and dirty work that radically questioned established caste hierarchies and realised a new 'ethos of service' (MW 126). In Indigenous contexts, they entailed social and cultural forms which reconnected with past traditions and practices, including the 'relearning of Indigenous languages and ceremonies' (MW 127). Williams argues that in such forms of prefiguration practices of justification play no foundational role; rather, they are to be seen as 'non-discursive practices that are understood by agents as performances of (or, in Gandhi's terms, experiments in) reciprocity and respect' (MW 127).

To be sure, Williams does not deny the important justificatory dimensions of saying 'no' to dominating forms of discourse as a demand for better reasons, better institutions and as a reaction to the failures of dominators to heed that demand (MW 128). These resistance movements manifest justificatory agency by rejecting false forms of discourse and justification. But in Williams's interpretation, these movements did not simply argue for other, new forms of justification. Rather, they tried to *substitute* them with non-discursive performances (MW 130). The reason for this brings us to the second interpretation of the dominating forces implicit in justificatory discourses that I mentioned above, namely the class-based character of according primacy to reason-giving and argumentation. Here, engaging in justification is no longer understood in terms of conformity to an imposed and alienating order; rather, it means conforming to some form of discursive rationalism which reproduces class structure. Such structures can be better overcome by 'displacing practices of justification with practices of service to community' (MW 131).

I recognise the importance of such radical forms of changing a caste social order through egalitarian practices; but I wonder whether they can really be interpreted as being non-discursive, not just in their 'no'-relation to the dominant orders of justification but also in their 'yes'-function in establishing new forms of egalitarian cooperation. For if the new forms of communal service and work were to realise and symbolise the equal worth of all as normative equals, the latter constitutes the general positive justification for these practices. And if this is so, how could work be *fairly* distributed beyond all traditional distinctions of caste in the absence of discursive forms of respectfully organising this work? Furthermore, as indicated above and as Aishwary Kumar[51] shows in his reading of Gandhi and Ambedkar, if these new egalitarian forms of social life were to prefigure true (or truer) *democracy*, how could they not entail forms of democratic decision-making which must be discursive?

Of course, this is not to deny the hierarchical risks and implications of discursive decision-making, which often privilege those who can speak well, have some (unwarranted but assumed) authority and so on. But what are the alternatives to that? That is, how great are the dangers of rule by charisma, of religious tradition, of social pressure against those who are assumed to be 'privileged' and so on? If we take realistic stock of the problems of discursive decision-making, then we should also be realistic and equally critical about other, less discursive modes of coordinating action.

Williams is the last of all scholars to overlook these dangers. As she remarks, revivals of older cultural forms often reproduce traditions 'structured by their own forms of domination, including gender-based domination' (MW 132), which is why discursive critique is required against the imposition of colonial as well as traditional forms of domination. Thus, I take it, turning away from justification can never be accepted uncritically, and *every* social form we turn to must be open to discursive criticism and cannot shield itself from criticism, whether by women, the young, the less educated, the non-religious or other groups.

It is here where the third candidate for an order of justification from which one might turn away becomes most relevant. According to Williams, 'when we treat our practices as objects of critical reason and argumentation, we are necessarily alienated from them; we are not wholly immersed in them' (MW 132). Thus 'full attention and care' in performing communal work is incompatible with discursive critique and argument. I am not sure I agree with this, but here we must first distinguish between argumentation as part of a practice and critical argument about a practice. As part of a practice of working together, communication and reasoning can never be excluded, for even work teams or sports teams that have cooperated for a long time need communication. So they are always discursively structured, I believe, and that is part of being immersed in them, not its antithesis.

If that is the case, the possibility of critically interrogating the practice is always present, and such critique can be situated on a spectrum ranging from small internal questions (is this the best way to do this?) to radical questioning (why do it this way, and who is to tell?). Some forms of critique belong to human practices, especially more complex ones. But some forms clearly have an alienating character, although quite often it is out of a spirit of commitment and care that such questions are asked. For any practice that is guided by a spirit of egalitarian reciprocity, as in Williams's examples, must open itself up to the question whether it is true to that *Geist*. Especially prefigurative practices, or so it seems to me, which *explicitly* try to create new egalitarian forms of social life, must be open to this. For manifesting a new spirit is their *justification*. It would be at odds with that spirit if engaging in these practices excluded asking critical questions.

This does not mean, to address a final worry expressed by Williams, that an egalitarian practice cannot be successfully performed on the basis of reasons that remain implicit (MW 133) and that have become, so to speak, people's second nature. It is not that a moral form of relationship consists of constant moral argument and discourse; rather, it presupposes respectful ways of treating others as equal normative authorities. So I agree that moral practices are multiple and need not always involve explicit justification, but Williams and I also agree that 'moral reasons must underlie the practice' (MW 133), and that is why I conclude that any implicit set of reasons must remain open to the possibility of explicit justification and not restrict or seal off the space of reasons. Most of the time justifications remain implicit in what Habermas calls lifeworld knowledge and action, and since treating others morally always means treating them in a morally *justifiable* way, whether this is the case can at any time be turned into an explicit question. That is what is implied by respecting the other as an equal moral authority. Hence we should be suspicious of practices that fear such kinds of questioning as alienating.

VI Heresy and critique (reply to Patchen Markell)

Patchen Markell's is one of the most original and important voices in current critical theory, since he illuminates how the very concepts through which we think about politics (and society) shape our views in particular ways and harbour effects of power. The way in which he combines theories as different as Foucault's, Arendt's and critical race theories in the light of the classical tradition of political philosophy is unique and exemplary for what critical political theory can be.[52]

Given that character of his work, I am especially grateful to him for subjecting my attempts to critical scrutiny. He focuses on the (possibly) different ways in which a critical theory needs to transcend conventional horizons of thought in order to determine what emancipation could mean.

Like my other critics, Markell worries about the narrowness of an approach centred on practices of justification. He fears that it remains bound up too closely with the limits of what can be thought and said in given orders of justification and thus loses the transcending power that critique must possess, such as the power of those who in the past were decried as heretics or as mad when they pushed the limits of the thinkable to make room for new ways of viewing the world. I believe that this understanding of what radical critique can do and ought to do is very much in line with my approach, which is one of the reasons why I differ from critics like Amy Allen or Seyla Benhabib in arguing for the possibility of radically questioning a *sittliche* form of social life, in a way that is not bound by 'immanent' standards of critique.[53] Yet Markell, if I understand him correctly, is nevertheless concerned that the rationalism of my approach underappreciates the world-disclosing aspects of a 'prior sense of what there *is* in the world to be reasoned *about*' (PM 140f.),[54] or what he calls a 'space of appearance' prior to and more basic than the space of reasons. Critical theory thus needs to understand and be able to intervene in that space, the space of what is socially thinkable – or unthinkable. I basically agree with Markell on this, although I have some hesitations about the (seemingly) strict dichotomy between these two realms that he suggests. And I have qualms about some possible implications concerning the standards of rationality that apply to 'ontological' forms of critique.

Before I go into this, however, allow me to preface my remarks with a brief biographical reminiscence. In the late 1980s in Frankfurt, a number of my friends and colleagues, inspired by Heidegger and Foucault especially, reflected on the 'world-disclosing' powers of language, as did Cristina Lafont, for example, in such illuminating ways.[55] Nick Kompridis later developed his own version of critical theory based on this approach,[56] and I recall attending inspiring seminars by Jürgen Habermas and Karl-Otto Apel with Hubert Dreyfus as well as Richard Bernstein in which this issue was discussed at length. The main worries at that time, when the National Socialist character of Heidegger's writings was also the focus of intense debates, were of course how one could develop a non-authoritarian, emancipatory notion of opening up a 'world', which Heidegger had interpreted as the 'strife' between the world of possibilities for a *Volk* appropriating its mission given its 'earthly' historical character.[57] Foucault's notion of truth-regimes (*epistemes*) of power served as an antidote to Heidegger's political-poetic, nationalist historical existentialism, and Foucault's search for new forms of social and individual life was seen by many as a better way to think about the practical work of freedom.[58] Following Foucault and Nietzsche, genealogy was deemed to be the appropriate approach to the critical reconstruction and unmasking of these effects of power.[59]

Markell is right to take up this point and remind me of this important dimension of language and of critique. He does so with the help of an intriguing reinterpretation of what Hannah Arendt means when she says that power 'survives or outlasts action' (PM 142) and that it 'keeps people together'.[60] In that paragraph, she refers to 'the foundation of cities' as creating the durable common public space for the appearance of words and deeds and as 'the most important material prerequisite of power',[61] thus stressing, like Heidegger, the importance of political founding and its sustainable results – but, in contrast to Heidegger, in a republican way. Markell invests this with a more ontological meaning which is also very much in line with a Heideggerian reading. He describes how the lasting effects of powerful actions or events configure a space of power by 'charging' a situation, because these actions and events lend possible future actions and events a particular meaning and in that sense make a collective future possible. According to Markell, power thereby acquires an ontological and epistemic importance by structuring or constituting 'the field of objects with which the subjects of practical reason engage' (PM 144). Similar to Foucault's analysis of subject formation, Markell uses Arendt to point to processes of object formation as grounding or configuring the space of appearance in certain ways. According to Markell, that space is prior to the space of reasons, because it determines what can appear as thinkable at all: 'It's not that we accept these features of the world because we have been socialised into a tacit belief in their justifiability, or because we think there is no alternative: we – all of us, or some of us – simply do not think much about them at all' (PM 144).

I believe that Markell is right to point to the limits of what is thinkable in any social realm, thereby delimiting the space of possible reasoning; but I think that the distinction he makes between the space of reasons and the space of appearance is too stark. For as he rightly notes, I analyse how the space of reasons is configured with the help of the concept of a 'justification narrative'.[62] Such narratives develop over long periods of time and construct – or, if you prefer, configure – the social space of meanings and interpretations, though often in multiple and occasionally contradictory ways. As an example I cite Max Weber's narrative of the Protestant Ethic and its importance for a modern economy and, more than that, for modern ways of thinking about what constitutes a good, socially valuable and rewarding virtuous life. If such narratives gain a firm grip on subjects and their noumenal economies, so to speak, they limit the realm of the thinkable as much as they structure it. So they mediate precisely between the space of thought and the space of what is thinkable; in fact, they basically connect these two spaces into one. I do not see the point of making a strict separation between what justifications can be about and what appears to be justified, for the two realms are closely interconnected. What appears, always appears within a horizon of understanding as part of narratives and structures of justification. In other words, we would undervalue the space of reasons and reasoning and interpret it too narrowly if we left larger narratives of justification and how they constitute what is thinkable out of the picture (which I take to be an important insight of hermeneutics, as I argued above in response to Bejan). So I do not agree that I theorise this space too narrowly; on the contrary, I think that Markell's interpretation of my theory may be too narrow.

In my view, the space of what is thinkable and how it is configured would not be adequately explained if we conceived of these developments as anonymous *Ereignisse* of world disclosure (*Weltentbergung*) that did not admit of any further explanation, like ontological revolutions *ex nihilo* (which, to be sure, is not what Markell argues). Such an extreme separation of the spaces of appearance and of reasons would imply that the former could not be evaluated in accordance with rational standards, since the latter would only apply within a particular ontological paradigm which it could never transcend. But such transcendence is what Markell actually appeals to when he uses the example of the racist character of the US penal system. A radical critique of this system – in particular, of the false and racially biased justification narratives on which it rests – presupposes an equally radical view that it lacks any proper justification. Markell agrees with this when he says that the demand for justification is 'an important part of the critique of these phenomena' (PM 145); but he then goes on to claim that that demand 'must be accompanied or even preceded by a struggle to reconfigure the space of appearance, to bring these phenomena to attention or to alter the terms of their public representation' (PM 145). I agree, but I do not see how one could alter such terms of representation other than by pointing out the lack of justification of the system that is being criticised. Such a critique might imply acts of 'disrupting ordinary life and sense' (PM 145) and of transcending conventional 'political common sense' (PM 146); but such disruption would remain a mere disruption if it were not accompanied by rational criticism which employs epistemic and moral categories that reveal the *injustice* of the existing system. The point is that the required switch in perspective must be a response to real injustice and not bring about a complete *Gestaltwandel* such that no one knows how the new way of seeing things was motivated. In other words, criticism calls for a justification narrative about why an older such narrative had to be overcome, because it provided an ideological justification of injustice and cruelty as something good, useful or unavoidable. Overcoming such strong narratives by offering an alternative is a form of rational critique and it changes the game of justification while playing it, rather than by somehow bringing about a whole different game. Transcending conventional limits of what can be thought and justified is part of the game of justification, not some *Ereignis* apart from it. Again, we would interpret the notion of the space of justifications too narrowly if we argued that such game changes could not be brought about *with reasons*. The space of reasons is infinite, and its (rational) revolution is part of that very space. In the example cited by Markell, moral reasons drive that revolution. If we could only recognise such reasons *after* the revolution in our *Weltbild*, then that revolution would have been unmotivated and groundless. But that is not how progress is made. (I will come back to this issue below in my response to David Owen.)

I agree with Markell that critical theory needs to reflect on its own supposed 'higher' wisdom and should enquire critically into its own institutional and noumenal conditions of possibility. That includes not just playing conventional games of justification but also reshaping our 'sense of what there is to be argued about' (PM 147). But in my view this is part of the practice of justification, including a historical-genealogical understanding of the narratives and discourses of power we might help in reproducing. One such discourse surely is the neo-Heideggerian one, and one needs to be aware of its authoritarian as well as its possible emancipatory implications, assuming it is redefined appropriately. The latter presuppose that we hold fast to principles of radical critique and moral equality, for being a heretic in itself is not a sign of higher insights into the limits of the thinkable that must be transcended. Markell might be right that Angela Davis is a Pierre Bayle of the twentieth century, but only because she relentlessly exposed the lack of social and moral justification for the existing, racially grounded penal system. For fascists also 'heretically' reject what they regard as 'conventionally' policed systems of justification and argue that they should be transcended radically by allowing for alternatives that democrats regard as 'unthinkable'. But then what are the standards for distinguishing emancipatory from regressive and oppressive forms of radical critique if not standards of moral justification? We need to examine these standards critically by asking how we apply them and what they imply; but we also need to uphold them and defend the right to justification as a basic right to non-domination.

VII Moral Darwinism (reply to David Owen)

For many years, my thinking about critique especially has developed in dialogue with my dear friend David Owen, and I owe him many important insights. His readings of Nietzsche are an exemplar of radical interpretation for emancipatory purposes,[63] and his version of the method of genealogical critique is very illuminating and brings together many different strands of philosophy, from Wittgenstein to Foucault, in an original way.[64] Like Markell and other critics, he is worried that my rationalistic picture of thinking and acting is too narrow to comprehend the workings of social power and develop a proper conception of social progress. I welcome these challenges, since they provide me with an additional opportunity to offer a better interpretation of my own views.

The first issue on which Owen rightly presses me is how to understand the second-order practical insight, as I call it, that makes us 'see' or 'recognise' a human being as a moral person to be respected as an equal normative authority, independently of further considerations about our particular relation to the other or contingent specific qualities that he or she may have.[65] This is a complex view, because it combines on the one hand seeing a particular as well as a general 'aspect' of others as humans and not being blind to them as having a 'soul', as Wittgenstein argues, and on the other a rational insight into the moral justification this entails for recognising the other as an equal moral person with an unqualified right to justification. The justification for morally respecting the other is simply that he or she is a human being and an authority equal to me, and it implies that to ask for further reasons is to ask one question too many. We all share the status of being normative equals in the realm of justification. In my view, that is a moral insight of practical reason in Kant's sense of the term.

I agree with Owen and Cavell that racist slave-owners probably do not regard slaves as not human at all but only as a different kind of human being (DO 152).[66] So when I said that 'soul-blindness' (Cavell's term) means having lost the capacity 'to perceive humans as humans'[67] I meant (and should have stated more clearly) 'as humans in the *full* moral sense', not as humans in any sense of the term that might allow for (immoral) distinctions. To treat another subject as a slave presupposes, I assume, regarding him or her as a second-class human being who can be used, steered and abused. I also agree, as Owen argues following Cavell, that those who (mis)treat others in such ways not only fail to comprehend something essential about these others, namely that treating them in this way can never be justified, but also something about themselves, namely that they fail to regard themselves as equals to these others in the space of justifications. In a recent paper, I refer to this a form of 'noumenal alienation'.[68] I also agree with Owen that someone who is morally blind to some groups of people can be selective in recognising other groups as equals; but I would not call that selectivity a partial morality (and I think Owen would not either). Rather, I would describe it as thoroughly immoral, since this selectivity destroys morality as a whole. And I did not mean to say that, empirically speaking, recognising some humans as equals means recognising all human beings as equals (DO 154). I only meant to say that this is what the second-order moral insight implies, normatively speaking.

Furthermore, I agree with Owen that there can be many ways in which a person comes to have such a second-order insight, and that contingent experiences play a major role in that process. There is no rational automatism that leads to this insight. Kantians like me emphasise the *capacity* for such insights and the importance of living up to this potential; but nowhere do they argue that the faculty of reason develops as an autonomous mechanism without proper cultivation. So it is indeed true that overcoming soul-blindness does not require 'additional facts' (DO 154), as Owen argues; but I think that it does respond to a normative reason, albeit one of a particular kind: in this insight, recognising the other as human means recognising the reason for respecting him or her morally. He or she *is* the reason. So, as Owen says (DO 155), the slave-owner who comes to have that insight has a new 'range of reasons for acting'; but in my view this implies that he now properly understands what underlies these reasons, namely the status of the other as a normative equal. The insight is at the same time one of reason and perception, and the contingent *genealogy* through which one comes to have this insight does not change the general *validity* of its structure as a matter of recognising oneself and others as having a right and duty of justification. I will return to the distinction between genesis and validity in a moment, since it is at the core of further discussions between us.

But let me first comment briefly on Owen's second point, which concerns my notion of power. We share a pronounced interest in this topic, and in our analyses of ideology, for example, we think in similar terms (I believe). Like Owen, I believe that a 'moral conversion' that came about contingently and not by rational argument is something of relevance for noumenal power, because it marks a shift in the economy of reasons and justifications for a person. But if this change was brought about intentionally by others, then there has been an *exercise* of power; by contrast, if it simply 'happened' without anyone intending it, I call it a case of 'influence' or merely an 'occurrence' within the space of justifications. A lot here depends on the word 'exercise', since I want to distinguish these cases.[69] I do not think there is any contradiction between this use of 'influence' and my formulation of the exercise of power based on the ability 'to influence' the space of reasons for others, for the latter is an intentional form of influence, whereas the former is not. If you like, you can also call the former cases of influence forms of 'power', because they reflect constellations in the realm of justification; but that would make the concept of power very broad, since lots of factors, such as the weather, influence how we think and act. I think we need more focused definitions. Thus I of course accept that how the space of justifications within a society is constituted in general finds expression in social and noumenal structures that shape individual or group actions (based on certain justification narratives), and that structural power 'works through an order of continuous aspect perception' (DO 156). But I disagree with Owen's conclusion that such kinds of structural power (which I call influence) are 'not different in kind to exercises of power by individuals' (DO 156). They both refer to changes in the noumenal realm for a person; but the ways in which these changes come about are different, and that is relevant for our analysis of power.

The third, and final, very important issue that Owen brings up is the question of general aspect changes that we look at and evaluate from a historical perspective. What role does justification play here? As far as I can see, there are two issues involved: what role does justification play in actual processes of development and progress, and what role does justification play from the perspective of *ex post* evaluation?

With regard to the first question, I agree with Owen and Bernard Williams that we cannot reduce complex historical changes to a discursive process of 'winning' an argument (DO 157f.). A large number of factors and causes play a role here, and social struggles are not like seminar situations in which we deliberate about the right argument and, if things go well, submit to the force of the better reasons. But it would be equally reductive to say that justifications and arguments play no role in these processes, since the parties to the struggle produce lots of justifications for their aims and their strategies, as the Cambridge School reminds us.[70] These justifications are usually highly specific, but they often transcend the realm of validity of their time and place, as I argued above in my discussion with Bejan. For example, revolutionary claims based on what were called 'natural rights' raise such a validity claim. So every social struggle is a struggle over justifications; but it would be wrong to infer that how social struggles unfold follows the force of better arguments or, even worse, that the better arguments always carry the day. In that respect, Williams is right.

But Williams, and Owen following him, make a much stronger point, and that brings up the issue of historical evaluation. For both subscribe to the idea that, *historically* speaking, a moral-political change, perhaps even a revolution – such as 'liberalism's historical victory'

(DO 157) – did not just not come about by winning an argument against the old regime (which is true). Rather, also with respect to the *justification* of the claims raised by liberals in non-liberal societies, for example, they claim that it is only *after* the change (and the victory) that the arguments can be seen as having deserved that victory. In a sense the positions in question *produce* the normative platform from which they are regarded as valid and justified; they create their own justification through their historical triumph. But since this is not the proper meaning of the term justification, Owen suggests that we call it vindication, which, although it does not derive from *vincere* but instead from *vindicare*, carries with it the idea of justification by winning, but winning not in the sense of winning an argument but of being successful in factually overcoming and defeating the opposition. Vindication, according to Owen, means that 'justificatory reasons cannot be given independently and in advance of the action or outlook in question' (DO 158). In other words, as the Gauguin example shows, the historical winner determines what does and does not count as vindicated.

As one might expect, I have some qualms about this view. For it entails the danger of a form of relativism that I would like to avoid, a form of what I call moral Darwinism.[71] If historical victory vindicates historical change by establishing new criteria of justification that were not normatively valid before the change, then a slave revolt was *not justified* before slavery had actually been overcome. And after it was not properly justified either, but only vindicated. That seems wrong to me, and it seems to contradict some of Owen's own earlier statements about the immorality of slavery. More than that, it does not allow us to take a proper stance with respect to historical struggles and it is Darwinist in giving priority to 'winners'. Furthermore, it leads to a self-congratulatory historical narrative in which liberalism, democracy, respect toleration or what have you presumably were victorious. But I think that these struggles to overcome domination in its various forms, including the domination inherent in some forms of one-sided liberalism, are ongoing, and it is not helpful to think of us as justifiably being democrats because democracy was vindicated by winning its historical battles.

The major issue, however, is that this idea of vindication combines genesis and validity in a particularly troublesome way. It says that in a radical historical struggle, we do not know which side has the better justifications for its claims, for only the winning team will be vindicated and then produces a new platform of justification. The latter, however, does not allow for judgements of moral validity concerning the past, and thus not concerning the future either, because there again historical victories will decide which justifications are plausible by vindicating some changes rather than others. This view not only paralyses the exercise of historical, but also that of future judgements. In fact, it negates the very possibility of agents fighting for their claims in the belief that they have good reasons for regarding them as morally justified and justifiable.

Do we really want to say that for us 'heirs of victorious liberalism', so to speak, the values connected with it are justified because of that victory? That the opposition to feudal orders by democrats was not justified given the oppression within these orders? That the French Revolution was not justified until it became successful? That Bayle's arguments were not more justified than those of Bossuet because the Bayleans first had to defeat the Bossuetians historically? Do we want to say that Marx was wrong when he argued that communists were fighting against '*Unrecht schlechthin*',[72] injustice *as such*, because what they were really fighting for was to make their conception of justice dominant without any general yardstick of what justice means, so there was no *schlechthin*? Was the struggle for gender justice or for racial justice only justified once it was achieved – and, again, has it been?

I fear that moral Darwinism is self-defeating if one wants to uphold a meaningful view of historical struggles that can lead to emancipation, properly understood. That of course does not mean that we cannot *explain* in historical terms why and how many people in earlier societies held very different views of morality or society, and that there existed very different narratives and standards of justification. But when these were *morally* questioned, we cannot stand aloof and say that the questioners (say, the slaves) did not have any justification on their side, even though we can understand from a historical perspective why they were seen as not being justified. And, again, to say that their claims were justified because they were successful would presuppose that we are simply repeating the standards of the victorious and that the losers were never justified since they were not vindicated. I think that we need to be careful to ensure that our judgements about historical progress are well reflected and do not produce victorious stereotypes, and in that regard Owen's reminder concerning relativity is important. But it is contradictory to warn against self-congratulatory historical assessments and at the same time recommend their very logic.

My view, however, carries a heavy burden of normative argument. For by what criteria are we supposed to judge whether slaves had a justifiable moral claim in a society in which they were not fully recognised as claim-makers in the first place? Are we not simply projecting 'our' views on them and their societies? This is something we should avoid, while accepting that there are major historical differences in the spaces of justifications. But I am committed to the idea that the radical question and demand for reciprocal and general justification is always *pro tanto* justified, because it uses the principle of justification itself to radicalise the standards that determine what is seen as justifiable. 'Radicalise' here means that those who were subject to certain normative orders that were meant to be *generally* justifiable with respect to, say, God's will, the common good or human nature, questioned and rejected that general justifiability by pointing out its particularity and exclusions. And they also did not accept the positive defence of such particularity – in, say, a Rortyan move – as a justification, since the general order had to rest on a justification that was general in nature. This is what Williams's notion of basic legitimation demands, and is itself radicalised by his critical theory principle that a justification does not count if it is produced by the very asymmetrical order that is supposedly being justified.[73] Thus I hold that there is a universal moral grammar built into any normative order that claims to be justifiable, as every order must, and this moral grammar allows for critique of any justification that fails to measure up to standards of reciprocity and generality. So when the dominated, in whatever historical period, asked for justifications they could accept, they may have stopped at some particular stage of justification. But they used a grammar that can always be further radicalised, in contemporary as well as future societies. We do not use 'our' allegedly vindicated standards of justification to assess past claims and developments; rather, we use the standards that those who were engaged in emancipatory movements used to establish themselves as agents of justification. And we should also use them to overcome our own exclusions and ideological normative orders of justification.

Despite my concerns about the notion of vindication, Owen is right to bring up a particularly complex issue connected with this to which I do not have a good reply. That is the question of which norms of justification can justify the means and strategies by which political movements fight for and construct new structures of justification. Could it be that the use of violence can be vindicated even though it is not justified in such conflicts and struggles? Owen calls this 'the Machiavelli question', i.e. the question of whether 'the performance of morally unjustified actions may be necessary for the establishment of good ends' (DO 160). And he suggests that some actions (although not all) that appear unjustifiable may still be vindicated by the good they bring about. Note that the notion of vindication at work here is different from the one discussed above, for in this case the point is not that historical change brings about a new platform of justification from which the results look justified because they have been vindicated; rather, here the question is whether the means required to achieve an end that is already seen as justified are themselves justified. So the question, I take it, is really still one about justification, although now about justifications of a particular kind, namely of those actions that lead to a new and superior structure of justification. And I admit that Kantians, as much as any other view of political morality, should have a response to this. But I do not have a well worked-out view of what has been called 'revolutionary ethics' or the ethics of effective social change through certain means including violence. I have some principles in terms of which I would think about this, such as the Kantian idea that our actions should not belie our moral aims or make future cooperation impossible, or some notion of proportionality, but not much more. However, I think that these questions still call for *justifications* and that retrospective vindication does not constitute an alternative to this. For otherwise we would open the door to all kinds of actions which we could see as vindicated in the end although they were not justified. And that could seriously damage the relevance and primacy of moral justification, whose acceptance we must insist on for social agents, including past ones. Maybe what they did ultimately brought about something good, as Gauguin also did; but that neither justifies nor vindicates their deeds if they carry the scar of immorality. I would prefer to separate the question of the justifiability of their actions from assessments of the good they brought about and not to use a notion of vindication that is situated uncomfortably between these two dimensions of evaluation.

In sum, I would like to combine issues of *dynasteia* and *politeia* in my view (DO 161), since my notion of political order is not static. Rather, I consider a normative order as always being in flux, as involving a constant struggle between conflicting forces. Democratic justice, if things go well, is a virtue of recuperation, because it transforms relations and structures of domination into relations and structures of justification. Justification is essential when playing the game of politics, since this game is a game of noumenal power. But it is also a game about justice, which is why I try to develop a descriptive, social-analytic language of justification *and* a normative one at the same time. Only in this way can we avoid positivism, i.e. the idea that we can provide a neutral description of social dynamics without evaluating it. And when we evaluate, we had better have standards of justification to hold onto. We are always observers as well as participants in these games when we engage in political philosophy in a critical mode. I believe that Owen and I agree here.

If I ever make any progress in that practice, it is due to great minds from whom I learn. And if such minds focus on my work to help me make it better, it is the greatest privilege one can enjoy in our profession.

So I thank my critics again from the bottom of my heart in the hope that I have learned something from their great comments, although probably not as much as I should have.

Notes

1. T.M. Bejan, *Mere Civility: Disagreement and the Limits of Toleration* (Cambridge, MA: Harvard University Press, 2017).
2. Compare *TiC*, p. 13.
3. T.M. Bejan, 'What's the Use? Rainer Forst and the History of Toleration' (ch. 2 in this volume). All the following numbers in brackets refer to the pages of this volume, referencing the respective comments of my critics with their initials.
4. K.O. Apel, 'The "Erklären/Verstehen"-Controversy in the Philosophy of the Human and Natural Sciences', in G. Fløistadt (ed.), *Contemporary Philosophy: A New Survey* (Chronicles of the International Institute for Philosophy II) (The Hague, Boston and London: Martinus Nijhof, 1982), pp. 19–50, and *Die Erklären: Verstehen-Kontroverse in transzendentalpragmatischer Sicht* (Frankfurt/M: Suhrkamp, 1979).
5. See the Rawls Papers, 'Essay and Notes on Toleration', 1950–1955, HUM 48, Box 7, Folder 16. Rawls here quotes Bayle in French, referring to Jean Delvolve, *Religion, Critique et Philosophie Positive chez Pierre Bayle* from 1906. Teresa Bejan thinks that the notes have been dated wrongly.
6. *TiC*, p. 151; J. Rawls, 'On My Religion', in Rawls, *A Brief Inquiry into the Meaning of Sin and Faith* (Cambridge, MA: Harvard University Press, 2009), p. 266.
7. See for example P. Balint, 'The Respect Conception of Toleration' in Balint, *Respecting Toleration: Traditional Liberalism and Contemporary Diversity* (Oxford: Oxford University Press, 2017), pp. 48f.
8. Bejan, *Mere Civility*, p. 160.
9. T.M. Bejan, 'Review Essay: Recent Work on Toleration', *The Review of Politics*, 80 (2018), 703f.
10. B. Williams, 'Persons, Character, and Morality', in Williams, *Moral Luck: Philosophical Papers 1973–1980* (Cambridge: Cambridge University Press, 1981), p. 18.

11 Bejan, *Mere Civility*, p. 160.
12 C. Kukathas, 'Let's Get Radical: Extending the Reach of Baylean (and Forstian) Toleration' (ch. 3 in this volume).
13 I wish a video existed of Chandran's great performance of that footnote in York, surpassing the Monty Python 'Dead Parrot' sketch this is drawn from by far.
14 Apart from his own writings on Bayle, Kukathas edited Bayle's main treatise on toleration including all four parts of the book – P. Bayle, *A Philosophical Commentary on These Words of the Gospel, Luke 14:23*, ed. J. Kilcullen and C. Kukathas (Indianapolis: Liberty Fund, 2005).
15 See *TiC*, p. 69.
16 See *ibid.*, pp. 253f.
17 P. Bayle, *Philosophical Commentary on These Words of Jesus Christ, Compel Them to Come In*, ed. and trans. A. Godman Tannenbaum (New York: Peter Lang, 1987), II.7, p. 147. See *TiC*, p. 255 on Bayle's discussion of the limits of toleration. As I explain there, it is true, as Horton (JH 70) remarks in 'Tales of Toleration', that Bayle had the Catholic Church in mind there, but only as a persecutionist institution (which it was when he wrote this, pursuing him and throwing his brother in jail instead), not as a ban on Catholics generally. He likewise criticises intolerant Protestants. Thus I do not see his reflections on the limits of toleration as being on a par with Locke's more sweeping considerations. That also holds with respect to atheists (or those who were regarded as such at the time).
18 Bayle, *Philosophical Commentary*, I.1, p. 30; *TiC*, p. 248.
19 Bayle, *Philosophical Commentary*, I.10, pp. 84–5; *TiC*, p. 251.
20 See my 'Two Pictures of Justice', in *JDRJ*, pp. 3–25.
21 I am tempted to say that the hope to find a conception of toleration in that approach is as futile as the attempt to buy any cheese in the well-kept 'National Cheese Emporium'.
22 See, for example, J. Horton and S. Mendus (eds), *Aspects of Toleration* (London and New York: Routledge, 1985) and Horton and Mendus (eds), *Toleration, Identity and Difference* (Basingstoke: Macmillan, 1999); J. Horton and P. Nicholson, *Toleration: Philosophy and Practice* (Aldershot: Brookfield, 1992).
23 J. Horton, 'Three (Apparent) Paradoxes of Toleration', *Synthesis Philosophica*, 9:1 (1994), 7–20 – and my discussion of it in my 'Toleration and its Paradoxes:

A Tribute to John Horton', *Philosophia*, 45:2 (2017), 415–424. See also *TiC*, pp. 21f.
24 See also his generous review of my toleration book in J. Horton, 'Rainer Forst: Toleration in Conflict. Past and Present', *Notre Dame Philosophical Reviews*, 25 September 2013: https://ndpr.nd.edu/news/toleration-in-conflict-past-and-present (accessed 3 December 2019).
25 J. Horton, 'Tales of Toleration' (ch. 4 in this volume).
26 See also my lead chapter in this volume and *TiC* generally, as well as my 'Two Stories about Toleration', in C. Ungureanu and L. Zucca (eds), *Law, State and Religion in the New Europe: Debates and Dilemmas* (Cambridge: Cambridge University Press, 2012), pp. 49–64.
27 See M. Bassiouni, 'Wie viel Meinungsfreiheit müssen Muslime tolerieren?', in C. Ströbele *et al.* (eds), *Kritik, Widerspruch, Blasphemie. Anfragen an Christentum und Islam* (Regensburg: Verlag Friedrich Pustet, 2017), pp. 211–229.
28 As is Glen Newey, see his *Toleration in Political Conflict* (Cambridge: Cambridge University Press, 2013), pp. 93–100.
29 For that distinction, see *RtJ*, pp. 174f.
30 *TiC*, pp. 556–564.
31 S. Macedo, *Just Married: Same-Sex Couples, Monogamy & the Future of Marriage* (Princeton: Princeton University Press, 2015).
32 Compare J. Horton, 'Realism, Liberal Moralism and a Political Theory of Modus Vivendi', *European Journal of Political Theory*, 9:4 (2010), 431–448.
33 Newey, *Toleration in Political Conflict*.
34 *TiC*, pp. 569f.
35 See for example his *Philosophy in an Age of Pluralism: The Philosophy of Charles Taylor in Question* (Cambridge: Cambridge University Press, 1994); 'Prospects for Transnational Citizenship and Democracy', *Ethics & International Affairs*, 15:2 (2001), 53–66; 'Liberalism, Multiculturalism, and the Problem of Internal Minorities', in A.S. Laden and D. Owen (eds), *Multiculturalism and Political Theory* (Cambridge: Cambridge University Press, 2007), pp. 244–264; 'Compromise, Pluralism, and Deliberation', *Critical Review of International Social and Political Philosophy*, 20:5 (2017), 635–655.

36 D. Miller, *Justice for Earthlings* (Cambridge: Cambridge University Press, 2013), pp. 16f.
37 D. Weinstock, 'Overcoming Toleration?' (ch. 5 in this volume).
38 For a good attempt, see L. Valentini, 'Ideal vs. Non-Ideal Theory: A Conceptual Map', *Philosophical Compass*, 7:9 (2012), 654–664. I discuss this in the Introduction to *N&P*.
39 *TiC*, p. 506.
40 *Ibid.*
41 Newey's work is a relevant example.
42 *TiC*, pp. 569–571.
43 See e.g. D. Weinstock, 'A Neutral Conception of Reasonableness?', *Episteme*, 3:3 (2006), 234–247; A. Shachar, *Multiculturalism Jurisdictions: Cultural Differences and Women's Rights* (Cambridge: Cambridge University Press, 2001) and her 'Two Critiques of Multiculturalism', *Cardozo Law Review*, 23:1 (2001), 253–297.
44 M. Williams, *Voice, Trust and Memory: Marginalized Groups and the Failings of Liberal Representation* (Princeton: Princeton University Press, 1998); J. Chan, D. Chull Shin and M. Williams (eds), *East Asian Perspectives on Legitimacy. Bridging the Empirical-Normative Divide* (New York: Cambridge University Press, 2016).
45 M. Williams, 'On Turning Away from Justification' (ch. 6 in this volume).
46 A. Allen, 'The Power of Justification', in R. Forst, *Justice Democracy, and the Right to Justification: Rainer Forst in Dialogue* (London and New York: Bloomsbury, 2014), pp. 65–86, and 'Progress, Normativity, and Universality: Reply to Forst', in A. Allen and E. Mendieta (eds), *Justification and Emancipation: The Critical Theory of Rainer Forst* (University Park: Penn State University Press, 2019), pp. 147–156. See my replies in 'Justifying Justification: Reply to My Critics', in *JDRJ*, pp. 169–216, and 'Navigating a World of Conflict and Power: Reply to My Critics', in *Justification and Emancipation: The Critical Theory of Rainer Forst*, pp. 157–187.
47 K. Olson, 'Complexities of Political Discourse: Class, Power, and the Linguistic Turn', in *JDRJ*, pp. 87–102. See my reply in 'Justifying Justification: Reply to My Critics'.
48 L. McNay, 'The Limits of Justification: Critique Disclosure, and Reflexivity', in E. Herlin-Karnell, M. Klatt and H. A. Morales Zúñiga (eds), *Constitutionalism*

Justified: Rainer Forst in Discourse (Oxford: Oxford University Press, 2019). See my reply in 'The Constitution of Justification: Replies and Comments' in the same volume.
49 C. Lu, 'The Right to Justification and the Good of Nonalienation', in *Justification and Emancipation: The Political Philosophy of Rainer Forst*, pp. 76–92. See my reply in 'Navigating a World of Conflict and Power: Reply to My Critics'.
50 *CoJ*, pp. 126–133.
51 A. Kumar, *Radical Equality: Ambedkar, Gandhi, and the Risk of Democracy* (Stanford: Stanford University Press, 2015).
52 See, for example, his *Bound by Recognition* (Princeton: Princeton University Press, 2003).
53 See my responses to Allen in 'Justifying Justification: Reply to My Critics' and 'Navigating a World of Conflict and Power: Reply to My Critics', and to Benhabib in 'The Right to Justification: Moral and Political, Transcendental and Historical', *Political Theory*, 43:6 (2015), 822–837; see also my 'The Justification of Progress and the Progress of Justification', in *Justification and Emancipation: The Political Philosophy of Rainer Forst*, pp. 17–37.
54 P. Markell, 'Power, Attention and the Tasks of Critical Theory' (ch. 7 in this volume).
55 C. Lafont, *Heidegger, Language and World-Disclosure* (Cambridge: Cambridge University Press, 2000).
56 N. Kompridis, *Critique and Disclosure: Critical Theory between Past and Future* (Cambridge, MA: MIT Press, 2006).
57 M. Heidegger, 'The Origin of the Work of Art', trans. A. Hofstadter with minor changes by D.F. Krell, in D.F. Krell (ed.), *Martin Heidegger: Basic Writings*, rev. and expd. edn (London: Routledge, 1993), pp. 143–212.
58 It was in the context of these debates that I wrote my first essay on Heidegger and Foucault, 'Endlichkeit Freiheit Individualität. Die Sorge um das Selbst bei Heidegger und Foucault', in E. Erdmann, A. Honneth and R. Forst (eds), *Ethos der Moderne* (Frankfurt/M: Suhrkamp, 1990), pp. 146–186.
59 See D. Owen, 'Criticism and Captivity: On Genealogy and Critical Theory', *European Journal of Philosophy*, 10:2 (2002), 216–230; 'On Genealogy and Political Theory', *Political Theory*, 33:1 (2005), 110–120. And M. Saar, *Genealogie als Kritik. Geschichte und Theorie des Subjekts nach Nietzsche und Foucault* (Frankfurt/M and New York: Campus, 2007); 'Understanding

Genealogy: History, Power, and the Self', *Journal for the Philosophy of History*, 2:3 (2008), 295–314; 'Genealogy and Subjectivity', *European Journal of Philosophy*, 10:2 (2002), 231–245.
60 H. Arendt, *The Human Condition*, 2nd edn (Chicago: University of Chicago Press, 1998), p. 201.
61 *Ibid.*
62 R. Forst, 'Noumenal Power', in *N&P*, pp. 37–51; 'On the Concept of a Justification Narrative', in *N&P*, pp. 55–68; 'Noumenal Power Revisited: Reply to my Critics', *Journal of Political Power*, 11:3 (2018), 294–321, wherein see especially my replies to C. Hayward's 'On Structural Power', *Journal of Political Power*, 11:1 (2018), 56–67, and to A. Azmanova, 'Relational, Structural and Systemic Forms of Power: The "Right to Justification" Confronting Three Types of Domination', *Journal of Political Power*, 11:1 (2018), 68–78.
63 D. Owen, *Nietzsche's Genealogy of Morals* (London and New York: Routledge, 2007); 'Nietzsche's Genealogy Revisited', *Journal of Nietzsche Studies*, 35 (2008), 141–154; 'Genealogy as Exemplary Critique: Reflections on Foucault and the Imagination of the Political', *Economy and Society*, 24:4 (1995), 489–506.
64 See D. Owen, *Maturity and Modernity: Nietzsche, Weber, Foucault and the Ambivalence of Reason* (London and New York: Routledge, 1994); 'Criticism and Captivity: On Genealogy and Critical Theory' and 'On Genealogy and Political Theory'.
65 See my *RtJ*, pp. 35–42.
66 D. Owen, 'Power, Justification and Vindication' (ch. 8 in this volume).
67 *RtJ*, p. 41.
68 R. Forst, 'Noumenal Alienation: Rousseau, Kant and Marx on the Dialectics of Self-Determination', *Kantian Review*, 22:4 (2017), 523–551.
69 See my discussion with Steven Lukes, 'Noumenal Power: Concept and Explanation', *Journal of Political Power*, 11:1 (2018), 46–55, in 'Noumenal Power Revisited'.
70 Q. Skinner, 'Meaning and Understanding in the History of Ideas', *History and Theory*, 8:1 (1969), 3–53.
71 See my reply to Benhabib in 'The Right to Justification: Moral and Political, Transcendental and Historical' and my 'The Justification of Progress and the Progress of Justification'.

72 K. Marx, 'Zur Kritik der Hegelschen Rechtsphilosophie. Einleitung', in *Karl Marx, Friedrich Engels: Werke* (MEW), vol. 1 (Berlin: Dietz Verlag, 1976), p. 390. In the English translation '*Unrecht schlechthin*' is translated with 'wrong generally' which is misleading, see Marx, 'Contribution to the Critique of Hegel's Philosophy of Law', in *Karl Marx, Frederick Engels: Collected Works*, vol. 3, Marx and Engels: 1843–1844, trans. M. Milligan and B. Ruhemann (New York: International Publishers, 2005), p. 186.

73 B. Williams, *In the Beginning Was the Deed* (Princeton: Princeton University Press, 2005), pp. 3 and 6.

Index

Abelard, Peter 28, 35, 175
abortion 3, 92n.33
acceptance 5–6, 8, 9, 26, 28–29, 39, 52, 58–59, 71–72, 89, 97–99, 143, 172, 190, 213
Addams, Jane 123
alienation 206
  alienating 197–199
Allen, Amy 23–24, 30, 37, 139–140, 143–145, 149n.19, 195, 200, 218n.53
Apel, Karl-Otto 201
Arendt, Hannah 140–145, 199, 201
Aristotle 193
atheist(s) 11, 30, 44n.49, 56, 215n.17
Augustine 9–12, 49–50, 57, 171
authority 10–11, 30–31, 49, 54–55, 61, 65, 73, 144, 146, 182, 184, 191, 197, 205
  normative 150, 199
autonomy 14, 56, 59, 119, 134

basic right to justification 23, 27, 35, 37, 44n.64, 77
  non-domination 205
Bayle, Pierre 9, 12–14, 16, 24, 27–28, 30, 32–33, 38, 44n.49, 46–57, 59–60, 67n.5, 67n.13, 70, 91n.3, 140, 147, 168, 170–177, 179, 183, 204, 210, 214n.5, 215n.14, 215n.17
Benhabib, Seyla 23–24, 30, 44n.53, 44n.64, 139, 200
Berlin, Isaiah 29
Bernstein, Richard 201
blasphemy 6, 18, 35, 182
Bodin, Jean 9, 13, 28, 170
Boggs, Carl 124

Bossuet, Jacques Bénigne 210
Bourdieu, Pierre 122, 131
Brown, Wendy 18n.3, 19n.14, 76, 91n.1

Cambridge School 208
Castellio, Sebastian 9, 17, 24, 35, 38
Catholic Church 11, 35, 187, 215n.17
Cavell, Stanley 151–154, 206
Christian(s) 3, 8, 10–11, 13, 16, 24, 37, 46, 49, 51, 54, 86, 175, 183, 185
colonial(ism) 125–127, 137n.34, 139, 195–196
community 37, 46, 56, 74, 126, 129, 131–134, 160, 168, 178, 187
comprehensive doctrines 15, 78
consequentialist 62, 96, 104–105
constructivist 23, 35, 117
  construction of justice 63
  construction of reason 65
  constructivism 40n.3
Coulthard, Glen 126–127, 130
critical theory 16, 25–27, 29, 78, 139–147, 154, 181, 193, 199–200, 204
  of justification 120, 122, 195
  principle 211
  of toleration 16, 18, 170
  see also Frankfurt School

Davis, Angela 147, 204
deliberation 160, 184
deliberative democracy 79, 119, 125
democratic 13, 18, 93n.40, 105, 124, 141, 151, 161, 178–179, 182, 184–185, 194, 197, 213
culture 36

Index

democracy 28, 79, 94, 119, 123–125, 151, 188, 194–195, 197, 209
justice 213
liberal 27, 31, 36, 105
society(ies) 27, 170, 181
toleration 4, 6
deontological difference 15, 177, 180–181
de-reify(ied) 37, 40, 41n.22, 182
Dewey, John 123
dialectic 4, 18, 129
Diderot, Denis 51
disobedience 126, 128
history of 8, 12, 18n.3, 30, 169, 171, 181, 194
diversity 7, 36, 38–39, 172
diverse citizens 38
diverse societies 25, 98
domination 4, 8, 11, 17–18, 23–24, 28, 119–120, 122–133, 139, 141, 143–144, 150, 159, 178, 181, 185, 194–196, 198, 209, 213
Donatist(s) 10–11, 46
Dreyfus, Hubert 201

Edict of Nantes 7–8, 55
education 88, 121, 145, 179, 184
emancipation 25, 38, 41, 120, 140, 195, 200, 210
Enlightenment 7, 23–24, 28, 31, 36, 51, 54, 130
triumphalism 23, 28
equality 9, 31, 73–76, 131, 150, 157, 178, 204
gender 88, 107

feminist 106–107, 189, 192, 195
Fish, Stanley 28
Fitzmaurice, Deborah 59
forms of life 3, 105, 196
Foucault, Michel 43n.33, 122, 131, 159, 161, 199–201, 205, 218n.58

Frankfurt School 23–24, 41n.13
fundamentum inconcussum 35–36

Gadamer, Hans-Georg 168
Gaita, Raimond 153–154
Gallie, Walter Bryce 26
Gandhi, Mahatma 125–127, 130, 196
genealogical 4, 169, 205
historical 204
God 10–11, 50–51, 79, 173–174, 211
Goethe, Johann Wolfgang von 4, 8, 29, 76

Habermas, Jürgen 18n.3, 29, 38–41, 45, 78, 117, 143, 177, 199, 201
Hegel, Georg Wilhelm Friedrich 129
Hegelian(ism) 11, 38, 105, 170
Heidegger, Martin 200–201
Heideggerian 204, 218n.58
Heiner, Brady 146–147
hierarchy 131, 157
higher order (reasons) 71, 97
Hobbes, Thomas 33, 36–37
Horkheimer, Max 146
human rights 6, 155, 159
humanity 119, 160
Husserl, Edmund 146

ideal (theory) 29, 78, 94, 96, 114n.2, 189
ideology 130, 207
ideological 17, 130, 139, 143, 146, 181, 203, 212
indifference 5, 7, 33, 35, 143, 190
inequality 8, 24
injustice 12, 122, 128, 203, 210
institutions 9, 46, 102, 104–106, 121–122, 139, 142, 144–145, 155, 196
intersubjective 15, 129, 130
Islam(ic) 3, 16, 49

justice 10, 12, 16, 38, 42n.23, 46–48, 55, 59–61, 66, 121–124, 128, 135n.15, 139, 150–152, 175, 177, 179–180, 187–188, 190, 193, 210
   construction 63, 150
   disagree(ment) 64–65, 95, 178–179
   distributive 23, 81
   divine 12
   full 121, 150
   fundamental(s) 121–122, 128, 150, 158, 178
   political 38, 81
   principle(s) 14, 81
   procedural 121, 158
justification for/of toleration 15, 56–57
justification narratives 30, 202–203, 207
   see also narratives of justification

Kant, Immanuel 4, 8–9, 12, 28, 31, 34, 36, 60–63, 68n.32, 76, 108, 154, 181, 205
Kantian(ism) 37, 57, 83, 98, 105, 117, 122, 160, 167, 171–173, 175, 177, 186, 190, 213
   neo-Kantian 39, 172
   proto-Kantian 175, 177
Kompridis, Nikolas 200
Kumar, Aishwary 197
Kymlicka, Will 56

Lafont, Cristina 200
Lessing, Gotthold Ephraim 9
limits of toleration 5–7, 54, 57, 59, 71, 77, 86–87, 89, 176–180, 186, 192, 215n.17
Llull, Ramon 28, 35
Locke, John 9–12, 18, 28, 31–33, 44n.49, 47, 56, 70, 91n.3, 168, 215n.17
   Lockean 27, 103
Lu, Catherine 195
Lukes, Steven 219n.69

Luther, Martin 10, 24, 30, 36–37
Lutheran 174

Machiavelli, Niccoló 159–162, 212
McNay, Lois 195
marriage 3, 13–14, 18, 85–86, 179, 185–186, 188
Marx, Karl 146, 154, 210
Merleau-Ponty, Maurice 146
method 23, 27, 124, 205
   methodological 25, 32
Mill, John Stuart 56, 61, 70
Miller, David 188
minority(ies) 3–4, 8, 14, 16, 55, 73, 100, 102, 109–110, 179, 184–185, 191, 193
modern(ity) 8, 27, 31–37, 41n.10, 42n.23, 45n.74, 47, 57, 79, 89, 132, 157, 202
modus vivendi 56, 73, 85, 113–114
Montaigne, Michel de 33, 171
moral Darwinism 209–210

narratives of justification 30, 143, 202
   see also justification narratives
Newey, Glen 27, 83–84, 186, 216n.28, 217n.41
Nicholas of Cusa 9
Nietzsche, Friedrich 5, 201, 205
non-domination 205
non-ideal (theory) 94–96, 110, 112–113, 114n.2, 188–189, 193
normatively dependent 13, 47, 59, 66, 72, 90, 97, 99, 177–178, 180
noumenal 17, 122, 131, 140–141, 156, 168–169, 202, 204, 206–208, 213

obedience 8, 36, 51
objection 5–6, 8–9, 14, 26, 29, 47, 51, 58–59, 61, 65–66, 71–72, 76, 86–87, 97–100, 172, 181–182, 186–187, 190, 192
obligation(s) 45n.70, 77, 127

Okin, Susan Moller 115n.22
Olson, Kevin 119–120, 195
O'Neill, Onora 61, 68n.32

Paine, Thomas 76
paradox(es) 5–6, 19n.10, 26, 29, 50, 58, 98–99, 115n.9, 180
paradoxical 111, 113, 176, 179
paternalistic 185
peace 6, 14, 56, 62–65, 68n.29, 73
Pettit, Philip 115n.21
political theory 23–25, 35, 39, 41n.17, 94, 161–162, 175, 188, 199
power 3, 8, 16, 18n.2, 23, 25–26, 31, 55, 60–65, 73–74, 83, 86, 100, 102–105, 110, 122, 126, 128, 140–146, 150, 153, 157, 159, 171, 181, 184, 189, 191, 204
 critique 17, 200
 critical 57
 effects 195, 199, 201
 justification(s) 29–30, 33, 119, 155
 normativity 160–161
 noumenal 17, 131, 140, 156, 169, 207, 213
 orders of 143, 195
 political 66, 109
 relations 17, 25, 121, 123, 130, 139–140, 146, 151, 154
 social 4, 122, 205
 structure(s) 122, 130, 156
 structural 100, 208
prefigurative practice(s) 123–127, 129, 132–133, 135n.22, 194–196
principle of justification 15, 18, 57
Proast, Jonas 10, 57, 91n.3
progress 3, 7–8, 11–13, 15–18, 30–31, 37, 43n.42, 128, 132, 169, 181, 204–205, 208, 211, 213
 moral 15, 139

racism 6–7
 racist 7, 103, 154, 187, 192, 203, 206
 tolerant racist 7, 58

Rancière, Jacques 156
rationalisation 4, 34, 180–181
rationalistic 118, 174, 205
Rawls, John 14, 20n.25, 27–29, 38, 40n.3, 41n.13, 70, 78, 113, 121, 161, 170
Rawlsian 27, 78, 121, 170, 189
realism 181, 189
realist(ic) 29, 186, 188, 197
reason 7, 12, 14–18, 36, 48–54, 60–65, 68n.32, 76–77, 83, 91n.3, 109, 111, 130, 132, 134n.5, 144, 170, 174–179, 183, 198, 201, 205, 206–207
 agreement of free citizens 61
 public 79, 119
reasonable disagreement 10, 14, 91n.3, 94, 170, 176
recognition 5, 8, 28–29, 61, 74–75, 108, 117, 129–130, 151, 154
reconstruct(ion) 9, 70, 117–119, 141, 167, 169–171, 194, 201
 reconstructive 173, 178
Reimarus, Hermann Samuel 28
rejection 6–9, 14, 26, 59, 71–72, 97–99, 104, 106, 110, 130, 192
revolutionary 24, 57, 124, 208, 212
Rex, Walter 50–51, 53, 54, 67n.13
right to justification 24, 27, 35–37, 46–48, 59
Rushdie, Salman 80–85, 182

Sangiovanni, Andrea 45n.70
scepticism 33, 50–51, 78, 110, 115n.9, 158, 174, 178–179, 181
Scheffler, Samuel 40
secular 9, 13, 16, 36, 182
Shachar, Ayelet 103, 193
Simpson, Leanne Betasamosake 137n.42
Skinner, Quentin 25, 41
slave(ry) 24, 129, 146, 152–155, 206–207, 209–211
space of justifications 17, 204, 206–207

space of reasons 111, 139–145, 150, 155–156, 158–159, 170, 202, 204, 207
Stoic(s) 34–35

toleration 3–18, 24–39, 47–52, 54–66, 69–75, 82, 84–90, 95–102, 104–114, 118, 120–121, 167–184, 186–193, 195
   coexistence conception 56, 73–74, 85, 90, 173, 183
   esteem conception 56, 73, 75, 87, 172–173, 190
   permission conception 7, 9, 13, 28, 34, 43n.33, 55–56, 73–76, 85, 91n.3, 170, 181, 187, 191–193
   respect conception 9, 12–16, 25–27, 29, 33, 35, 38–39, 55–56, 73–76, 78, 86–87, 89–90, 91n.3, 109, 169–170, 173, 175, 187, 189, 190–194, 209

Toleration Act 8, 32, 55
Tully, James 25, 135n.22

universalistic moral point of view 24, 139

violence 7, 12, 46, 49, 52, 54, 60, 66, 95, 131, 141, 159, 176–177, 212
virtue of justice 47–48, 175, 178, 190
Voltaire 31

Weber, Max 202
Williams, Bernard 157–158, 160, 173, 208, 211
Williams, Roger 28, 32–33, 45n.72
Wittgenstein, Ludwig 151, 205

Young, Iris Marion 40

Zemmour, Éric 115n.24